Elena Sommers is a visually impaired writer. Writing has been her passion since she was a little girl. The legendary writers: Philip Pullman, JK Rowling, Leo Tolstoy and Pushkin inspired her to write. Elena was born in the picturesque city of St Petersburg and grew up among the magnificent, baroque-style castles. Later, she visited gorgeous Windsor Castle, Buckingham palace and Aspen house.

The castle inspired her to write about royalty and the marvellous idea came to her mind to write about Russia and its royalty, Nicholas the second, his family, love, life, murder, mystery, sex and political arguments.

Do you wish to discover more?

Would you like to read it?

Elena Sommers

NICHOLAS AND ALEXANDRA MAJESTIES AND MASSACRE

AUSTIN MACAULEY PUBLISHERS™
LONDON * CAMBRIDGE * NEW YORK * SHARJAH

Copyright © Elena Sommers 2023

The right of Elena Sommers to be identified as author of this work has been asserted by the author in accordance with sections 77 and 78 of the Copyright, Designs and Patents Act 1988.

All rights reserved. No part of this publication may be reproduced, stored in a retrieval system, or transmitted in any form or by any means, electronic, mechanical, photocopying, recording, or otherwise, without the prior permission of the publishers.

Any person who commits any unauthorised act in relation to this publication may be liable to criminal prosecution and civil claims for damages.

A CIP catalogue record for this title is available from the British Library.

ISBN 9781398440135 (Paperback)
ISBN 9781398440142 (ePub e-book)
ISBN 9781398448193 (Audiobook)

www.austinmacauley.com

First Published 2023
Austin Macauley Publishers Ltd®
1 Canada Square
Canary Wharf
London
E14 5AA

Table of Contents

Chapter 1: Nicholas and Alexandra … 7

Chapter 2: Grigori Rasputin … 16

Chapter 3: The Future Czar and His Mistress Matilda Kshesinskaya … 25

Chapter 4: Grigori Rasputin and His Prediction … 35

Chapter 5: A Visit to Germany and the Funeral of Alexander III … 43

Chapter 6: Wedding Day … 51

Chapter 7: St Petersburg at Last … 60

Chapter 8: Coronation and Khodynka Tragedy … 68

Chapter 9: Nicholas and Alexandra, Their Young Family and Holiday to France … 77

Chapter 10: Grigori Rasputin and His Wish … 86

Chapter 11: Czarevich Alexei … 94

Chapter 12: A Bomb Explosion … 103

Chapter 13: Revolution 1905 … 112

Chapter 14: A Blue Room … 120

Chapter 15: Grigori and His Influence … 128

Chapter 16: Visit to England and Alexei's Birthday Celebration … 137

Chapter 17: Murder of Mr Stolypin … 146

Chapter 18: First World War … 155

Chapter 19: Unkillable Monk … 165

Chapter 20: Revolution 1917	**174**
Chapter 21: Massacre	**184**
Epilogue	**196**
Quotes and References	**204**

Chapter 1
Nicholas and Alexandra

As soon as both Elizabeth and Sergei answered 'yes I do,' they swapped the diamond rings and pronounced additional wedding vows. The bride was wearing a snowy white dress with a long train. The sparkling pearls and aquamarines glistened in her tiara. The groom had a military uniform and looked stately and handsome in white, red and blue.

'I'd love to have God at the centre of our marriage,' the groom begun. 'I promise to look after you in sickness and in health. I will be faithful and loyal to you for the rest of my life, Princess Elizabeth. I will love, admire and cherish you, darling, forever and will make your dreams come true,' he said confidently and looked at his beloved bride. Everybody clapped.

'It would be wonderful to have God at the centre of our marriage and experience, whatever challenges and blessings He prepares for us,' the bride commenced her speech. Her voice trembled across the chapel in Winter Palace. 'I promise to love and cherish you forever, Grand Duke Sergei. I'd love to be loyal and faithful to you for the rest of my life and make your dreams come true,' Elizabeth announced in her angelic voice and gave a marvellous smile. The audience applauded once again.

'I pronounce you husband and wife. The groom may kiss the bride.' Sergei did not keep the public waiting on this occasion.

'My sister is so stunning as a bride,' Alex said to Nicholas. They were both standing opposite the newly married couple. 'She looks simply magnificent.'

'I do agree, my uncle is enjoying his wedding day. It took a few months to prepare and rehearse it.'

'What are you doing in your spare time, Prince Nicholas?' twelve-year-old Alex asked him with real interest.

'I have no free time, Your Highness. Unfortunately, I must prepare to be an emperor, I have to learn even more than previously; English, Russian, German, Spanish, French, geography, etiquette and history,' Nicholas complained.

'I can't speak Russian at all and my French is not brilliant, but I love to speak, read and write in English and German,' Alex replied. Nicholas was busy taking pictures. The wedding photographs were taken by professional photographers – indoors and outdoors – however, Nicholas used his own camera, he found it quite amusing to take black and white pictures during special occasions. The chapel looked predominantly stylish with thousands of candles, specifically prepared for the wedding day.

Gradually, it was time for the wedding breakfast. The wedding guests gathered in the dining area. They indulged in sturgeon and royal oscietra caviar toasts for starter, lobster with thermidor butter sauce for main course and a seven-layer wedding cake for dessert.

'Fifteen of June 1884 is the best day of my life,' Elizabeth whispered to Sergei. The bride was simply magnificent.

'I wish it would last forever,' her husband replied. The guests found this royal wedding utterly marvellous.

Princess Alex truly enjoyed her first visit to Russia. She made friends with Prince Nicholas. Alex thought that if she had the chance to travel to Russia once more, she would take this opportunity as soon as possible.

Four years later, the opportunity arose. The princess received an invitation from the Russian royal family. Almost instantly, she posted her acceptance of their invitation and ordered her suitcases to be packed and departed in the direction of Petersburg. Princess Alex had been in her royal carriage for quite a long time, accompanied by her three ladies-in-waiting, coachmen and two armed bodyguards. Her elegant carriage made of red wood had her coat of arms on each carriage door and was pulled by five speedy Arabian beauties. She brought seven suitcases full of stylish hats, elegant dresses, shoes and jewellery, just in case. The endless birch trees, oak and pine trees passed by monotonously in front of her eyes. Russia always gave her both exhilaration and fear, because from what she could see, Russia was a real world of contrast. As she had been there before, Princess Alex knew what to expect; however, they were looking for a potential bride for Prince Nicholas and Alex might, therefore, be on top of their list. Her level of anxiety went up and up. Alex compared herself with another German princess, Catherine the Great, who made the same trip from Germany to Russia

140 years ago to see Peter. Catherine the Great inspired Alex, because in her long and successful reign she was an outstanding empress.

Maybe, if I am an empress, she thought, *I'll be as successful as Catherine, maybe not. It's all about correct and wrong decisions. The main thing is that I am eager to see the heir apparent once again and build our love and friendship.* The 17-year-old princess felt so grown up, making the most serious life-decisions almost alone. After losing her mum and her siblings in a diphtheria outbreak, she assumed that the whole world was on her shoulders once more. Unfortunately, in this situation, Princess Alex was not able to ask her mother for advice. After hours of running, the horses slowed down a great deal. She was definitely late, but couldn't do anything to change it. Slowly and gradually, the brightly orange sunset appeared in the sky. Shortly, the hours of woodland gradually changed in front of her eyes and village after village after village passed by. Finally, they arrived at a fabulous city with townhouses, magnificent castles, churches with golden rooftops and modern theatres. The wealthy and poor crowds of people alike wandered around the streets of St Petersburg. It was already dark outside; however, there were the most modern electric lights present on central streets and Nevsky Prospect.

'We have almost arrived, Your Highness,' one of her ladies-in-waiting announced in German, bringing Alex back to reality from her deep thoughts. They rushed through Nevsky Prospect, crossing over several bridges, turned right and ended up in front of an arch. Two solemn soldiers, dressed in red, white and blue, blocked their way.

'Alex, Princess of Hesse by Rhine,' said one of her ladies-in-waiting in a horsey voice, looking at a yawning soldier.

'An invitation, please?' he replied. A piece of paper with a royal stamp was shown and they went through an arch and stopped in front of the magnificent baroque castle, the Winter Palace with a two-tier colonnade all throughout the building, designed by Giovanni Rustrelly. Alexandra entered the sumptuous and majestic building once again; it reminded her of her sister's wedding. The Winter Palace was one of the most luxurious castles in the world. She entered the main hall.

The kings and queens from the past stared at her from the portraits and paintings on the walls, as if wanting to say something important. She felt so small and lost in this luxurious building with thousands of candles, gas lamps, electric lights and so much gold. Two or three very well-dressed couples walked past, talking about something trivial.

'Hello, my dear sister, the other guests and I have been waiting for you.' A stunning-looking lady in a peach-coloured dress glided towards Princess Alex and gave her a gentle hug. That was totally unexpected to see her sister so soon.

'Hello, Elizabeth, dearest. How are you? I'm so delighted to see you,' she said with a smile while returning the hug.

'My husband and I had been working in charitable organisations and monasteries to help the most unfortunate and disadvantaged of our society, for four years in a row,' she explained in her delightful voice and her eyes sparkled like diamonds.

'I'm glad you are helping others,' Princess Alex answered without interest. 'I wish I was as kind as you, my honourable sister.' They walked slowly towards the grand reception. The classical music became louder and louder.

'Alex Princess of Hesse by Rhine with her sister Grand Duchess Elizabeth of Russia,' a butler announced loudly when they entered.

Fashionable, glamorous and privileged people were gathered in the golden ballroom. Almost all of them looked at them when they entered, including the empress Maria Feodorovna herself, who poised proudly in the centre and looked splendid in her silver dress with multiple diamonds. A legion of pugs ran around the place, making a bit of noise.

'Hello, Your Imperial Majesty!' She gave a courtesy and smiled, looking straight at the queen.

Her light blue dress was simple, but elegant.

'Hello, Princess Alex. I am delighted to see you; however, you are awfully late. The ball is almost over.'

'Apologies, Your Majesty. The roads in Russia are endlessly long. My horses were so slow.'

'Maybe you should choose a better dress and faster horses, Your Highness, next time,' the Countess Suvorova said coldly. Her exquisite outfit was from the latest French fashion. Alex totally ignored her remark.

'Many years ago,' the queen continued, 'when I was a little girl, about six years old, Hans Christian Andersen used to visit Yellow Palace in Denmark and read us his fabulous fairy tales. From that time, I always remember a phrase from *The Ugly Duckling*, "It doesn't matter being born in a duck yard, as long as you are hatched from a swan's egg".'

'Yes, Your Majesty,' Alex blushed, not knowing where to look. A bitter flavour suddenly stuck in her throat; she tried to ignore it, swallowed and nodded politely in reply. She became shy all of a sudden.

'I'm just wondering whether she is a good match for my boy, if she positively hatched from a diamond egg and whether or not she has enough wisdom to become an excellent empress in the near future. Her Royal Highness might have misunderstood my comment,' the Queen stated, changed the subject and started to talk to someone else entirely.

'Are you all right, sweetheart?' Elizabeth asked, watching her reaction when they walked slightly away.

'I am fine, thanks, Elizabeth, just a bit tired.' She took a glass of champagne from a passing servant and sipped the cold refreshing liquid as if dying from thirst. *I might not be from the richest royal family in the world, but my grandma Queen Victoria is prosperous,* she thought and it made her feel a bit better. However, Alex was too shy to say it to the queen. Instead, she made herself busy talking to her sister.

'How is your marriage with Grand Duke Sergei, dear sister?' she asked with great interest.

'My marriage is wonderful. We love each other so much, the only problem is we don't have any children. Hopefully, with God's blessing, we might have them one day.'

'Lots of blessings to you both!' she exclaimed. 'My dear sister.'

Four gentlemen came into a ballroom at that precise moment, Laughing; Alexander III, Grand Duke Sergei, Grand Duke Nicholas and Grand Duke Nikolai Nikolayevich. All four of them were dressed in the latest fashion. Nicholas was wearing gloves.

'The King of Denmark's cigars were rather nice,' Alexander III remarked matter-of-factly. He was over six feet tall and had that domineering appearance about him. He was like a Russian bear.

'Yes, they were indeed, Your Majesty,' Grand Duke Sergei laughed in reply. He was 6 feet tall, young and handsome.

Princess Alex walked towards His Majesty, gave a courtesy and smiled.

'My greetings to you, Your Imperial Majesty of Russia, I am so delighted to see you.' In that moment, the princess looked simply magnificent.

'Hello, Your Highness Princess Alex of Hesse by Rhine. Are you enjoying the royal ball?'

'Of course I am, the ball is simply delightful. My apologies for being late.'

'No worries,' he coughed. 'Would you like to marry Nicholas?'

The question put Alex on the spot. She thought for a few seconds and answered.

'To be truthful, I haven't thought about it yet.' Alex looked straight into his eyes.

'As a couple, you both have plenty of time to decide. Nicholas has not yet proposed. Thank you for being honest.' He signalled to the butler to carry on dancing.

'Voices of Spring Waltz by Johan Strauss Jr,' was announced by the butler. The couples began to twirl around the gold drawing room.

'Would you like to dance, Princess Alex?' Nicholas asked her.

'I will be delighted, Your Highness,' she replied, as a large smile appeared on her face and they started to waltz.

The music carried them around the golden dance room with confident steps. The bright candlelight reflected in multiple mirrors. It was breathtakingly thrilling. Nicholas and Alexandra had their first dance.

'Alex, you look magnificent. I love dancing with you, it is so awesome.'

'The dance is so delightful, as if it is a real heaven.'

They twirled and twirled and twirled.

The ball finished gradually and Alex finally managed to go in her guest parlour. The rooms were impressively well-furnished, with modern-designed Victorian furniture. Even the latest innovation, a wooden and brass shiny telephone was resting on a stylish dressing table. There were two enormous windows in her bedroom, with a view of the River Neva. She opened one of them. A gentle, warm breeze moved the curtains left and right. It was nearly midnight. She suddenly realised that she hadn't eaten anything for many hours, except tiny snacks and champagne, because she was too late for the banquet. Alex lifted the phone up and ordered a meal in her parlour. When her midnight feast was delivered, it was 1 am. While she was feasting, the princess thought about the future czar. The love was born in her young heart. Alex recollected in her mind how delightful it was to dance with Nicholas.

Next morning, Nicholas asked Alex to go for a walk in the Winter Palace garden. She agreed and they adored each other's company. The weather was warm and pleasant. Stylish water fountains stood here and there, spraying water in sophisticated patterns. The carpets of red, pink, white, purple and yellow roses bloomed in geometrical patterns. The aromatic perfume of flowers and other plants created an unforgettable aroma in the garden. Nicholas cut seven red roses off with his silver knife, formed a stylish bouquet and gave them to Princess Alex.

'Thank you so much, dear Nicholas, they are wonderful,' she beamed.

'It's my pleasure, dear Princess,' and unexpectedly for both of them, they gave each other a gentle kiss.

The kiss was so sweet and tender. It was simply magical and they had butterflies. It was the first ever kiss for both of them. They walked back to the castle laughing.

'Look, Nicholas, your fingers are bleeding, you might have cut them by accident with that knife,' Alex said softly.

'I'm not very good at gardening,' he laughed and wiped his fingers with a white handkerchief. 'Seven roses and blood, what does it mean?' He thought it might be a warning from God, which he completely ignored.

Next day, Nicholas thought about Alex the entire day and made his mind up to write a love letter in English and invite her for a ballet performance in Mariinsky Theatre, thinking that it might be a fabulous experience for both of them.

Dearest Princess Alex,

Your sweet face is in my imagination continuously. I am simply unable to stop thinking about you.

I am fond of you, my beloved Alex. Please let me be your dearest friend constantly.

I'd love to invite you to the theatre today. There will be the entire society. With warmest wishes

Yours devotedly,
Nicholas

Alex was in her bedroom when the letter arrived. She opened it immediately. The two goldish-brown tickets were in the envelope. She read it again and again and a lovely smile appeared on her face. She felt a bit nervous and began to write her reply.

Dearest Nicholas,

I am truly delighted to receive a love letter from you. Exclusively, after the ball I suddenly realised that I have the warmest adoration towards you. I feel so happy in your wonderful company. Shall we write to each other regularly from now on? I do prefer to write in English. French is not the best in my opinion. It's easier for me to express myself in English and it could be our secret language, because not many people are able to read and write in it around us. I'd love to accept your invitation to the theatre. I will be there today to enjoy Swan Lake.

Yours devotedly,
Princess Alex

She put her stamp on it, folded the letter, put it in the envelope and asked it to be delivered promptly. When Alex's carriage slowed down in front of the Mariinsky Theatre, the well-dressed opulent public were already gathered in front of the building, talking about "Swan Lake" and Peter Ilyich Tchaikovsky. The building of the theatre stood grand and proud with an imposing front façade. Bright electric lights illuminated it in a magical way. Princess Alex gracefully came out of the carriage, wearing the latest fashion – a turquoise dress, an elegant hat and a tiny handbag. She was followed by her ladies-in-waiting and two bodyguards. Nicholas was wearing a white suit and looked truly imperial. Two bodyguards followed him constantly.

'Good evening, Princess Alex of Hesse by Rhine. Thank you kindly for accepting my invitation.'

'Good evening, Prince Nicholas of Russia and Poland. I am truly delighted to see you this evening.'

Together they entered the magnificent building in the first-class-only part. The carpet in the theatre was dark red. The bright chandeliers gave off a lot of light. They glided upstairs together towards their balcony and began to get ready for the performance. The theatre was bursting with people. The czar and czarina occupied an opposite balcony. The members of well-known aristocracy and well-to-do merchant families had the other balconies; the members of the middle-class occupied the multiple rows below.

The performance begun shortly, the music was magnificent, the stage was brightly lit. The fabulous, pretty professional ballet dancers pirouetted on a colourful and brightly lit stage, wearing beautiful dresses and jewellery. The point work was truly superb with imperial quality. Swan Lake was simply magical, exciting, provoking and disturbing. During an intermission, Nicholas ordered a bottle of champagne.

'I would like to raise a glass, for a long friendship and relationship between two nations,' Nicholas smiled.

'With greatest appreciation, I'd love to accept the union and friendship,' Alex agreed.

'Princess Alex, after your trip to Russia, are you planning to go back home to Germany?'

'No, Nicholas, I'm planning to visit Queen Victoria first,' she replied.

Shortly after the second part of the performance, they wished farewell and left the theatre in personal vehicles. Both Nicholas and Alexandra without realising it had fallen madly in love. Princess Alex departed Russia shortly; she was sure that her visit was quite successful despite the conversation with Queen Maria Feodorovna. Alex knew there would be something to talk about with Queen Victoria.

A few days after the visit to the theatre, Grand Duke Nicholas made his mind up to propose to Princess Alex, whenever they would see each other again.

Chapter 2
Grigori Rasputin

Grigori had been woken up by the running in and out of a toddler. It was already midday.

'Get out, Dmitry! I'm still asleep,' he shouted to the kid. He was annoyed because his sweet dreams had been interrupted. He put a pillow on top of his head. The child looked at his father and ran outside again. He was dreaming about royalty and talking to the czarina herself, but she looked kind of different.

'Rubbish, it's only a dream, I'll never be in the castle for real.' He tried to go to sleep again, but failed. He got up and walked out of their wooden bungalow in a quite large and stinky farmyard. His wife Praskovia was washing children's clothes with a slippery piece of brown soap. She was a strong, tall and broad Siberian woman. He would tell everyone that she could give birth without shouting.

She had a toddler and was already pregnant with another one. Grigori hated a lot of noise. Praskovia got up with the roosters today – collected eggs, milked the cow, pulled weeds out of their vegetable plot and fed the pigs.

'Do you want sex?' he asked his wife and walked towards her closer and closer.

'Get off me,' she laughed and pushed him away. 'You pervert, the neighbours are looking, go and clean up after the cow and the pigs, instead.'

Grigori was disappointed and walked towards the animal shed in total silence. He grabbed a shovel and started to clean the dung. The manure stunk and made him feel sick. He detested doing that.

I'd rather my wife does it instead of me, he thought and stopped breathing. *My life is trash; no sex, no sleep, a lot of manure, I'd rather go somewhere else and come back with the cash to pay somebody else to do it. I'll tell my wife that*

I received a message from God to become a monk. When he finished, Grigori slammed a door of the shed and stomped away.

He walked through a green field, the cows were grazing here and there. Pokrovskoe looked normal today, nothing out of the ordinary at all. Then he turned towards a little apple orchard and suddenly noticed a young peasant girl, about eighteen, picking the apples. Grigori recognised her straightaway; her name was Nina, she was a farmer's daughter. Her strong arms and pretty breasts attracted his attention. Grigori decided to use his hypnotic powers. He stared straight into her eyes. His dark eyes were large and powerful and she couldn't escape his gaze. Nina went into a stupor-like trance.

'Nina, you look pretty today,' he whispered quietly.

'No one ever called me pretty before,' she said slowly as if on drugs. Grigori grabbed a basket full of apples from her hands and put it on the ground in front of the birch tree and gave her a kiss.

'Do you know the story about Adam and Eve?' he asked, hugging her closer and closer.

'Yes,' she mumbled and he started to take her clothes off, making sure that no one was around.

'Here! Bite this apple for me.' The girl obeyed him. 'The story says who eats a fruit from a forbidden tree will be vice forever, you will be vice pretty soon.'

Grigori pushed her body against the tree. Finally, he managed to release his sexual energy. He left the girl where he found her. She couldn't even remember what happened to her and how she lost her virginity.

When he returned back home, Grigori was much happier. His wife told him that their neighbour Raisa Sobakina had an epileptic fit once more. Grigori walked slowly to the neighbour's house and found Raisa lying down on the floor, shaking all over. Calmly and quietly, Grigori walked around her and lifted her head into his huge hands and turned it on its side. Her lips were tight and blue. He had done the same with the body. Then he put three pillows around her head and began to talk.

'Raisa, can you hear me?' she mumbled. 'God tells me you will be fine soon.' He used his hypnotic powers to bring her back to reality, staring into her eyes. Gradually, she returned back to normal and begun to talk.

'I am thirsty,' she whispered. Everyone in her house were pleased to hear that. They gave Rasputin some money and thanked him with milk and eggs. Grigori was pleased and sprinted all the way home.

'It's much better to treat patients instead of cleaning poop.' He had definitely made up his mind.

Next morning, Grigori was up at five and started to pack his bags.

Praskovia opened her eyes.

'Are you going somewhere?' she asked him quietly.

'Yeah,' he said softly. 'I just had a dream.'

'What was your dream about?' she asked with interest.

'The Virgin Mary came to me in person. She had a halo on her head. She was wearing a yellow and red garment and had baby Jesus on her lap.'

'Wow bless! What did she say?'

'Go, Grigori, to the Znamensky Holy Monastery and stay there for a few months, praying to God asking for forgiveness. Your road will be clear and you will have no misfortune on your way.'

'God be with you,' whispered his wife, kissed him goodbye and he softly closed the door behind him.

Grigori took his favourite wooden walking stick, a huge backpack full of food and his husky dog named Alaska, mainly for protection and to hunt. When he began his journey, he decided to walk all the way through to the monastery, no matter how long it might take him. At first, he marched confidently through familiar fields and woodland. He knew the way very well. Tall, hundreds-of-years-old pine trees and birch trees stretched directly upwards; there were thousands of them in all directions. One almost certainly could get lost very easily without local knowledge. He had a strong body, and he checked every day how tough and resilient it was. Grigori made himself suffer from hunger and thirst on purpose. His 6-foot-tall body became thinner and thinner.

When his food ran out entirely, Grigori stopped occasionally to make a crackling bonfire and cook a fish he caught in a river or lake or to fry a juicy rabbit he shot with his bow and arrow. For months on end, he hadn't seen a single soul. All of a sudden, Grigori thought he was dreaming. He spotted a large gathering of people around an enormous bonfire. The sounds of drums filled up the air. The members of the group were totally naked, they walked around the fire, all in a hypnotic trance and on drugs. Rasputin dropped his bags by the tree and joined in. It was true freedom. He had never experienced anything like this before. When all of them were in a stupor of trance, including Rasputin, they began to have sex with each other. Each man chose a girl he liked. When they reached ecstasy, they swapped partners and again and again and again, until they became one by one able to achieve a state of euphoria. It was stronger than an ordinary orgasm and only monks or shamans were able to do that.

'What a beautiful bliss, no sin, no repentance,' Rasputin said with a huge smile on his face.

In a few days, he left the sect and continued peacefully on his way forward towards the monastery, but he never forgot the forbidden Siberian sect and achieving euphoria there. At night, because of the wild animals – wolves, tigers and leopards – he made a blazing fire in a field and hung a hammock over a branch of a fir tree. His dog was beside him constantly when he slept, barking and distracting the wildlife. The wolves howled every night, but he ignored them and prayed. He prayed to God to be safe and sound, reaching the abbey. In three exhausting months, he arrived at the monastery. His tall figure looked even taller, because he had become so malnourished.

Grigori rang the doorbell, pulling a string. A loud, reverberating sound spread all over the quiet convent. Nobody answered the door for a long time; he was so exhausted. Grigori pulled the string again and again and finally a short monk in a black robe answered the door. Grigori put his bags down and prepared to talk. He knew at once that it would be wise to use his hypnotic power, because his story sounded a bit absurd even to himself. When the man opened the door, he stared at him for quite a while, using his power.

'Hello, Father Superior!' he said finally. 'My name is Father Grigori'

'Hello, Father Grigori, I am Father Peter. Father Superior is away tonight,' he replied.

'I was sent here by Virgin Mary. She came to me in my dream,' Rasputin responded.

The monk was trying to digest the information; because he was under a trance, his thoughts were confused and slow.

'Please, come in,' he said finally, stretching the words. 'I was waiting for you for three weeks in a row. Jesus told me about your arrival in my dream.'

'God bless your soul,' Rasputin growled as they walked along the corridor towards the monks' quarters.

'Please take this room, Father Grigori,' Father Peter said, pointing to a very basic private room with a single bed, rough wooden table, old chair, tiny stove and brown wooden box to keep his clothes in. It was basic even for a peasant like him, but he was pleased regardless.

'It's nice,' he just replied.

'You can keep your dog with you in your room, if you like,' he said kindly. The bright scars from the burns covered his face.

'Cheers, it's very kind of you,' Grigori mumbled. He dropped all his bags in the room.

'You look rather tired, Father Grigori, please come with me together with your dog.'

They walked slowly towards the kitchen, through a long corridor. The kitchen felt so warm and welcoming with a blazing fire in a fireplace. A long scratched wooden table stood straight in the middle of it and two benches alongside it for the monks to sit on and eat. A row of icons hung above the table for the men to pray. Father Peter dropped two ladles of the warm and steamy porridge for Grigori and gave him a wooden spoon.

'Bless your soul,' Grigori thanked him and began to eat, as if he never had before.

Then he gave two ladles of the same porridge to the dog. Grigori thanked Peter and carried on eating. Alaska copied the master, making loud slurping sounds. Rasputin slept very well in the convent, without fear of being eaten by wolves. The dog kept him warm through the night.

The day in the monastery began at five. The annoying, loud bell woke them up in the morning. Then, after washing with freezing water, they all went outside and ran around the entire building in a large circle, five times, in order to keep fit. Next, there was a morning prayer in a little chapel until eight. After that, it was time for breakfast. The monks served themselves a bit of rice porridge with a blob of raspberry jam and sat down around the wooden table to eat. The blazing fire kept them warm.

'Are you a new arrival?' Father Superior asked after a little prayer.

All eyes looked directly at Rasputin.

'My name is Father Grigori. I did arrive yesterday. I was sent here by Virgin Mary. She came to me in my dream and asked me to go to Znamensky Holy Monastery to pray and ask God for his forgiveness.'

All the monks seemed to take it very seriously. They looked at each other a few times with a kind of acceptance. He couldn't believe his eyes. Grigori didn't even need to use his power.

'No drinks, no meat, no sex, work and pray every day. If you're caught, you will be out.' Father Superior stared at him.

'Sure, can I keep my dog in my room?' he asked just in case.

'Yes, of course, no problem.'

Grigori was very pleased.

Soon after breakfast, all monks worked in the garden, pulling weeds from the vegetable patches. It was easy for Grigori, he knew it very well. Then it was time for reading and prayer, until two o'clock. In the library, a number of monks took their chosen books outside to read, a quarter came back to their rooms and a third of them stayed in the library. Father Peter decided to be in the library. He grabbed a blue Bible to read. Grigori copied his behaviour, but he didn't read it, just flicked through the pages.

'Why are you not reading the Bible?' Father Peter asked in a high-pitched voice.

'You know, a long time ago, I fell off a horse, hurt my head and since then I have lost my memory, so I can't read any more,' he lied and showed him a large scar on the back of his head to prove it. Grigori didn't want to admit to anyone in this place that he was just an illiterate peasant from Pokrovskoe.

'How peculiar, this is wicked, because I lost my memory of my family after a fire in my old private estate.' Father Peter showed him his burns.

'Poor, poor you. With God's help, I will help you to restore your memory. I have done that before,' Grigori said with great confidence.

'Certainly, yes please, it would be marvellous. I will teach you to read and write again, if you wish,' and they began immediately. Peter showed him an alphabet and explained about phonics. Then he gave him homework for the following day. There was no one in the library at this precise point. Risking being noticed, Grigori put Peter in a deep hypnotic trance.

'What is your name?' Peter's round eyes rolled from side to side.

'Count Paul Vronsky,' he answered in a sleepy voice.

'Do you remember what happened to you yesterday?' Grigori asked and Peter's eyes rolled from side to side once again.

'I spent a day in a convent with monks and met a new arrival, Father Grigori,' he replied.

'God speaks from my head. Your memory is returning to you. What happened the night before the fire?' Peter's eyes rolled up.

'I don't remember it.'

'Tell me, what did you do in the morning, before the fire?'

'I remember riding a horse with my five-year-old daughter, Sophia. She had learned so much. Sophia was adorable, smiling and talking non- stop.'

'Great, what happened next?'

Peter's eyes rolled up and up.

'I remember getting ready for a ball and I recollect giving orders to my servants.' Then he stopped.

'Go on, what's next?' Silence followed.

'The guests arrived and we had a lovely ball. There were about twenty people staying overnight. I woke up at 2 pm. The screaming was unbearable. The impenetrable smoke filled the air and the bright flickering fire was around me. I tried to locate my wife and my daughter, but I couldn't find them anywhere at all. I yelled their names, but there was no response. I remember saving five people through the window, using tied-up sheets. After that, it's only darkness. Most of all, I would like to find out what happened to Sophia and Margaret.' His face became sweaty and his breathing increased. Then he fell asleep.

'Peter, wake up, wake up, it's time to go for a meal,' Grigori said firmly and Peter awoke without any recollection about what had just happened to him.

The dinner was much better than breakfast. They had Greek salad, vegetarian borsch and apples. Grigori remembered his wife's pork chops and it made him a bit homesick. Peter behaved as if nothing had happened. After dinner, the monks were free to do what they liked inside the monastery. Grigori decided to talk to Father Superior.

'Can I talk to you about something in private?' he asked, when Peter walked out of the door.

'Of course you can,' he said quietly. 'Let's go to my private quarters.'

His room was a little bit better furnished than the rest of them, but still on the plain side. The monk made two hot cups of coffee: one for him and one for Grigori. Grigori had never had a coffee before, because it was too expensive for him.

'It's Father Peter I would like to talk to you about,' he said, looking at the floor.

'His behaviour has changed so much since your arrival. I don't know what you have done, but it's a true miracle. The fact that he can talk to you so easily, without concentrating on the past.'

'We were talking like friends, he told me a little bit about the fire, but he still doesn't remember all of it. Jesus tells me that his memory will come back in three or four months.'

Father Superior was surprised to hear that.

'You can carry on talking to him about the fire; you both can use the room from the library on the left to be more private.'

That suited Father Grigori very well. Now he could carry on his hypnotic sessions and learn how to read and write without prying eyes.

'Father Superior, I know very little about this fire. How did they rescue him?' he said, drinking coffee.

'When he lost his consciousness from the smoke, rescuing the people, his butler put him on his back. It's good he wasn't heavy, he managed to go all the way down to the ground using the rope made of sheets.'

'What about his wife and his child? Were they rescued too?'

'No, they both perished. We couldn't tell him, we were scared that he would go back to hysteria, anger and panic attacks.'

Grigori thought that it would be better to tell Peter the truth, but he didn't want to argue with Father Superior; he made his mind up to tell them when he was ready.

'What happened to his villa?' he asked instead.

'It burned to the ground. Ash and stones were all that were left after the fire. Would you like to have a look?' And he gave him a piece of paper with an address written on it. Obviously, Rasputin couldn't read it. He took it regardless.

'I'm going to visit that place,' he replied.

'When he arrived here after the fire, he was really poorly. His relatives didn't want him to be in a mental asylum, instead they decided to keep him in brotherhood. I think it was the right decision.' A couple of tears appeared on his face.

They finished their coffee and Grigori went into his room, thinking about Father Peter. The dinner was at seven and sleep time at eleven.

In the morning, they had a writing lesson and Rasputin put Peter in a trance again, in order to improve his memory. After dinner, Grigori took the last coins he had saved for later and decided to spend it on a cab to go to Peter's estate. He showed a piece of paper with an address on it to the driver and asked him to go there and back.

'The master's house has burned down. Why are you going there?' the driver asked with surprise in his voice.

'I'm going to pray for your master,' he answered shortly. They were both silent all the way there and back.

When Grigori walked around the ruins, it was depressing to look at. The walls were black, the roof fallen down and grey ash was all over the place. Father Grigori knelt and prayed to God.

After six months being in the monastery, Grigori had learned how to read and write, thanks to Father Peter. They became great friends. Gradually, the memory returned to Father Peter.

One sunny day, they had been learning writing, when Grigori noticed something heavy bulging out of Peter's pocket.

'What is in your pocket, bulging out? It looks quite heavy,' he asked his friend.

'It's a bottle of an expensive cognac. My auntie purchased it for me in France, in case I become totally desperate,' he laughed.

'Share,' Grigori beamed.

Peter poured out the golden liquid of the bottle into two glasses, one for him and one for Grigori.

'For the future and for our friendship,' he exclaimed. The glasses clinked and the men drank the whole bottle in one sitting The cognac was outstanding and they had so much fun.

'Do you know, Peter, your memories are returning to you because you had remembered where you left the cognac. They laughed.

'I do remember that night without doubt,' and he told him everything he knew about it.

Grigori pretended that he was hearing it for the first time in his life.

'When, I arrived in this monastery, after the fire, I had hysteria and panic attacks. I wanted to kill myself at one point.'

'What would you do, Peter, if I tell you the truth about your wife and your kid?' Rasputin asked seriously.

'In any case, I will try to build my life from scratch and I will not go crazy,' he said honestly.

'Well, they are with the angels,' he replied softly.

Peter burst into tears and shortly stopped.

'Thanks for letting me know. Now I am going to my property in St Petersburg and will try to build a new life. You're welcome there at any time. Here is my business card. You can read it without doubt.' They laughed.

Grigori left the monastery shortly after Peter. Father Superior wrote him an outstanding review.

Chapter 3
The Future Czar and His Mistress Matilda Kshesinskaya

Every week, for a couple of years, Nicholas Romanov visited and participated in army training. His training took place in an exercise battlefield. The soldiers ran, jumped and exercised for a warm-up and had gunfire drills as a main bit. He wasn't too bad at shooting, but disliked the training in general although he couldn't avoid it, because it was the emperor's order. About fifty, full-of-testosterone, sweaty boys ran around the field in military uniforms, thinking about girls. The lads were aged between eighteen and twenty-five. The boys were from all walks of life, mostly local youngsters.

'Have you ever had a girlfriend, guys?' Maxim Sokolov asked in the changing room.

'Yeah,' most of them replied and some answered, 'no'. Nicholas was silent.

'What about you, royal boy? You probably had a lot of ladies already?'

All the boys burst into laughter, including Nicholas.

'No, I'm still a virgin,' he replied and boys bellowed with laughter once more.

'How old are you?' Sokolov asked.

'I am 22,' Nicholas answered. 'I'm looking for one, honestly,' he lied. They guffawed even more.

After this funny story, Nicholas thought that it might be a lovely idea to find a mistress after all, before marriage. However, he did not wish to search for one on purpose; only if it happened naturally between them both. On the way home, from the window of his carriage he looked at the stunning girls of Petersburg and thought that his girlfriend must be the most beautiful girl in Russia.

A few months passed. The Romanov's family, including the Emperor, received an invitation to the Mariinsky Theatre for the ballet school final examination. The entire family decided to accept.

A panel of five judges was placed beside the stage. The stage was brightly lit. The Romanovs were seated in the first three rows and the students and their teachers behind them. There were no members of the public. The future ballerinas appeared one by one and performed their prepared examination piece. Each of them was given a score of their performance and the girl with the highest score would have a medal and a job at the Royal Mariinsky Theatre itself. All of the ballerinas were wonderful. They worked hard through their entire childhood, but the girl who stood out most was Matilda Kshesinskaya. She was magnificent. Nicholas couldn't stop looking at her. Her technique was outstanding. She received the top mark and a shiny medal. The small audience stood up, clapping. Nicholas walked onto the stage and shook her delicate hand.

'Congratulations, Matilda! You will be the glory of the Royal Ballet.'

'I'm so honoured, thank you so much Your Royal Highness!'

Their eyes met for the first time. A radiant smile was on Matilda's magnificent face. Nicholas realised that he must be first with his compliments, otherwise some of the male members of the Romanov family would almost certainly be interested in such a glorious star.

After this performance, the heir to the throne invited Matilda for a luxury dinner in the most affluent restaurant in St Petersburg. She accepted his invitation without a second thought. Nicholas had never experienced it before and was a bit anxious and excited. He was in the restaurant fifteen minutes prior. He was wearing a navy suit and looked stately royal. When Matilda arrived, she looked glamorous. She was wearing a white dress with pearls, white gloves and a delicate hat with feathers. A cylinder-shaped white handbag was in her hand.

'Hello, Madam Kshesinskaya,' he kissed her hand. 'You look even more magnificent than this morning. Please sit down and share a meal with your royal friend.'

'I'll be truly delighted to share this dinner with you, Nicholas, and I'll keep it in my memory for the rest of my life. It's like a fairy tale.'

'It's a fairy-tale dream, just for the two of us. Please accept a tiny gift from me, my little "K" and a perfect ballerina.' Nicholas presented a wrapped-up little pink box in front of Matilda. The girl smiled and opened the box. She pulled out an expensive pink pearls and diamond necklace. It sparkled majestically in the candlelight.

'I'm so honoured to receive it. Nicholas, you are spoiling me.'

'Would you like to try it on, Matilda? It will complement your outfit perfectly, I presume,' he inquired.

'I'd love to, it would be marvellous.'

Nicholas stood up and connected it gently on her neck, Matilda stood up and pirouetted in front of the mirror, beside Nicholas. The jewellery sparkled majestically with diamonds and pearls.

'Wearing this necklace, Nicholas, I am the most beautiful 18-year-old in St Petersburg,' she beamed.

'You are the most beautiful ballerina in Russia or even the world, Matilda. You look simply superb. For our unique friendship and a real fairy tale.' Two crystal glasses were raised with champagne.

'For fairy tale forever,' Matilda answered and sipped her champagne.

'Tell me a little bit about your life, Matilda, it's perhaps more exciting than mine,' Nicholas asked while eating his starter.

'My dear father just bought me a perfect house for graduation, he is so proud of me, all my hard work has paid off. Please tell me about your life, Your Highness, it must be simply superb.'

'My life is challenging at times. Sometimes, I wish I wasn't born royal, I'd rather have a life of an aristocratic person like you, I would have had more freedom.' Matilda was surprised to hear that.

'I wish I was a princess,' Matilda giggled.

Rather soon, Nicholas and Matilda finished their dinner and two bottles of champagne.

'Would you like me to order you a carriage?' Nicolas asked Matilda.

'Perhaps I had too much champagne, but I'd like to invite you in my house, for a coffee, Your Highness. What do you think about my idea?'

'I simply love it.' Matilda's invitation was a marvellous surprise for Nicholas. 'Would you like to go in my royal carriage? It's waiting outside.'

'Of course, Nicholas, I'll be delighted.'

The bill was paid, too young souls sat opposite one another near the bright window of the royal carriage, holding hands and looking straight into each other's eyes, their lips touched gently and the powerful feeling of love penetrated through their bodies. They gave each other a kiss. The first proper kiss for both of them. The powerful burst of adrenaline went through their young souls. Matilda wasn't shy or stupid and she made that decision consciously. She was an adult and a confident one.

'I love you, Nicholas,' Matilda whispered quietly in his ear.

'I love you too, my perfect "little K".'

The carriage went past the Winter Palace, turned left and stopped shortly in front of Matilda's house.

'What a pretty house. We are almost neighbours. It even has modern electric lights,' Nicholas commented when they stopped in front of a security gate. After a short conversation with a security officer, the carriage passed through and they ended up by the front door. The front door was opened wide by Matilda's butler. Nicholas and Matilda walked into a spacious reception area with a delicate set of marble stairs, large windows, pictures by Rembrandt and golden chandeliers.

'It's good enough for royalty,' Nicholas laughed.

'Thank you for the compliments, Your Highness, I'm truly delighted that you like my new home.' Matilda smiled and asked her butler to bring two coffees and cakes. Then she gave His Royal Highness a tour around the house.

At first, she showed the sitting room, dining room, drawing room, professional ballet studio and a library downstairs and then eight guest bedrooms upstairs, finishing in her own bedroom. The room was very modern, in a Victorian style. It had a four-poster bed, two dressing tables, a little table with two armchairs, a walk-in wardrobe and a luxury bathroom.

'Would you like to stay overnight, Your Royal Highness?' she whispered in his ear.

'I would be delighted,' Nicholas whispered and she locked the door.

From that moment, the entire world belonged only to the two of them. At first, Nicholas thought that he might be shy, but he wasn't. It was so natural. They embraced and kissed each other again and again, passionately with trepidation, gradually removing each other's clothes. Nicholas realised that Matilda was breath-taking when she was wearing glamorous dresses; however, he understood that her body was human perfection when she was without them. She stood in front of Nicholas naked, like a Greek goddess of love. Matilda was thrilled to bits that she was going to lose her innocence with the heir to the throne and he was so handsome. Gently, Nicholas entered a cave of wonders. They discovered each other's bodies in a way they had never experienced before, like two young acrobats, changing positions again and again and again. They managed to reach multiple orgasms. On that night, they both thought that they were the happiest couple on earth. They stayed awake until sunrise.

'Matilda my love, would you like to become my mistress?' Nicholas asked and kissed her.

'Of course, I would be delighted. I will tell all my friends that my boyfriend is Nicholas Romanov, how charming is that?' And she squeaked in delight. 'The only problem is that we can't get married, I'm not a princess.'

In a few days, Matilda organised a sleepover party with all her ballet friends, including Pavlova, in her new house. Matilda was one of the richest girls out of them all so far. She was really proud and her popularity grew bigger and bigger. At first, they had endless amounts of food. The long table was served with a buffet. The table was full of exotic food and tons of cakes and ice cream. The girls were eager to try everything. They had boundless amounts of alcohol during the party, whatever they wished. The teenage girls were really pleased and wanted to try everything.

'Nicholas Romanov is my boyfriend; can you imagine that?' Matilda smiled.

'Unbelievable. How did you manage to achieve it?' one of the girls replied.

'The main thing is, don't be scared and you can do anything in your life.'

'Did you enjoy the physical connection?' Pavlova asked with interest.

'It was fantastic,' and everyone laughed.

'I'm engaged to the second-in-line in the Dutch royal family, we may get married in autumn,' the stunning blonde girl with large blue eyes pointed in a pompous way.

'I always thought you would be quite successful, my darling. Your parents are so wealthy,' Matilda answered in an intriguing way.

'Matilda, sweetheart, please coach me in ballet, you are a superstar,' Anna Pavlova asked with a sweet smile.

'Of course I can, anything you like today. Would you like more champagne?'

The girls giggled loudly.

'Thank you, thank you, Matilda. I'll be your best friend forever,' Anna Pavlova laughed.

The party lasted until morning. The house was turned upside down. The girls, especially Matilda, had a lot of fun.

A few months past, Matilda coached Anna Pavlova for the role of Nickya in La Bayadere in her private studio. This performance was scheduled for May. The tickets were all sold out. Matilda thought that a not very strong ballerina like Anna would not upstage her and agreed to coach. Anna worked really hard; she spent a considerable amount of time training. The theatre was totally filled up during their performance. The public loved Anna more and a new ballet star, Anna Pavlova, was born. After this performance, Matilda was sure that she would never teach Anna again and they became distant friends.

One day in the beginning of winter, when roads were especially icy, the phone rang continuously in Nicholas's bedroom. He lifted the phone up and talked to the person. It was Matilda's butler.

'Matilda's sledge overturned on the way to the theatre and she's in pain,' he shouted.

Nicholas rushed into her house and found her sleeping in bed. He sat down beside her in an armchair and began to wait. When she awoke, she saw Nicholas and smiled.

'Nicholas, dearest, I'm so delighted to see you.'

'What's happened with my poor little K?' he asked and kissed her.

'My sledge overturned and I lost your baby.'

'It doesn't matter, the main thing is you are alive.'

In a couple of weeks, Matilda recovered from her injury. Nicholas spent almost all his time by her side.

For about a year, the relationship between Nicholas and Matilda continued without any complications. The private collection of jewellery from Nicholas grew bigger and bigger. Matilda received golden bracelets with rubies, diamond earrings, pearl necklaces and diamond chokers. Matilda always performed on stage, her glorious ballet performances, wearing real jewellery. They went out in public together and showed the society that they were together. Nicholas took Matilda to theatres, boutiques, the jewellery shops and royal balls at the Winter Palace. His parents, however, were icy cold about their relationship.

'Be careful, son, do not create a scandal please,' Alexander III warned him in private.

Nicholas was not amused about that. In contrast, Nicholas invited Matilda to the palace the next day. The entire society was present there. Everyone was waiting on what's going to happen next, because people love gossiping about latest news and drama.

Grand Duke Andre Vladimirovich, Nicholas's first cousin, was openly and passionately talking to Matilda about something. They were both engaged in conversation, so passionately, as if they were in love or a married couple. Nicholas was irritated and decided to talk to his cousin in private.

'Matilda and I are still a couple,' he said to Andre.

'We'll see about that,' he replied coldly and walked away.

It became apparent to Nicholas that there was something serious between Matilda and Andre. Nicholas returned to the room, stared coldly at Matilda and poured himself a shot of vodka.

'Do you know, Your Highness, that Madam Kshesinskaya is in a relationship with Grand Duke Sergei?' Countess Suvorova informed him. 'They were seen together in public.'

'Do you mean with my cousin Andre?' he asked in surprise.

'Yes, with them both,' she replied, 'I'm afraid.'

Nicholas was terribly cross and drank his shot of vodka. He walked towards Matilda and interrupted their conversation in a forceful way.

'Matilda, there is something seriously wrong. Let's go in your room and discuss it in private together.'

He was so forceful that she could not dare to deny his request. She said goodbye to Andre and they both marched out of the room. Nicholas was furious. They walked into Matilda's library and stood opposite each other.

'Can you be honest to one man? It's a scandal! I'm breaking up with you.'

'It's my choice to sleep with one man or all of Petersburg,' she answered coldly. 'Nicholas, I am with child again.'

He was surprised to hear that. 'Could I be the child's father?' he only asked.

'I'm not entirely sure who it is out of three. The baby will have triple HRH title.'

'Matilda, why didn't you tell me earlier?'

'Because it started not long ago.'

'How are we going to solve this problem?' he said in a deep voice.

'Don't worry, I'm engaged to Grand Duke Andre, already,' she sighed, 'although I am in love with Sergei and going to carry on the relationships with them both. Sergei and I are going on holiday on Thursday to Venice, Paris and Rome. Nicholas, it's impossible for us to get married, so I have to build my life with other people. Please do understand that.'

'When you marry him, we can remain distant friends. I grew up with Andre and don't desire to become enemies because of this situation. By marrying you, he saves me from trouble. I'd like to look at the baby when he or she is born. Goodbye, Matilda. We had a great time.'

He walked away without looking at her and slammed the door behind him. Nicholas was truly saddened. He decided to walk and send his carriage away. He wandered endlessly through the snowy streets of St Petersburg without any purpose at all. The deep snow was on the ground. He had mixed feelings whether this child could be his after all. It suddenly became very cold. Nicholas couldn't bear it any longer and decided to visit Elizabeth and Andre. They were both at home.

'What's wrong, Nicholas? You look so gloomy. Would you like a drink?' Andre asked in a friendly way.

'Some vodka, please,' he answered shortly. He told them almost everything – excluding the subject of the baby – about what had just happened to him.

'Don't worry, mate,' Andre said in a friendly manner. 'Everything will be different in a few days.'

'I will talk to Alex to accept your proposal,' Elizabeth added softly with a tiny smile on her face.

'Thank you both, you are my real friends. I feel much better now.'

'It's my pleasure,' Elizabeth responded in her angelic voice.

'I do not like sharing Matilda with anyone else. She can be with two of them or just me only. There is no other option.'

'Now you can see it so well what's right or wrong. The mighty God opened your eyes,' Andre replied.

'Well, it's getting late.' He looked at his watch.

'I'll take you home in my carriage,' Andre promised and they both walked outside into a snow storm.

When Nicholas arrived back at the castle, he was a bit drunk and tired.

'What's wrong, son? You look like a thundery cloud,' the queen stopped him.

'Nothing,' he replied with a deep sigh.

'You must stop this relationship; Matilda is with child,' the queen said in a serious voice.

'Do you know about the baby already? That was prompt.'

'The entire capital has been informed, it's not a secret. How are you going to solve this problem?'

'The problem has been solved, ma'am. She is engaged.'

'Who's the lucky candidate?'

'My cousin Andre,' he said quietly.

'Great news, Nikki, I suppose,' the queen smiled.

'Yes, it undeniably is.' They gave each other a hug.

'Nicholas, have you been writing to Princess Alex?'

'For about a year, Mum.'

'I'm delighted to hear that. Good night, son, you are dismissed.'

It was a difficult day for Nicholas, yet a feeling of anxiety remained in his heart.

A couple of weeks later, Nicholas received an invitation to one of his relative's wedding reception. He was delighted and decided to be there.

The wedding took place in a small chapel in the outskirts of the city. There were only two hundred guests invited. It was quite small by royal standards. The bride looked wonderful in her white dress with pearls, a bouquet of pink roses and a stylish veil. The groom looked glamorous in black. The wedding day was lovely. All guests were talking about the bride and groom. Unexpectedly, Nicholas noticed Matilda among the guests. She was all in lilac, and on her neck she was wearing a pink pearl and diamond necklace. Nicholas recognised it immediately and a great big smile appeared on his face. After the ceremony and wedding breakfast, there was a moment when they stood alone in one of the corridors.

'I'm glad to see you, Madame Kshesinskaya,' he gave a tiny smile.

'It's lovely to see you, Your Royal Highness,' she gave a courtesy and looked at him.

'You look wonderful, as usual. This necklace suits you. When are you going to have your wedding day with Grand Duke Andre?' he asked with interest.

'Unfortunately, we can't get permission from the Emperor yet. As soon as it occurs, I'll inform everyone,' she sighed deeply.

'I am sorry to hear that. Hopefully it will happen soon.'

'I hope so, the baby will be born in July.'

'Matilda, sorry for making a scene,' he sighed.

'Sorry for everything,' and they gave each other a friendly hug. 'I can see a tear in your eye; but you never cry.'

'No, it's just one tear.'

They walked slowly towards people dancing and enjoying the wedding. It put a nice final stop to their relationship and Nicholas didn't feel anxious any longer.

Matilda's baby was born in July. His name was Prince Vladimir.

Matilda was delighted to look after him.

'Look, he's so pretty and strong,' she laughed. 'A real triple royal.'

The boy never knew for sure who his father truly was.

Chapter 4
Grigori Rasputin and His Prediction

When Rasputin left the Znamensky Monastery, he was glad that everything went according to plan. He even managed to make a good friendship and now he had somewhere to stay in Petersburg. This fact on its own made him thrilled to bits. The only problem was, at this point, he had no cash. Rasputin was on a hunt.

Good for Rasputin, healthcare in Russia was appalling. The people of the country relied upon the old-fashioned way: the healers, monks, shamans, church leaders, midwives or just knowledgeable elderly ladies. The people gave each other help and advice by word of mouth whom to invite on their property when they become ill. Nobody seemed to do anything about it, especially Alexander III.

Rasputin wandered through the streets of the local town for a while, until he reached the wooden building of an orthodox church. A lonely, thin-looking priest in light brown robes was reading a christening book when Rasputin came in. Multiple candles were lit up in the church, but there were no people in the building. The priest ignored him. Rasputin coughed.

'My name is Father Grigori, God be with you. I am here on a mission to help the poor and poorly of your neighbourhood,' and he bowed deeply and courteously.

'Hello, Father Grigori, God be with you. I am Father Ivan. Come and share dinner with me and I'll give you some information.' They shared a simple meal: milk, bread, butter and eggs. Grigori told him about his visit to the monastery. The priest seemed to believe him. Father Ivan gave him a list of addresses of people who needed help. There were ten of them in total; luckily Rasputin was now able to read.

The first patient was an elderly gran. She was lying down in bed, shaking all over and looked really ill. Rasputin made eye contact with the patient and put her under a hypnotic trance.

'God speaks through my head. Relax, relax, relax,' and he lifted his arm up, releasing the energy, calming her down. In half an hour, she was considerably calmer, her shaking reduced and she began to talk.

'God bless you, son; I haven't felt this good for years,' she said to Rasputin.

Her family was very happy. Despite being quite poor, they gave him money and food. There were about ten people in a two-bedroom bungalow, all members of the extended family of the grandmother.

The second patient was a 19-year-old girl in labour. She had been in labour for nearly three days. The midwife was there, but she couldn't do much. The girl was in agony.

'I'm glad you came, Father Grigori. Her baby is stuck. I don't know what to do.'

'Did you give her any drugs?'

'She had a tiny bit of morphine a long time ago and it isn't helping anymore.'

'The baby is nearly out. She must sit in a squatting position and push. I will try to reduce her pain.' When the girl was in that position, he placed both of his hands on the girl's back.

'With God's help. Your pain is going away. Push, push, push.' The girl stopped yelling and paid attention to them both and with the last scream, her baby was born. Everyone was pleased. The midwife attended the baby.

'It's a nice healthy baby boy.'

Rasputin was paid very generously. It was the largest amount of money he had ever received. He was absolutely sure that he had healing power. People started to talk about him as a healer. One by one, he visited all his patients, except one.

The last patient was a young wealthy lady who wanted to commit suicide after her husband died. She lived in a townhouse and had a personal servant. Rasputin went upstairs to her bedroom. The lady was crying when he came in. Rasputin found her quite appealing. He hadn't had sex for a long time. He locked the door behind him when he came in. He kneeled down beside her and begun asking questions and putting her in a hypnotic trance.

'You look pretty! What's wrong? My name is Father Grigori. I'm here to help.'

'My life is over. I don't want to be around without him,' she sobbed.

'God says to me that you need to find a new husband. Don't cry and be strong.'

Very slowly, her sobs subsided and Rasputin kissed her. He put his arms around her body and they began the process. The girl seemed to be unaware of what was going on, but she kind of liked it. Suddenly, Rasputin heard something, perhaps the door shut.

His intuition was never wrong. After he reached satisfaction, he slowly crept out of the room and came downstairs. The front door was locked. He unlocked the window on time and climbed out. Grigori untangled a knot in the lead of his dog and began to walk away. At this moment in time, a not very tall policeman appeared in front of him, together with the house servant. He probably had guessed what was going on and called the police.

'Father Grigori, I'm arresting you on suspicion of rape,' the policeman shouted.

Rasputin set his dog on him and ran away. Luckily, all his belongings were with him at that moment. Unexpectedly, he appeared in front of the train station at the moment the train was about to depart. He jumped in, panting.

'Do you have a ticket?' a train assistant asked him.

'No, no, no. What is the name of the station, two stops from now? I forgot.'

The assistant answered him in his squeaky voice.

'I want to have a ticket to that stop.' When he bought a ticket, he sat down, stopped panting and relaxed.

Rasputin knew that the train was going in the direction of St Petersburg. His fame as a healer was increasing rapidly and he was sure that he would never be hungry again. Grigori's negative reputation, however, as a rapist was following behind him. Just in case, he changed his appearance in the train's toilet. He looked now exactly like a shaman.

Soon, he arrived at his destination, the night almost finished. The beautiful red sunrise appeared in the sky. He had a sleep on the train and appeared fully rested. Rasputin wandered through the streets of the empty village, together with his dog. In a couple of hours, people appeared on the streets and his appearance attracted their attention.

'Are you a real shaman?' children asked with open mouths.

'Yes, I am. I was sent by God into your village to give you all future prophecies.' Rasputin had some knowledge about shamanism. He had some experience when he was a boy. He knew exactly how to run the service. The children brought some adults with them, who were interested.

'Come altogether at sunset to the large field over there and bring a bucket of water, an item of food, a stone and a stick. God will give predictions using my voice.'

Meanwhile, he collected an enormous pile of wood for a bonfire. When the evening began, a large crowd of people gathered on the field nearby. Rasputin started a gigantic bonfire, and began to play a drum. The blazing fire became brighter and brighter.

'Build a huge circle around the bonfire with your stones.' They obeyed him. 'Build a circle around the stones, hold hands and walk around listening to the drum.' The drum sounded monotonous and people started to feel drowsy. Rasputin set some herbs on fire as well. 'Take your sticks and set them on fire and walk around with them. Throw them in the fire. Take a bucket of water and pour it in the fire.'

The fire wasn't bright any longer and tall, white smoke rose into the sky.

'Leave an item of food to sacrifice to God and keep walking around.'

The drum got louder and louder. People were under a trance or spell.

Suddenly, Rasputin begun to speak with a different voice. 'There will be First World War and revolution and all of you, standing here, including Father Grigori will be dead. Millions of people will perish and Russia will be in crisis. Let everyone know. Father Grigori must find his way to St Nicholas Monastery.'

The deep voice stopped. Rasputin lost consciousness. People looked at him in disbelief and fear. Everyone thought that it was the voice of God and all of them had been ghosts. A deep fear went through their souls. No one out of those people checked up on Rasputin; they were all frightened of him. His dog Alaska licked his face. Rasputin opened his eyes and stood up. His memory was temporarily distorted. People began to walk away in fear and Father Grigori was standing alone in front of the intense fire.

'That was strong,' exclaimed a teenage boy behind him, making him jump. 'Can you teach me? I love strong stuff like that.'

Rasputin turned around and looked at him. He was a tall, good-looking lad, about 18.

'Do you know where St Nicolas Monastery is?'

'Yeah I do.'

'Show me the way and I'll teach you,' he promised. 'What's your name?'

'Stepan, I am from this village, from a peasant family. I want to be a shaman or a monk and I will follow you.'

Rasputin was amazed to have a follower.

When the fire was no longer burning, Rasputin changed his shaman's outfit into a black robe of an ordinary monk, grabbed all his belongings and both men and a dog began to walk towards the monastery. They made their mind up to walk almost all the way there. Rasputin loved walking along the road; tall ancient trees surrounded them on both sides, the birds sung high-pitched tweets, the wild animals hooted and barked, here and there, it was so surreal and tranquil. At those points, Grigori thought that he was close to God.

In a few hours, they reached another village. In the middle of the village was a little market. They bought bread, milk and pancakes and sat down to have a picnic beside the tree. An elderly man with a long beard stood beside the wall. He overheard their conversation and asked whether he could join in and walk with them all the way to the monastery.

'The more the merrier,' croaked Rasputin. 'Only we walk fast.'

Now he had two followers. His group was growing fast. They stayed overnight on the field by the lake. The night was warm and quiet. In the morning, all refreshed and with new strength, the three men walked towards a local town. Alaska ran ahead, wagging his tail. The enormous fields of sunflowers, wheat and oats stretched in all directions. So, with God's help, they reached the town. It was a small town with a mine. Right on the outskirts of it, they met a homeless person. He asked whether he could join their party.

''Course you can. We are going to share our food with you,' Rasputin promised. There were four of them, walking along the dusty streets now. In a few yards, they saw a tavern.

'Guys, do you want to have a pint and food?' he asked loudly. 'I haven't had a beer in ages.'

They all approved and came into the small, shabby, stinking-of-beer place with dark brown walls. About twenty people were already there, half-drunk and very loud. Rasputin ordered bangers and mash for all his companions and two or three pints of beer each. He never paid for anybody in his life in a pub before. He couldn't afford it. Always folks bought him a drink in the bar. He was very proud, at last, to pay for other people. The guys were very pleased and praised him loudly. Soon, the whole pub paid attention to Rasputin and everyone joined their conversation. They laughed so much.

'I had sex with 20 girls and some of them were wealthy.'

People laughed, but no one believed him. In reality, it was true. Rasputin was wondering why when he spoke the truth, no one believed him, but, when he was lying, everybody thought that he spoke the truth. There were three brothers in the pub, drinking, ex-miners. They had lost their jobs.

'We have nothing to lose,' said one of them. 'Is there any chance we can be a part of your group?'

'Seven is better than four, go on.' Grigori was grateful to God for his six supporters.

They walked slowly after the meal, enjoying a precious moment. In the evening, they were out of the town, heading towards a woodland area. They stopped there for the night. Next day, the heavy rain began; everyone was miserable and cold.

'How far is it to the monastery?' Grigori asked Stepan. 'It might be awful if we got lost right at the end of our journey.'

'If we walk fast, we might be there today. I know my way, I told you, I have been there,' he said with irritation. The entire day they wandered through the woods with gloomy faces. Finally, they saw the white walls of the holy monastery in front of them. Everyone was pleased to see it. Unexpectedly for all of them, the sun appeared on the sky and golden images of the monastery glistened on the sunshine.

'I told you I know the way,' Stepan exclaimed with excitement.

'With God's blessing and your help, we have reached this monastery.'

'One day, I will walk to Greece to see Mount Athos,' he answered.

'I'll come with you. Whenever you go,' answered one of the men.

Rasputin was silent, admiring the view.

'Do you know folks, women and female animals are banned from Mount Athos. The most sacred place in Eastern Orthodoxy.'

'No,' the majority replied. 'I wonder why?'

'The Virgin Mary flew there 900 years ago and fell in love with that place. Now it's considered to be her sacred land. Now, no females are allowed, only female cats, because they are sacred.'

'I'm glad my wife is banned from Mount Athos,' the homeless guy replied. Everyone laughed.

They approached the entrance of the holy monastery and knocked at the door.

The 70-year-old abbot opened the door straight away. He was wearing a long purple garment and his head was totally white.

'Hello, holy father! God bless you; my name is Father Grigori. I brought six believers with me,' and he gifted him with two loaves of bread and red wine.

'Hello, Father Grigori, God bless you too. I am Father Alexander. New people in the monastery are always welcome. Come in, all seven of you, thank you for the gifts.' He let them pass through. They appeared in a little courtyard.

'Father Albert, show the new arrivals their praying cells and the dormitory.'

The seven followed him through the maze of corridors. It felt so cold in the building, the thick stone walls were hiding the sunshine, everyone was shivering, except the monk. Finally, they came into the dormitory area. All seven of them were given a cell. Each cell had a wooden single bed with a thin mattress, a table with a single candle in the middle of it, a chair and a small box to keep their belongings. There was a corner with the icons for a monk to pray. The homeless person was so pleased at last to get his own room. He thanked Father Grigori, Father Albert and God. Grigori was very proud that he had managed to help him. He had never had a chance to help anyone to improve their life-situation.

'Can I keep my dog in my room?' Rasputin asked Father Albert.

'Yeah, as long as you clean after him,' the monk replied.

The general rules in St Nicholas Monastery were quite strict: all the monks were vegetarian, didn't drink alcohol, were not permitted to have intimacy, they had to pray a lot and work in the monastery. Each holy father was given a task which they had to complete every day. Soon after, all new arrivals were shown the way to the dining area. The room had two large windows, which let in a lot of light, a long wooden dinner table with long benches on both sides of it and an empty fireplace and a row of icons hung above the table for monks to pray. When they entered, the table was already served for them; the monks sat down around it. Then, Father Alexander read a dinner prayer. When he finished, the monks began to eat. They had fish and chips and strawberries for pudding – products from their own garden. Father Grigori and his companions loved the food.

'Why did you come to this monastery?' Father Alexander asked Father Grigori.

'I was directed here by God and Virgin Mary,' explained Father Grigori. 'I want to learn more about orthodox religion and during my stay in this monastery, I wish to visit the holy places, like Mount Athos in Greece and others.'

'What can you give back to the Abbey?' Father Alexander asked him with interest.

'I am a healer and treat patients with God's help and I have excellent review papers from the other monasteries.'

'What can you do for the monastery?' Father Alexander asked an elderly man with a white beard.

'I am a carpenter and I can make or repair the furniture.'

'What about you three brothers, what can you bring to the table?' he carried on asking.

'We can help with gardening,' they replied.

'What about you, young man, do you have any talent?'

''Course I do, I'd like to learn everything about religion and become a real monk and stay here forever. I will work really hard,' he promised.

'What about you, a poor person, what can you do for us, young man?' he asked a homeless guy.

'I can do anything you like, please don't kick me out.' Some people laughed.

'You can all stay,' announced Father Alexander.

Shortly after, the monotonous life in the monastery began for the new arrivals. Because of their routine, every day looked identical to the other.

Rasputin managed to make the holy pilgrimages into the other monasteries and holy places, as far as Greece. He learned a great deal in the monasteries and became, overall, a better person. Grigori's dream to visit St Petersburg grew into a massive and unbearable ambition.

Chapter 5
A Visit to Germany and the Funeral of Alexander III

Rather soon, on 19 April 1894, the wedding took place of Ernest Louis, Grand Duke of Hesse, with Victoria Melita of Saxe-Coburg and Gotha in Noyce Palace in Darmstadt. Ernest was a brother of Princess Alex. The ceremony took place in a small chapel of the Noyce Palace. Victoria was wearing an elegant white dress with pearls and Ernest was in military uniform. They both looked happy and delightful. It was a small wedding ceremony, followed by a lavish wedding banquet. The invited guests were from royal families from all over the globe. Both Nicholas and Alex were among the invited guests. They had a chance to have a conversation during the wedding banquet. The black-and-white images were taken right at the end of the wedding day by professional photographers.

Succeeding it, the future Czar Nicholas II stood on one knee, in front of Princess Alex, and gave a little speech.

'Our love is powerful and it's only the beginning of a new chapter in our life,' he began. 'No one will value and cherish you more than me. I need your support to create our future together, Princess Alex. God gives a lot of challenges and blessings to all of us. I know, as a couple, we can go through the greatest and happiest times together, staying strong and positive, forever. Let's dance together on our wedding day. I'd love to share an infinite future with you. I'd like you to be the mother of my children, my queen, my wife and my console. Would you like to marry me?' After he stopped, there was total silence.

'No, I'm not yet prepared, I'm afraid, to accept this proposal,' Alex said with a sigh.

Everybody gasped. Nicholas looked a bit lost and disappointed. He couldn't understand why. He thought that it might be because of his connection with Matilda K. Luckily for him, no one was able to read his thoughts.

'Alex, sweetheart, why did you reject this proposal?' Queen Victoria asked her granddaughter, looking straight into her eyes.

'The main reason is my religion, Grandmother. I do not wish to become orthodox. I have been a Lutheran all my life, it might take a lot of persuasion for me to change my mind.'

'In my personal belief and experience,' Queen Victoria answered, 'Russia is a dangerous country. Your personal safety will be my greatest concern. Although, if there is love and admiration between you and Nicholas, you might consider accepting his proposal, because, when two people are in love, life is charming and delightful and you can go through difficulties with ease.' The queen's voice was calm and authoritative.

'Both orthodox and Lutheran religions are Christian,' Princess Elizabeth explained quietly. 'God, Jesus and the Holy Spirit are in both religions. There are some differences in communion, praying and service; nevertheless, the differences could be learned over time. Moreover, the Slavonic language is used during the holy services. Remember, it's not the same language as standard Russian. Over the years, being in Russia, I managed to learn the language and now, I do appreciate the orthodox church services. I am a deeply religious person and would not survive without God by my side. My dear sister, I do understand your concern.'

'Dear Princess Alex, I know it's your duty to marry Nicholas and the duty comes always first.' William II spoke in German with his low, stately voice. In only two months, in June, he would become the German Emperor.

'Think with your heart, my dear sister,' the groom concluded. 'It's my wedding day and love is in the air,' he laughed.

'Thank you kindly, my honourable relatives, for the most valuable advice. I take it into consideration and at this precise moment, I am ready to accept the proposal from Nicholas.' The wedding guests applauded loudly.

'Grand Duke Nicholas, dearest, would you like to repeat your proposal, please?' Queen Victoria asked him.

Nicholas stood on one knee in front of Princess Alex and began to say his proposal once again. 'Our love is powerful and it's only the beginning of a new chapter in our life,' he started. 'No one will value and cherish you more than me. I need your support to create our future together, Princess Alex. God gives a lot of challenges and blessings to all of us. I know, as a couple, we can go through the greatest and happiest times together, staying strong and positive, forever.

Let's dance together on our wedding day. I'd love to share an infinite future with you. I would like you to be the mother of my children, my queen, my wife and my console. Would you like to marry me?' Prince Nicholas opened the box and put an engagement ring with three blue sapphires – one emerald and 17 diamonds – on her left hand.

'Yes, yes, positively, I will, was there ever any doubt? I'd love to spend my entire life with you, my priceless Nicholas.' Everyone clapped.

'I can't believe it,' exclaimed Nicholas. 'We will be married soon and you will be the future empress.' They gave each other a gentle hug.

'Congratulations for your engagement!' Princess Victoria of the United Kingdom applauded them.

'Thank you, Auntie Victoria, it's so kind of you.'

'Feeling so much joy for you today, superb achievement,' Grand Duke Sergei and Elizabeth congratulated them.

'It is a time for celebration!' Queen Victoria saluted them.

'It's a happy day for you and for us,' Ernest and Victoria smiled.

'Magnificent decision, Princess Alex! Best wishes!' the future emperor William II announced in his low voice.

'Thank you all so much for all your wonderful positive remarks, I feel truly delighted,' Nicholas answered. He couldn't yet believe that Alex had accepted his proposal. Nicholas stayed in Germany for a few days.

'Do you know what I truly like about Germany?' Nicholas asked Sergei and Elizabeth, when they strolled along the quiet suburban streets of Darmstadt.

'The beauty of it perhaps?' Elizabeth replied.

'Not only the fact that, we can walk along the streets here freely, without security and constant fear of being attacked.' After his grandad Alexander's brutal murder with a horrifying bomb explosion by a member of a terrorist organisation Narodnaya Volya, Nicholas was simply terrified walking along the streets of Russia without security.

As soon as Nicholas returned to Russia, to his terrible regret, he found out that his father – Alexander III – was dangerously ill with glomerulonephritis. The nephrons of one of his kidneys became inflamed, his urine red. The damage to his kidney was not able to clean up the waste products. At the moment Nicholas saw him, he was in bed with a high fever, a strong pain in his kidney, a constant urge to pee and swelling. His wife was continuously beside his bed, looking after him. Alexander opened his eyes; everything was blurred and his children and wife were beside him. They were saying something to him, but he couldn't understand them. They were far, far away.

'Just sleep,' said the queen and stroked his hand gently.

'When the doctor was here last time, what did he say?' Nicholas asked his mother.

'The doctor was here in the morning, he gave him some morphine for pain relief, placed leeches all over his body to reduce inflammation, gave him a jug with a herbal concoction to reduce his temperature and prescribed to avoid salt in his diet.'

'That's good, hopefully with God's help he will be better soon. From now on, with your permission, until he's better, I'm going to complete all the state work that has to be done immediately,' Nicholas promised.

'Yes, please dear,' Maria Feodorovna sighed.

'The state work will be completed as necessary,' Nicholas assured her and left the room.

His father's condition appeared after the tragic train accident of 1888, due to overexerting one of his kidneys. The tremor in the train travelled with great speed for hours. Almost the entire royal family was in one of the carriages. At one point, the vibration of the train became unbearable. No one knew what was going on. It was really noisy and no one was able to talk normally. Suddenly, the ear-piercing screech of metal on metal scratched through their souls. The treacherous train derailed and dragged itself through earth, grass and gravel with the force of gravity. People and items were falling on top of one another, squashing, breaking and smashing. Some windows were smashed into pieces and glass was everywhere. Abruptly, with an ear-piercing crash, the train stopped and became quiet. Only people moaned here and there.

The emperor got up and looked around; there was no way out from the terrible train. The metal of the structure was squashed and bent. Because Alexander was six feet tall, he was able to reach the roof. Alexander's physical strength was excellent. He lifted the roof up and asked someone to put something in between the roof and the train structure. That way, everybody was able to climb out of the train carriage, including the emperor.

Miraculously, no one was seriously injured from that particular carriage, except small cuts and bruises. People from other carriages, however, were seriously injured and 21 people died. From that moment onwards, his kidney started to bother Alexander III, but it was never serious like that. After the tragic train accident, people praised the emperor for his bravery during the crash.

The Orthodox Church thanked God for the miraculous survival of many passengers, including the royal family.

In a few months, Alexander's condition improved a little. He was strong enough to talk, eat, read and write, but he was not strong enough to come out of bed. Alexander began to realise that his death was quite near and he asked Princess Alex to visit him and receive his blessing with Nicholas. Alexander III demanded to wear his military uniform before the event, which exhausted him enormously. Princess Alex arrived promptly from Germany and they both visited the Emperor.

'Hello, your Imperial Majesty,' Alex curtsied and Nicholas bowed.

'Come in, my children, splendid to see you both. Congratulations on your engagement.' He was lying down in bed, trying to collect all his remaining strength.

'Thank you. Hopefully, Father, you will feel better soon.'

'Quite quickly, my crown will go from my head to yours and you will be crowned Nicholas II. You will have absolute power; sharing the power, like constitutional monarchy, may lead to disaster. I'll give you this country in its entirety and in peace. There were no wars during my reign. Rule wisely and with God's help the Romanovs will be in power for another 300 years. Please protect and support the queen mother. The splendid royal wedding will take place and your wife Alex will give you children and all the support you need for the years to come and shall become your consul. God bless you both and the entire Romanov family.' This speech made the czar extremely tired and he closed his eyes.

'Much obliged, dear Father, I'm going to follow your wise guidance,' and Nicholas kissed his father's hand.

'Princess Alex, which name will you take, after being converted and christened as an orthodox?'

'I like the name Catherine, like Catherine the Great. What if my name will be Ekaterina Feodorovna?' she considered.

'I do prefer Alexandra, because it sounds similar to Alex,' Nicholas answered fast. The princess considered both options in total silence and then replied.

'My name will be Alexander Feodorovna. I'll choose the name that Nicholas likes.' They both said goodbye and left the czar sleeping. This event had made him so exhausted.

Dinner was served in the luxurious stately dining hall, just for the two of them. The portrait of Catherine the Great during her coronation stared at them. The golden chandeliers gave a soft light and it felt romantic and dreamy. A large square table made of polished red wood stood in the centre. Their supper was served on golden plates.

'This is our first meal together, darling, after our engagement. You look breathtakingly gorgeous,' Nicholas said and raised a glass of white wine.

Alex felt overwhelmed again. Her surroundings were extremely luxurious. She wasn't used to such extravagance. Nevertheless, she tried to hide it from Nicholas as much as she could.

'Thank you, dearest. I'd love to announce a toast,' Alex raised a glass of champagne. 'For our future family and hopefully it will bring a lot of children and happiness,' she gave a tiny smile.

'It's a wonderful toast and hopefully your wish will come true. I have a little engagement gift for you, my dear princess, a diamond tiara. It was delivered for me specifically from France.' He placed the tiara in front of Alex. It had a golden platform with seven green emeralds, one red ruby right in the centre and hundreds of diamonds, they were arranged in a sophisticated pattern. The diadem glistened magically with all its precious stones. The princess lifted it up and the diamonds played with the candle light like a clear waterfall.

'This diadem is simply magnificent. Hopefully, I'll have a special occasion to wear it in the future,' Alex twirled it in her hand. 'Thank you, my fiancé. I love you so much,' Alex beamed and they gave each other a kiss. Love between Nicholas and Alexandra increased day by day.

In contrast, Alex couldn't find anyone in Russia who would just simply talk to her, friendly and easily, like a soulmate. The princess made herself busy, studying religion, French and Russian in order to avoid being truly depressed. She was too shy to ask people for communication and they misunderstood her shyness with arrogance.

On 1 November 1894, Alexander III passed away in the arms of his wife Maria Feodorovna. An orthodox priest recited the Trisagion hymn. The closest people to His Majesty surrounded him. They said goodbye and closed his eyes.

At the precise moment he died, in the line of succession, his oldest son became the Emperor of Russia, Nicholas II.

'The emperor is dead, long live the emperor,' people proclaimed. 'God save the czar.'

Nicholas was honoured to hear it for the first time in his life, although he had a close connection to his father and looked really upset.

'Dear, dear papa, what will I do without you?' he said in despair. The burden of power fell on his shoulders. He made some orders regarding the funeral and gave a hug to his mum. The queen was truly in despair. She sobbed bitterly, leaning against his shoulder.

'I loved him,' she sobbed. 'He was the best husband anyone could wish for.'

'He will remain in our hearts and memory for the rest of our lives,' Nicholas said quietly, trying not to burst into tears. When everything had been arranged regarding the funeral, he walked towards his room. He saw Alex going down the stairs.

'Be strong, Your Imperial Highness, I swear to support you through happiness and sorrow alike.' She greeted him like this for the first time. They gave each other a friendly hug. Everybody was in black. When Nicholas reached his bedroom, he locked the door behind him. He laid down in bed, cuddled his pillow and burst into tears.

'If only my papa had lived ten years longer, I would have been wiser and would have acquired more knowledge. I'm only 26. I'm not ready to be the czar yet. The biggest question is, what will happen to me, Russia and my family? Well, with God's help I'll try my best.' Gradually, his sobs subsided and he poured himself a drink.

The lengthy burial procession stretched along the streets of St Petersburg. Hundreds of people in black wanted to say goodbye to the previous czar. People in the line were sober and mournful; everybody was singing the hymns with the priests. The procession walked slowly into the cathedral. 18 November 1894 was a sombre day for many people.

After the long procession, the body was transported to the cathedral. Saints Peter and Paul Cathedral stood utmost supreme; it was decorated with hundreds of candles. The public gathered indoors for the burial of the ex-Czar Alexander III of Russia. Everybody sung religious goodbye anthems in sober unison. The pastors in light brown uniforms were conducting the service. The lid of the coffin became open and two jars, white lilies and a lit candle were placed above his head, one with oil and another with honey. The oil signified the cycle of life. The honey represented the sweetness of heaven. The white lilies indicated peace. At the end of the service, everyone was given a large lit candle to hold. The candle embodied the life and death of the deceased person. They had to hold it to the end of the service. The time came to say goodbye, some people began to cry. The lid of the coffin was finally closed.

'Goodbye, dear papa, you will remain in my heart forever,' Nicholas sighed. 'I may be buried here in Saints Peter and Paul Cathedral in 50 years' time and we will see each other again in heaven.'

Then the burial itself took place. The wake followed and closest relatives only attended it. By tradition, orthodox believers had to wear black for 40 days; during these 40 days, the soul of the deceased person wanders around, coming back to where they used to live and to visit their own grave.

The wake took place in a spacious hall. All Alexander's favourite food was served on the long tables in order to please his soul.

'The most wonderful thing Alexander III attained was peace through his reign. He is known as peacemaker,' Maria Feodorovna announced.

'Yes, the world will remember him for this achievement,' Nicholas remarked. 'I would like to erect a statue in his honour to commemorate his achievements.'

'A marvellous idea,' she replied.

'He was a powerful autocrat, physically strong, six feet tall and like a Russian bear who ruled over his subjects, it was his highest success,' Grand Duke Nikolai Nikolayevich announced loudly.

'Yes, I do agree,' Grand Duchess Elizabeth commented softly. 'His biggest success was the six brilliant children he raised.'

'Our children were also my victory,' the queen remarked. Some people laughed. 'He was the best father and husband anyone could wish for.'

All through the evening, people were trying to remember everything positive about Alexander III. The majority of the time, Princess Alex was very quiet.

Chapter 6
Wedding Day

It was planned that the wedding day of Nicholas II of Russia and Princess Alex of Hesse would take place on 26 November in the Grand Church of the Winter Palace. Both of them were truly excited before their wedding celebration. It was decided that there would be no honeymoon and no reception because of the funeral. Nevertheless, they both were looking forward to the wedding day. The invitations were sent to their closest relatives on both sides and the members of foreign royal courts.

Finally, the wedding day arrived. Nicholas was getting ready for the wedding in Anichkov Palace with his 16-year-old brother Michael and his best man. Exclusively, for the ceremony, he was wearing a Hussar's uniform and stately crown, which symbolised immortality, glory and resurrection. His handsome appearance was flawlessly royal. When he was totally prepared, at 11:30 his brother Michael and the czar drove out of the palace in an open landau.

'Today, I will be married. It still sounds rather unreal. My dream came true. Princess Alex is my bride. I do desire to see my wife-to-be as soon as possible,' he was telling this all to Michael, while they were moving towards the Grand Church of the Winter Palace.

'You will be married in two or three hours, brother,' Michael laughed.

Princess Alex was in Andreevsky Palace with her sister Elizabeth and Grand Duke Andre. Elizabeth helped Alex to get ready for her wedding day. The princess was wearing a white wedding dress with pearls and diamonds, her mum's veil, a ring from Queen Victoria, a state crown with thousands of gems and diamonds, matching diamond necklace and earrings, which belonged to Catherine the Great. She was proud to wear the jewellery from Catherine because Alex was an admirer of the empress. Besides, she demonstrated her appreciation to Queen Victoria, that she was honoured to wear her gift during her special day.

Moreover, the veils reminded her of her mum and during this marvellous celebration the princess' look was simply splendid, charming and glorious. She had never looked better than on her wedding day. Alex was almost ready when the Queen Maria Feodorovna announced her arrival in a golden royal carriage. The entire delegation drove to the Winter Palace. The bride was thinking about the groom.

Swiftly, the tuneful and melodic bells began to ring, announcing the beginning of the wedding procession. The Queen Dowager Maria Feodorovna was leading it with Princess Alex. Nicholas II walked behind them, followed by King Christiane IX of Denmark, Queen Olga of Greece, Queen Victoria, George the Duke of York, Grand Duke Sergei and Elizabeth, Ernest Louis Grand Duke of Hesse, Michael, Grand Duke Sergei, Grand Duke Michael and Grand Duke Kirill slowly entered the church's building. The entire procession was simply magnificent. The church was decorated with hundreds of lit candles and looked heavenly beautiful. The pastors conducted the ceremony from this point. Nicholas and Alexandra were blessed by the priest in golden robes. The silver tray with the wedding rings was brought in and the rings were exchanged by bride and groom three times.

'Nicholas II of Russia, would you like to take Princess Alex of Hesse by Rhine to be your wedded wife, to have and to hold, to cherish and honour from this day forward?' the priest asked him loudly.

'Yes, I do.'

'Princess Alex of Hesse by Rhine, would you like to take Nicholas II of Russia to be your wedded husband, to have and to hold, to cherish and honour from this day forward?' the priest enquired again.

'Yes, I do.'

The common cup of sweet wine was brought to both of them to drink together. They drunk it jointly to share their successes and failures, hopes and fears, happiness and sorrows during their married life.

Grand Duke Andre, Grand Duke Kirill, Grand Duke Michael and Prince George of Greece lifted up their dazzling state crowns in order to crown them in their marriage. After being crowned, the couple kissed the golden cross and slowly walked out of the holy building. They were pronounced husband and wife and the bells of the church began to ring again. They were holding hands, walking out of the building, smiling and looking at each other. On the steps of the church, they gave each other a kiss.

The official photographs were taken by their professional photographer in Anichkov Palace. It was also organised that a family supper would take place in the Palace, not as a celebration of marriage, but as an evening meal. It was a double happy moment, because the queen mother had her birthday on 26 November, the same day. The closest family and friends gathered in the royal dining hall of the Anichkov Palace.

'My warmest congratulations, Nicky and Alex,' Maria Feodorovna said warmly and gave them a gift. 'Hopefully, you will have a male heir, rather soon.'

'Thank you, dear mother. Happy birthday, it was a wonderful day, I will never forget it.' They gave each other a friendly hug.

'Are you planning to go on the balcony tomorrow with Nicholas to wave to your subjects?' she asked Alexandra.

'I haven't made my mind up yet,' the czarina replied quietly.

'It's glorious, I absolutely adore doing that. Russian people love me. They cheer, welcome and give a standing ovation,' the queen announced in her imposing, confident voice.

'Oh, goodness gracious, I will join Nicholas this time,' Alexandra promised. However, in her heart she was truly scared.

'Best wishes from our family,' smiled Elizabeth. 'Here is our gift. Hopefully, your marriage will bring many children.'

'Thank you, my dear sister,' they gave each other a lovely smile.

'Enjoy your first married night, Your Majesties,' Grand Duke Andre Vladimirovich said to them both, giving them an enormous gift.

Alexandra became all red and couldn't say a word. Nicholas took the present.

'Cheers, mate,' the gentleman laughed. Alex tried to recover from her episode of shyness.

'My loveliest congratulations,' Princess Anastasia of Montenegro squeaked loudly. 'There are two dictionaries, Russian and French. Hopefully the books will be helpful,' she whispered quietly to Alex.

'Your French teacher must have been German, Your Majesty.' The sisters laughed. Alex became even more embarrassed.

'Thank you, sisters,' she answered with her dry voice, and looked away in an arrogant way.

After the main course, they shared a cake. It had seven layers. The pile of presents in front of them grew bigger and bigger. After a couple of champagnes, Alex recovered a bit from her embarrassment and became a little bit more cheerful and began to make jokes. Nevertheless, deep down in her soul, she had a bit of resentment.

The evening meal gradually ended and only Nicholas and Alexandra remained in the dining hall. Ten luxurious royal rooms of different purposes were given to them by the queen, until they chose their preferred palace in the near future. They both could not wait to be totally private today. Alexandra was delighted to walk slowly upstairs with Nicholas. It was a long day and she was a bit tired. Mostly, she was exhausted from being among so many people at once. She was truly delighted to be alone with Nicholas, because she loved him. Nicholas was the only person, except Elizabeth and her husband, who truthfully understood, cherished and admired her so well in the entire country.

Nicholas was so pleased that the time had come for the special moment. His wife Alexandra was the object of his real devotion, attachment and admiration for a long time. This sexual desire towards Alex was hidden far away in his heart, hidden even from himself; now they were married and allowed to be as close as they wished. Nicholas stepped towards an enormous window. It was snowing outside; large white snowflakes danced their magical dance in front of his eyes. He drew the curtains closed. A blazing log fire crackled in the delicate fireplace, opposite the four-poster bed, creating a warm and cosy feeling. The subtle aroma of flowers and lit candles created an unforgettable romantic atmosphere. Nicholas turned on a brand-new gramophone. The tuneful sweet music by Mozart filled up the room.

'My lovely bride, would you like some champagne?'

'Yes please, it will be wonderful,' she whispered quietly. The bubbling wine tasted cold and refreshing.

They gave each other their first adult kiss. The powerful burst of adrenaline rushed through their bodies, they embraced and their sexual desire reached maximum. They both began to remove each other's clothes one by one, until they were both standing totally naked in front of each other, their feet sunk in the fluffiest carpet. Nicholas lifted up Alexandra and placed her gently on top of the four-poster bed.

'Do you mind if I do it, my lovely princess?' he whispered, kissing her.

'Not at all, please do, I dreamed about it.' Slowly and gently he entered the dreamland. They moved in unison for a while. Soon, they reached an orgasm, almost at the same moment.

'It was marvellous. Thank you, my love. Queen Victoria was right saying that there is something to enjoy during the marriage, if you are in love.'

'Thank you, sweetheart, it's entirely my pleasure. Maybe soon we will have a baby boy.' They fell asleep, thinking about each other. The consummation of marriage was left for whoever to look at.

Their breakfast the next morning was served in the small breakfast area. It was a table for two. It was the first breakfast of their married life and it felt weirdly unusual. They were still high from the adrenaline they received from the previous night.

'There is such a difference between being married and single,' Nicholas mentioned, 'and only married people are able to understand that.'

'Being single means to be totally alone, being married means to be together. I'm delighted to be married and share my life with you, Nicholas,' she gave him a huge smile.

'I am going to work until 8 pm almost every day. Would you like to go on the balcony with me today to wave to our subjects? I'll give a little speech.'

'As I promised to your mother, I'll do it this time,' she fiddled with her napkin.

'Splendid. Presently, my mother and I are going to work in partnership on the majority of the government work.'

'I have a feeling,' Alexandra said quietly, 'that people in the Russian Royal Court are not welcoming me at present.'

'Perhaps you are taking it too seriously, sweetheart, too close to your heart. Turn it all into a joke and people will laugh and accept their queen,' he looked at Alexandra.

'I will try my best, thanks for your support.'

'We cannot forbid people talking, like Ivan the Terrible. He chopped their heads off.'

'Like the Queen of Hearts from Alice in Wonderland, "off with your head!"' They laughed.

After a few hours of state work, Czarina Alexandra joined Nicholas II to go on the balcony and wave to the public. Nicholas was proud to show the Russian people his beloved wife. Alexandra, however, was scared that something would go wrong.

As they stood on the balcony, Nicholas began to speak. Thousands of eyes stared at them; without warning, Alexandra became so embarrassed that her face turned red. She just stood there quietly, like a statue. He completed his speech. People cheered and clapped. Then they walked back indoors.

'Alex, why didn't you give a speech or even wave? People were waiting. You have to learn how to grow out of your shyness.'

'I'm sorry, it just happens to me. It might be beyond my control.' Two large tears appeared on her beautiful face. Nicholas gave her a hug of reassurance.

'Perhaps next time. Please don't cry. I love you, my sunshine.'

However, the public reacted in a different way. Almost everyone thought that Czarina Alexandra was arrogant, haughty and conceited. That she didn't want to speak to the public, because it was beyond her dignity.

In an hour, Nicholas joined Maria Feodorovna to complete the government documents and continue the ongoing projects. Both of them began to work enthusiastically together. It was a superb relief for Maria Feodorovna that she could assist Nicholas and forget about the death of her husband, at least for a minute or two. Queen Dowager gave her son the most valuable lessons about state work and she was tremendously proud to provide him help and advice in the beginning of his reign.

Nicholas truly appreciated his mum's help, because he felt, at times, that he was unprepared.

'I presume, maybe you should keep your father's ministers,' she suggested. 'So that they can carry on their duties freely, without major interruption.'

'I suppose you're correct. The ministers will remain at present, but I will replace them one by one as required.'

'The major school reforms must take place in Russia, because the current situation is dreadful,' the queen suggested.

'Let's look at how we can improve the education itself across the country,' the czar replied.

They spent the majority of their time talking about education reforms and giving orders to their secretaries.

'My father started to build a railway across Russia; compared to other developed countries, the length of the Russian railway is rather insignificant. I'd love to build a trans-Siberian railway connecting the west and east of the country,' Nicholas said enthusiastically.

'A brilliant idea, Your Majesty,' his mum replied. 'To build a new railway, you require a combination of metal: aluminium, iron, copper or steel. Consequently, the new factories and mines have to be built to increase the general metal production.'

'Factories will need electricity and coal. Consequently, the new small electric stations have to be built to power them,' he supposed.

'Building the railway will boost the economy and create new jobs,' Maria concluded. The railway engineers were invited to suggest their fresh ideas and launch the miscellaneous projects.

'Finally, for today, the preparations must begin for the coronation,' Nicholas announced.

'We have to send thousands of invitations,' his mum replied.

At the end of the day, after everyone left the office, except Nicholas and his mum, he talked to her privately, 'Thanks, ma'am, for your valuable support. I truly value and appreciate it.'

'I know, it's my duty; country first, self second,' the queen announced proudly.

'Apologies for the weird question, but Alex asked whether you can give her any of your jewellery?'

'She must be joking. Of course not. I bet she is too embarrassed to ask me in person,' she became cross. 'Princess Alex has been 29 days in Russia, out of which, eight days as empress. She would like everyone to accept and value her in the royal court; she wants the Russian people to be proud of her and value her as an empress. She also wishes to have your love and my jewellery. In fact, she's not doing anything to deserve it. If you arrive from another country, you have to earn the love and respect of your subjects with your hard work and dedication.'

'No worries, I think, Alex has plenty of time to change everyone's opinion about her. She just needs more time. Is there anywhere I can find any other jewellery, mum?'

'Yes, there are plenty of miscellaneous items of jewellery in different castles. She'll just have to find them. I'll give you the instructions shortly about where they are.'

'Much obliged, Your Majesty. See you tomorrow.'

'Goodbye, Nicky dear.'

After the evening meal, Nicholas and Alexandra went outside to see her sister Ella. St Petersburg was covered in snow and the Russian winter had begun. The real fur coats kept them warm. Czarina Alexandra was wearing a stylish, white full-length lynx fur coat and Czar Nicholas was in his trendy, full-length, black sable fur coat. The young royal couple had an authentic sophistication and elegance. The sledge they were in ran speedily. There was a good layer of snow on the ground. The troika ride was a new entertainment for Alexandra. She screamed from excitement. The snow was falling fast, the streets looked festive and cheerful.

'Awesome, I love it. It feels so exciting in a sledge.'

'Yeah, the Russian people and I adore winter.'

'Nicholas, dearest, I have made my mind up not to participate in the government work yet. I'll study languages and will visit all significant official balls and events that I cannot avoid.'

'Anything you like, I do respect your decision.'

'Thanks for your understanding. When are we going to look for our new place to live?'

'You and I are going to start looking at different options as soon as possible. It might take up to six months, until the decision is made.'

'I'm sorry, but I find it a bit stressful sometimes to share the same castle with my mother-in-law. It would be marvellous to have a castle just for two of us.'

'We'll see what I can do, Your Imperial Highness,' and he gave her a kiss. Nicholas had a strange feeling. He was in between his mum and his wife. He loved them both and they both complained about each other.

In the middle of April, Alexandra woke up feeling sick. She stopped eating and was really tired. She hadn't been that unwell for a long time. Alex remained in her room, sleeping.

'Where is your wife today,' Maria Feodorovna asked Nicholas.

'Alex is in bed with sickness and tiredness,' he explained.

'Are you absolutely sure?' A huge smile appeared on her face. 'She is expecting a baby. It's time to open a bottle of champagne.'

'Wonderful, I'm going to be a father,' he exclaimed. 'We must pray for this baby.'

'Please wait, I must ask Alex about something first.'

They rushed upstairs, knocked and entered the room. Alex opened her eyes.

'Alex, darling, when did you have the lady's business of yours last?' the queen demanded.

'Two months ago, I think, why?' she replied.

'You are going to have a baby soon,' she declared. The three of them clapped and cheered.

The pregnancy went very well without any complications and on 15 November 1895, Alexandra was in labour; the labour lasted about ten hours. Alexandra had five or six glasses of wine as pain relief and with a scream and a last push, a baby was born. The midwife cut the umbilical cord and looked at the baby, making sure that the infant was healthy.

'It's a girl,' the midwife announced and gave her to Alex to hold. A little girl looks so gorgeous. A tiny little angel.

'Hello, darling, sweetheart.' The baby waved her hand. 'I'm going to breastfeed you.' Breastfeeding went very well and Alexandra and her daughter loved it. Czarina Alexandra realised that some people from the Russian court would not like this idea and Queen Victoria would be cross, however, she was the boss, it was only for her to decide how to feed her baby. Czarina was so proud and delighted to be a mother at last. Her dream came true. Alexandra gently handed their daughter to Nicholas.

'She is so gorgeous. I can't believe I am a father. Her name is Grand Duchess Olga Nikolaevna Romanova.' The church bells began to ring all across the country, informing everyone about Olga's birth.

When Alexandra had fallen asleep after childbirth, Nicholas wrote a letter to Queen Victoria, informing her of the birth of her great-granddaughter.

Chapter 7
St Petersburg at Last

Grigori arrived in St Petersburg by train. He was wearing black robes and carrying his luggage in a brown sack made of leather. He marched along the platform, looking left and right. Rasputin had no dog with him this time. He had left Alaska in Pockrovskoe. The sun was shining bright and the tall buildings of the apartment blocks looked still sleepy, but cheerful. Rasputin took a business card out of his pocket from his friend Count Paul Vronsky. The address was written on it. The man was able to read it, but he had no idea how to find it. All the buildings looked identical to him. He wandered around the city for an hour and then decided to ask. A tall policeman with two German shepherds walked along the street.

'Sir!' he shouted from the other side of the road, his loud voice echoing along the street. 'I'm lost. Can you help?'

The policeman gave him a suspicious look.

'So, what would you like to find?'

Rasputin showed him the business card. The policeman gave him another suspicious stare.

'Why are you going to this address? It's quite a posh area,' he explained.

'The owner of the house promised me a job,' he lied. 'Tell me how to find it.' Rasputin begun to use his hypnotic power, staring at him non-stop.

'First, walk along this street for 20 minutes, then turn left and carry on walking for another five minutes, then ask someone if you're still unsure,' the policeman explained in a sleepy voice.

Grigori ran all the way there. He noticed that people in the capital were wearing better clothes and the girls were prettier too.

One day, one day, I might sleep with one of them, he thought and it made him feel happier.

The house he was looking for stood imposing and luxurious. A lovely front garden was in front of it. The pink and orange tulips bloomed 'round it; a large metal fence encircled the building. Grigori knocked at the door, but no one answered.

I must be stupid, thinking that Paul will be in, he thought.

A sudden idea came to his mind. Rasputin decided to have lunch on the bench across the road, then visit Alexander Nevsky Monastery. His simple lunch consisted of bread, eggs, cheese and baby potatoes. Grigori was so engrossed in his thoughts that he did not notice anything around him. A not-very-tall gentleman in grey overcoat, grey suit and fedora hat strolled towards him with his bulldog.

'Good afternoon, Father Grigori,' Paul said and looked straight into his eyes, smiling.

'Hello, Father Paul, buddy, great to see you,' Grigori smiled. 'I didn't think I would see you today,' and they shook hands. The dog growled. The owner rapped the dog's head and it stopped.

'Please welcome and be my guest, Grigor,' and he pointed in the direction of his mansion. They both passed through the high metal gate, walked through an elegant garden and entered a green front door with a family coat of arms on it. The bright front room had a grand piano, a marble staircase, pictures on the walls and crystal chandeliers.

'This is the most beautiful house I have ever been in,' Rasputin admitted to his friend, looking around.

'Thank you so much, I'm glad you like it. It took a few years to improve. Would you like me to show you your room?'

'Please, you have done it before, in the monastery.'

'Certainly, it is déjà vu with one difference, that the room I'll show you now is of much better quality.' They laughed.

They went upstairs and Paul entered one of his guest bedrooms. The bedroom looked ultra-modern. It had a double bed, two dressing tables, a walk-in wardrobe and a Roman-style bathroom.

'God bless you, Peter. It is awesome.' He left his bag on top of the bed and looked through the windows. The view was simply superb.

'Would you like a bottle of drink?'

'Maybe a bottle of Madeira red wine,' he answered; it was his favourite.

'I have to go down the cellar. Maybe I have one or two.'

They both ran downstairs and entered a cold, dark and dusty cellar. The rows of bottles and barrels stretched across the walls.

'Here you go, I can see it.' An old dusty bottle of Madeira stood on the bottom shelf.

'Time for a party,' Grigori answered and they both laughed.

'Help me to carry all the food to the dining table and we will have a feast.'

After the first glass of wine, Rasputin decided to tell Paul the truth about himself. For some reason, he felt a bit guilty.

'Paul, you can hate me after that, but I want to say the truth to you only. I haven't been a holy person all my life; before, I was a peasant from Pockrovskoe.'

'Goodness, that's why you couldn't read and write.' Rasputin nodded. 'I don't mind that. You will be my friend regardless, even if you were a criminal.'

'I just realised that, Paul you are my real friend and I have never had a friend before.' They raised their glasses for friendship.

'Honestly, Grigori, I'd like to tell you my personal secret,' he said softly. 'I am a bisexual person, gay and straight in combination.'

'Well, it's your choice, isn't it? We will be friends no matter what,' he replied in surprise.

'Gracious, I'm fond of you. I fell in love with you in the monastery, when I saw you for the first time. I didn't tell anyone, because it was inappropriate. You are truly tall. You have such a strong masculine body. You have powerful eyes and when you look at me, I want you like a man. Grigori, would you like to spend the night with me? I'm serious.'

Rasputin was silent and his mouth was opened wide.

'Yes, Paul, I agree,' he said finally. 'I have never had a connection with a man before.' He drank half of his glass of wine in one go. 'I'm happy to do it with you, before it's too late. You are really clever and handsome.'

They gave each other long eye contact and kissed. The snog was powerful and brought a lot of pleasure to both of them. Suddenly, the dog began to growl.

'Can I feed Midnight?' Rasputin asked him. 'You gave food to Alaska.'

'Of course you can, no problem at all.' Grigori filled up a plate of food from the table and gave it to the dog. Midnight began to eat. While the dog was busy eating, they went upstairs into the guestroom and began to explore each other's bodies. Rasputin discovered new ways of having sex. Paul thought that it was better than he expected. When they both were satisfied, they went downstairs to have more wine. They both got pretty drunk, enjoying each other's company. At about 2 am, they fell asleep and got up at midday.

'That was awesome. I absolutely loved it, I must admit. Let's go and have breakfast!' Paul exclaimed.

'Yeah, I'm no longer a virgin, I'm afraid.' They burst into laughter.

In the kitchen, Paul made two coffees and brought into his breakfast room, one for him and one for Grigori. In the monastery, he learned how to be self-sufficient, without servants.

'Two coffees and cake,' he smiled. 'I have something important to tell you today.'

'Cheers mate.'

'Would you like to stay in St Petersburg for the rest of your life, Grigori?' he asked him with interest.

'It was my dream, since birth. I didn't tell anyone, because they might have thought that I was crazy.'

'I'd love to give a donation towards the apartment you wish to buy, because you agreed to spend the night together.' He signed a cheque and gave it to Rasputin.

Grigori was thrilled to bits. His eyes widened. Rasputin thought it was happening to a different person, not him.

'God bless you, Paul, you are simply the best and it was my pleasure.' They gave each other a kiss.

'Moreover, I received the insurance money for my burned-down villa in order to rebuild it. This house is in the process of being sold. Not long ago, I went to London and bought a stunning property there. Now I have free cash that I can share.'

'Peter, do you want to stay in London forever?' Rasputin asked with curiosity in his voice.

'Absolutely positively, my plan is to move there permanently. I would like to make a proposal to all of the ladies in the British royal court,' he smiled. 'Everything here still reminds me of my wife and daughter.'

'God be with you. Hopefully she accepts your proposal. How many languages do you speak?'

'I can speak three languages: French, English and Russian. French and Russian are compulsory in the Russian Royal Court.' Grigori's eyes widened.

'Wow, that sounds cool. Bless you with your venture. So clever, to speak three languages, I can't even speak Russian.' They burst into laughter. 'Paul, do you know someone in the Russian Royal Court?'

'Certainly, I do, I'll give you one royal connection.' He went upstairs and brought a silver business card. 'Anastasia of Montenegro' was written on it and he gave it to Rasputin. He couldn't believe his luck. Potentially, he might be able to see the royal family.

'Bless your heart, Paul Vronsky, with all your beginnings and I will pray for you.' They gave each other a hug.

'I'm going to London tomorrow by train, and will be back at some point to sell this property. Here is my London address.' And he gave him a new business card. Please call me and update me when you have bought your property. It was my real pleasure to see you around mine and spend time together. For the rest of my life, I will remember this night.'

They said goodbye and gave each other their final hug. Rasputin marched out of Paul's property, both happy and sad. He was happy because he spent a lovely night in the company of his friend and his generous money donation. He was unhappy because he might never see Paul ever again in his life.

There were two people in this world who truly loved him; the richest and the poorest. The richest was Paul and the poorest was his wife Praskovia. Was it strange? He was absolutely sure that Praskovia would remain loyal to him, regardless of his behaviour, for the rest of his life. So far, St Petersburg met Rasputin with love. What will happen after?

Because Rasputin had valuables with him, he didn't want to be robbed. Grigori turned into a wild beast and switched on all his instincts. He was walking along the streets watching for an attacker. No one confronted him this time. Children and adults in rags begged on Nevsky with hungry eyes. He knew, very well, that he was not part of this crowd. Rasputin walked along the Prospect for a while and entered the first bank he saw. Grigori opened a new bank account and put almost all his money in it. The man still couldn't believe that he had a huge sum of money. It could have taken years for him to make this amount. The people in the bank were unusually polite and courteous to him. Now, it was time to look for an apartment in St Petersburg and he was also able to purchase his village home in Pockrovskoe.

He bought a new bag, new clothes, a golden chain and a golden orthodox cross to be more modern and presentable, especially for the capital. Grigori gave his picnic and old stuff to a penniless beggar by the front door and entered a restaurant; the poor man was very pleased. Grigori still couldn't believe that his life had changed all of a sudden. Rasputin's rise to prominence commenced. In the restaurant, while he was waiting for food, he noticed that he began to look at men with a different perspective. It was probably always with him; however, he didn't realise it.

After a lovely meal, without alcohol, Grigori decided to visit Alexander Nevsky Monastery. Providentially, he had an outstanding recommendation letter from the previous abbey with him. Grigori thought that he had to go to the monastery today, because it was his lucky day and he must use it wisely. He paid for the meal and after a few minutes of hiking, Rasputin reached the monastery. Grigori had no trouble finding it, because people on the streets knew exactly where it was. The fabulous building of the Alexander Nevsky Monastery spread across a massive land in front of him. Father Grigori was astonished at its size and beauty. From outside, the buildings looked like a royal palace, probably even better indoors. The door was wide open. Grigori walked in the large church building with his mouth hanging open. A porter sat quietly by the front door. Rasputin didn't even notice him at first.

'What is the purpose of your visit?' the man asked him abruptly.

His voice echoed in the cathedral building.

'Oh, nothing special, I just would like to see Archimandrite Feofan,' he pronounced in such a tone of voice like it wouldn't really matter at all if he didn't see him.

'Do you have a recommendation letter, by any chance?' the porter asked in an aristocratic manner, stretching his voice.

'Here you go,' and he placed a brown folder in front of him.

The man examined the papers for a while and finally said, 'It's outstanding. Follow me.'

They walked through a few large chapels of the monastery and everything was simply splendid around him. Rasputin thought that he had never seen a royal castle before; however, he would have imagined that it might have looked like this monastery.

'Please, sit down here,' the porter said finally. 'He will see you in a minute or two.' And he shuffled away like a mouse.

The waiting area was very comfortable and a Bible and a jug of water were set in the middle of a brown table in front of him. Grigori took the Bible and began to read. Thanks to Paul, he had no trouble reading now.

'Father Grigori!' a voice announced.

Rasputin stood up and saw a tall gentleman gliding towards him. He rose up and both holy men shook each other's hands.

'Nice to see you, Archimandrite Feofan,' Rasputin greeted him. His office was absolutely fabulous. It had a dark brown polished table, comfortable armchairs, a window with a magnificent view and golden icons on the walls. This room, in his opinion, could have belonged to the czar.

'What are your talents and expertise, Father Grigori?' he asked him with interest.

'Simply, I treat patients with unknown diseases,' he replied.

'What is unusual about my condition?' he asked all of a sudden.

Rasputin lifted his arm up and released some energy.

'With God's help, your pain is vanishing. You have joint pain in both of your wrists and you broke your left arm not long ago.'

Feofan opened his eyes wide.

'I must admit, my pain disappeared and how do you know all about my problems?'

'Well, I just look at a patient and I know, it is so easy. High and mighty opens my eyes. Give your broken arm more exercise.'

Feofan was simply astonished. 'Undeniably wonderful. I'm going to give you a room in this monastery and you will begin your shift tomorrow. There will be patients from all walks of life, including the royal family. What do you think about that?'

'The Creator guided me here, like a sheep, for an important mission. So, I'm here to fulfil God's wish.'

Feofan rung a silver bell on his desk. A monk with blond hair and blue eyes walked in.

'This is our new medical adviser. Show Father Grigori his room.' And he gave Rasputin a silver key. They walked upstairs and along the corridor. The room was comfortable and luxurious. It reminded him of Paul's guest bedroom. It had a double bed, a couple of bedside tables, a praying corner, a wardrobe and a tiny bathroom.

'This is the best cell in the monastery I have ever been in,' Rasputin commented to his companion.

'The furniture comes from the royal castles, the royal families have been donating their unwanted furniture for hundreds of years.'

'Do the members of the royal families visit this monastery?'

'Yes, they do; some of them visit to pray and some of them to receive a blessing or advice.'

'Maybe I will be lucky enough to see a member of the royal family one day,' Rasputin replied.

'Maybe.'

Day by day, Father Grigori began to get used to his new routine. He learned that there were three meals every day, breakfast, lunch and dinner. Sometimes, the food was vegetarian; however, it was very good quality. Every monk had his role to play in the monastery and that role was always the same. So everyone knew whom to ask if something happened.

Fortunately, he managed to make friends with Feofan and he commenced to advertise Rasputin's name in his social circles.

Father Grigori, as promised, begun his medical assistance and some of his patients were inside the monastery, some of them outside. And he started to learn more about different people and unfamiliar medical problems. Everything was almost perfect for him, although he disliked some rules. For instance, he couldn't invite anybody to the monastery. So, there was no chance of any social contacts from outside. For that reason, in his free time, he began slowly and gradually to search for an apartment to buy. No matter how hard he tried, he was wasn't able to find a suitable one so far.

Chapter 8
Coronation and Khodynka Tragedy

For the last few months, the entire Russian royal court had been preparing for one of the most vibrant and vital public events for the royal couple. It had been rehearsed several times. Hundreds of invitations and telegrams were posted to the governments of the majority of countries and other royal courts. The royal manifesto was written to announce this public event.

Manifesto
The consecrated coronation of the Emperor Nicholas the II and the Empress Alexandra Feodorovna will take place in Moscow on 14 May 1896 at 10 am in Dormition Cathedral.
From 6 of May till 26 of May will be an official coronation public celebration and holiday.
Nicholas II

On Nicholas's birthday, 6 May, the royal couple arrived in Moscow, Smolinsky railway station. The crowds of people gathered in front of the station. They cheered, clapped and waved to their czar and czarina. It was fabulous to see, for once, a cheerful crowd of people. Grand Duke Sergei and Elizabeth met them at the station.

'Happy birthday, Your Majesty. I hope your coronation goes well,' Grand Duke Andrei shouted through the noisy crowd.

'Thank you, Your Highness, hopefully with God's help the coronation will proceed according to our preparations and arrangements.'

All five of them proceeded to Petrovsky Palace. The weather was rather pleasant and everyone enjoyed the journey. The empress looked slightly nervous and talked to her sister non-stop.

'Grand Duchess Olga looks so sweet. How old is she now?' Elizabeth asked with interest. The baby gave them an adorable smile.

'She's six months old,' Alex smiled. 'She is such a delightful child. Queen Victoria will be appalled to discover that I'm still breastfeeding her.'

The sisters laughed.

'Unfortunately, two children, our distant relatives, became orphans all of a sudden. As a couple, we decided to adopt both of them,' Elizabeth informed her.

'How marvellous, it's so kind of you, my dear sister,' the czarina answered. 'Bless you mighty God.'

'Gosh, there are so many destitute children suffering across Russia. They need help. I brought 300 Christmas gifts last year into an orphanage in St Petersburg, but they need help all year round. I'm just wondering whether there is anything we can do to improve their lifestyle?'

'Perhaps, in the future, but at the moment we are awfully busy with our coronation, my dear sister.'

At the same morning, the Empress Dowager Maria Feodorovna arrived at Smolinsky station. The vast crowds of Moscow people met Her Majesty cheering, clapping and waving. The queen was very popular and people loved her. The queen's popularity increased day by day. This fact did not amuse Czarina Alexandra, however; Her Majesty's popularity was absolutely normal for Nicholas, her son, because he grew up there and considered it to be just a norm.

In the morning of 14 May, the holy coronation began. The weather was pleasant and the entire royal procession, which consisted of: members of royal families, church, social and military leaders and a dragoon of Cossacks, headed towards the cathedral. The entire parade was in full regalia and dazzled with gems and diamonds. The most fortunate local members of the public and local and international reporters managed to photograph and even video record this, the astounding royal parade, which moved slowly towards the Dormition Cathedral.

Nicholas II was paraded in his military uniform and had an imperial appearance. Personally, he enjoyed the ceremony and thought that it was truly a highlight of his life.

The Empress Alexandra was wearing an embroidered white coronation dress with white pearls and diamonds and a lengthy train. She felt a bit like a bride once again. Alexandra began to get used to Russia and was not as shy as she often used to be. A dazzling smile appeared on her face and she appreciated the entire coronation procession.

The Metropolitan of St Petersburg conducted the orthodox service. He handed Nicholas and Alexandra a golden holy cross to kiss by the front door of the cathedral. Three raised-up thrones were prepared at the head of the building.

The first throne was for Nicholas II, the second throne was for Empress Alexandra and the third throne was for the Queen Dowager Maria Feodorovna. Three emperors were seated upon them.

Next, a coronation shield, silver sword, royal sceptre and coronation orb were presented to Nicholas II symbolising royal power. Finally, the emperor lifted the state crown and placed it gently upon his own head. The crown shone brilliantly with 4,936 diamonds, 76 pearls and one red ruby. It was rather heavy, nearly 5 kg. The royal crown symbolised the imperial power, glory, immortality, righteousness and resurrection. Following Byzantium ancient tradition, when the future emperor places his crown on his own head, the unlimited power is given to him by the Mighty God.

The Metropolitan declared loudly, 'Forefather, the son and the Holy Spirit, amen. The Czar of all Russia, Nicholas II, you have been crowned by God and have absolute power over all your subjects.'

The church choir begun to sing.

Then, the newly crowned czar placed his crown briefly upon the Czarina's head to share his power as his console. At the next moment, he placed the smaller crown upon Alexandra's head to remain upon it. The next step of the coronation proceeded with anointing both monarchs. The special mixture of oil, a true secret, had been prepared years ago. The priest brushed the oil on their foreheads under the canopy.

Then Nicholas II walked through the golden holy royal doors of the cathedral, which were usually reserved for priests and bishops only and separate ordinary people and divinity. The coronation finished with a Holy Communion. The body and blood of Christ was received by them.

After the ceremony, the royal coronation banquet with Russian traditional food was served in the Kremlin. Long banquet tables stood in the luxury reception areas, with crystal chandeliers and portraits and paintings. The best cutlery and crockery arrived from St Petersburg with them, specifically for the coronation dinner; they were arranged with geometrical precision. The most delicious open sandwiches with royal oscietra, royal beluga, royal salmon and

Siberian sturgeon caviar were served with champagne, white wine or vodka for the first starter. The Olivier Russian winter salad, Greek salad or salmon salad was given with the second starter. There was a soup option between solyanka soup, okroshka or borsch for the third starter. The food was cooked by the best chefs in the country and looked and tasted absolutely superb.

'I'm still in a state of incredulity that my oldest son has been crowned today,' the Queen Maria Feodorovna announced loudly. 'I remember him being a baby not long ago and now he is the czar.'

'Yes, let's drink to the czar,' Grand Duke Andre answered, raising his glass.

'Hip, hip, hurray; hip, hip, hurray; hip, hip, hurray!' everyone roared in unison.

'A new future czar will be born soon,' Alexandra announced when it went quiet again.

'For the future male heir,' Anastasia of Montenegro declared firmly.

Three starters followed the main course. The Czarkoe beef stew, beef stroganoff, salmon with herbs or shashlik were prepared by chefs for the main course. There was a choice between the sweet pancakes, Pavlova cake, Napoleon cake or coronation cake for dessert, followed by coffee. Everyone enjoyed the coronation banquet and went out for a walk after the meal. The weather was warm and pleasant.

When the sun went down, the fireworks began. The members of the public were busy watching flying, crackling rockets. The royal couple stood on a balcony, alone and undisturbed. The Catherine wheels twinkled, glistened, dazzled and blazed in the darkness in red blue and green.

'How delightful, the fireworks are in our honour.' Nicholas embraced Alex and they gave each other a kiss.

'The coronation day was perfect, charming and magnificent. I will remember it my entire life. Nicky, I love you so much.'

The fireworks flashed, fizzled and glistened, brightening up the walls of the grand Kremlin. The popping rockets swished and swished, thumped, whistled and cracked and rattled. The night was simply perfect for the two of them.

On the morning of 18 May, the newspapers and magazines published the royal coronation speech. It was simple and straightforward. However, the opinions were polarised. Half of the people in the country liked the speech and truly agreed with the czar, and half of them disliked the speech and thought that it was propaganda in the interests of the ruling class only.

The Coronation Speech
The mighty God gave me an unlimited power to rule over the entire Russia and its subjects. As the czar, I will preserve the power of autocracy, as my beloved father had done in his fabulous reign before me. Those who believe that they can share my government and create democracy dream senseless dreams. The Romanovs were in power for 300 years and they will continue to rule for three more centuries.
Enjoy my gifts and the coronation festivities.
Bless you mighty God. The Czar Nicholas II

The same morning, 18 May, on Khodynka Field, at 6 am, the distribution of gifts was arranged by the royal family. The field where they arranged it to take place was covered with trenches and craters. Normally, it was used by the army for training and exercise. Grand Duke Sergei was in charge of the event. At 6 o'clock in the morning precisely, the crowd of half a million people gathered on that treacherous field. A coronation cup with sausage, gingerbread men and biscuits was supposed to be given at the end of the field in the specially arranged area. The people who were gathered there were middle-class people, working-class people, students, peasants and even children. The number of them wanted a little souvenir to commemorate the coronation. A few of them wished to sell their cup and make money. The percentage of those people wanted to get a cup in order to give a gift to their loved ones. Suddenly, someone from the crowd began to shout.

'Each cup contains a gold coin.'

'There are not enough cups for all of us.'

The density of the crowd was between six and seven people per square metre and the stampede begun. Each person was totally blocked on all four sides. They were so squashed that the crowd became like one being and behaved like a liquid. If one person fell, the gap was filled in automatically by other people. People began to get squashed. They started to put their children on top of their heads and asked them to run away on top of the crowd. A number of children managed to run away to safety without being squashed. The trenches and craters of the field filled in with dead bodies. 1,389 people died from suffocation, some of them are squashed by standing up. Over 1,300 people were injured, but survived. The police were trying to do something about it, but couldn't do much. The crowd was totally uncontrollable. Finally, the cups were given to people and they walked away and the mass dispersed. All injured people were taken to Moscow hospitals. The bodies were cleaned away very fast. At 2 o'clock, when the royal couple arrived, the field was empty and hygienic.

'How awful, all these people died trying to obtain a coronation cup,' Nicholas said to Alexandra, walking around the field.

'It is so sad,' answered Alexandra. 'It's not a cup of happiness, but a cup of sorrow.'

From that moment onwards, those cups people began to call cups of sorrow and Nicholas became known as Nicholas the bloodiest. Both Nicholas and Alexandra went on a balcony on that field and gave a little speech; nevertheless, it couldn't solve a problem.

'With the most horrible sorrow my wife and I have discovered about this tragedy today. We are awfully remorseful about the victims of this appalling tragedy. 1,389 people lost their lives in the human stampede. All victims of this appalling tragedy will receive a large financial compensation. God will help us in this dreadful situation and we must pray to the high and mighty, that the stampede will not happen again.'

Despite them both being remorseful, they didn't arrange national mourning for the stampede victims. People disliked that fact. In contrast, all planned celebration activities would still take place, regardless of the tragedy. Both Nicholas and Alexandra rushed to see Grand Duke Andre to enquire about the disaster. He was busy answering phone calls regarding this matter, and looked terribly sad.

'Do you know why this tragedy happened in the first place?' Nicholas asked him, entering the office.

'Because someone shouted that there was a gold coin in each cup and there were not enough cups for everybody. Subsequently, the crazy crowd began to push forward and people died.'

'The field, where it was arranged, is awful with trenches and ditches. Why didn't you think about safety before planning it?'

They stood opposite each other and Nicholas was cross.

'No one could have predicted that, Your Majesty, it's just a tragedy and it's not my fault.' They stood quietly for a few seconds.

'No, I suppose it's not your fault. Well, it's a bad omen. Conduct the investigation and make the people who were responsible answer for this tragedy,' he sighed.

'I have already begun the thorough research; all responsible will be definitely punished.' Elizabeth and Alexandra entered the office.

'Knowing about this tragedy, would you still like to go to the ball in the French embassy, Nicholas and Alexandra?' Elizabeth asked them both.

'Of course we will, the French–Russian relationship is quite strong at the moment. I wouldn't dream of spoiling it by ignoring the invitation. The French ambassador is expecting us and we will be there,' Nicholas replied.

'It's not much time left before the start. We have to go now. See you at the embassy,' Alexandra responded and they rushed outside.

They just about had enough time to get ready and arrive at the French embassy right on time.

The ball was simply wonderful. The French do know how to organise fantastic festivities. The French buffet table was served with fancy French cuisine. Félix Faure the President of France greeted the royal couple in person.

'Do you like French food, Your Majesties?' he asked them both with a smile.

'It's truly scrumptious. Yes, we do, Mr President,' Alexandra answered and grinned.

'It's fabulous, I'd like to invite the royal family to Paris to stay in my official residence for a week in September and you will be able to enjoy French cuisine.'

'Marvellous idea, I would love to accept the invitation, Mr Faure. It will be my first visit to France,' the emperor replied.

'It will be a great honour for me. I'll be truly delighted to show you Paris in person,' he exclaimed, gesticulating left and right.

'It's so awful, Your Majesties, what's happened today on Khodynka Field,' the French ambassador commented with a tragic expression.

'Yes, it's truly horrifying. So many lives lost without a trace,' the czarina sighed.

After the buffet, the ball was opened. Everybody danced until late into the night. The general atmosphere during the ball was quite sombre because of the tragic event.

The next day, in the morning, the royal couple arrived at one of Moscow's hospitals. Because of the tragedy, the hospital was totally jam-packed. All the beds were taken. The poor patients with horrific injuries had to lay down in corridors, using chairs, benches and the floor. Some of them were occupying only mattresses; luckily it wasn't cold. Some people had brain injuries, punctured lungs, heart attacks, broken bones, crushed skulls, crumpled faces and broken arms. They moaned, wailed, cried, shouted, sobbed and yowled. Pain relief had been given to them already; however, they were still in fear, in pain and in disbelief that they were still alive. The doctors and nurses ran from bed to bed, trying to comfort them and giving them necessary treatments. Both Nicholas and Alexandra hadn't seen anything like this before and they were in total shock. Alexandra volunteered to help the nurses and talk to patients. Nicholas arranged a meeting with the top doctor of the hospital instead. The doctor was pleased to see him. They shook hands. The doctor was tall and bald, wearing white robes.

'Do you have enough medication for all patients and all injuries?' the czar demanded.

'No, Your Majesty, most of it is out of stock. The hospital is on the edge of bursting. The doctors and nurses are doing their jobs as best they can.'

'Write me a list of medications the hospital requires. I will provide them for you as soon as possible.'

'Yes, Your Majesty.' He opened the glass cabinet, opened the folder and retrieved a piece of paper and gave it to the czar.

'The patients from the corridors must be moved to another hospital straightaway.'

'I'll do it today.'

'Each patient will receive financial compensation and each doctor and nurse will have a pay rise.'

A tiny smile appeared on his tired face. 'Thank you, Your Majesty.' They shook hands and Nicholas left the office.

Alexandra managed to talk to the patients. They told her about their ordeal the previous day. Her eyes were full of tears on the way home.

'Shocking experience,' she whispered and sobbed. 'If I wasn't born royal, I would have probably become a nurse.' Alexandra lifted her eyes full of tears and looked at Nicholas.

'Don't cry, Alex. We will do what we can to improve their condition,' he said and he gave her a hug of reassurance.

Nicholas received several reports regarding the matter. No one was eager to admit that it was their idea in the first place to use that nasty field. Consequently, it remained unknown whose idea it was. Grand Duke Andre resigned a few low-rank people connected to the organisation of this event, including a number of police members. The money was paid to the victims or their relatives, regardless of whether they were still alive or deceased. All hospitals in Moscow received the supply of medication and a staff pay rise. Despite all of that, people remained anxious and apprehensive and prayed to Jesus Christ.

Chapter 9
Nicholas and Alexandra, Their Young Family and Holiday to France

Rapidly after the coronation, they began to search for a suitable castle for them to call home. Three main possibilities were Winter Palace, Alexander Palace or Peterhof Palace. Winter Palace was too luxurious for Czarina Alexandra. It was so massive, that one could get lost, easily, among the portraits, paintings and superfluous furniture. The czarina wished for a small and cosy place, which they all would love and call home. Alexander Palace was a smaller option; however, both Nicholas and Alexandra were not hundred per cent sure about it. The third option was Peterhof Palace. It was quite small and delicate. Czarina Alexandra truly adored it. The palace was private, secure and secluded. It had gorgeous gardens with this kaleidoscope of stunning fountains. A perfect palace for a perfect family.

What do you think about Peterhof Palace, darling?' Nicholas asked her, wandering around the building, in his mysterious voice.

'In my opinion, this palace is quite charming and delightful. It has everything that our family may ever require,' she pronounced and her eyes sparkled like diamonds.

'It's away from the hustle and bustle of St Petersburg. The castle makes a safer place for our children.'

'It's a secluded haven for our growing family. Shall we make it our home?' Alexandra asked with excitement.

'Surely, we shall. Anything for you, my queen,' and they gave each other a kiss.

'It's time for a celebration.'

Alex was rather delighted that she didn't have to share a castle with her mother-in-law any longer and in this castle, she could do what pleased her, without being judged. To run the palace and for her personal and family needs, she was given a generous amount of money, monthly. She spent it prudently and economically. Alexandra had very little money while she was a child. Consequently, she learned how to spend it wisely.

The furniture of the castle was rather old-fashioned and awfully superfluous. Alex wished to create a warm homely atmosphere. In order to achieve it, she purchased new British furniture in latest Victorian style and decorated the castle in the British way. The result was fabulous. From now on, the royal family spent their quality time in Peterhof Palace and her new furniture reminded Alex about her grandma.

From time to time, Czarina Alexandra received jewellery gifts from Nicholas and other people for birthdays, Christmas, coronation and the birth of her children. She also found the miscellaneous diamond items of jewellery in different castles and began to collect them. Her diamond collection grew bigger and bigger. She had a secret place in her room where they were hidden. Occasionally, it gave her real pleasure to admire the diamonds when she was totally private and undisturbed. The items of jewellery mysteriously sparkled when she twirled them in her hand.

Czarina Alexandra employed a British governess just to help her from time to time to look after her sweet little darling. Together, they constructed a routine timetable for her little one. The baby grew into her routine quite quickly and behaved like an angel. Both Nicholas and Alexandra truly enjoyed being parents and the Grand Duchess Olga received lots of love.

In September 1896, when the little princess was ten months old, the three of them went on holiday to Paris. They used one of their royal trains to travel to France. The building of the trans-Siberian railway continued and the miles of rail track appeared rather rapidly. The royal carriage was fast and comfortable and they reached Paris in no time. Princess Olga enjoyed it all the way through. A group of French people greeted them on the platform and the president of France, Mr Faure, himself met them at the station.

'Hello, Your Majesties. I'm glad to see you both once again and your pretty daughter. Welcome to Paris.' They shook hands.

'Hello, Mr Félix Faure. It's fabulous to see you and admire the capital of France for the first time ever,' Nicholas answered in an official tone of voice.

They were driven to Mr Faure's formal residency in Paris. The weather was lovely and warm, and everyone enjoyed the journey. After settling in, they were invited for dinner in a French restaurant in the newly opened Eiffel Tower. The tower was built ten years prior to that, to commemorate the centenary anniversary of the French Revolution and to represent the world influence of France. When everyone who was invited assembled in front of the Eiffel Tower it was dark outside and the thousands of gas lamps were lit up on the tower. The view was simply breath-taking.

'This is the tallest man-made tower in the world. It is 324 m tall and only one person died through its construction,' Félix Faure explained proudly to a small group of well-dressed people in front of him. 'Ladies and gentlemen, please follow me.' They walked into a medium-sized lift and came out on the second floor of the structure. The group marched into a stylish restaurant. Paris sparkled with all its lights at them.

'If I was not yet married, I would have wished to have my wedding day up here. It's so wonderful,' Czarina Alexandra remarked.

'Yes, it would have been a marvellous idea. The Eiffel Tower is without doubt, one of the most impressive structures in the world. It might appear in the list of Seven Wonders one day,' Nicholas answered.

'It only took two years to build it,' Félix Faure added proudly. 'French people are simply superb at building and record-breaking,'

Alexandra replied quietly.

'Currently, Russia is in the middle of building its trans-Siberian railway,' Nicholas said to the French president. 'I'd love to build the longest rail track in history, nearly 10,000 km long, connecting the east and west of the country. Almost one billion roubles in gold is going towards this project. There is a significant difference that Russia has more casualties than France on their building site, it is due to immense impenetrable woodland, treacherous marshland, an unqualified workforce and severe Siberian weather conditions.' Everyone was listening to him with great interest.

'I hope you will be successful, Your Majesty, in your remarkable project,' Félix Faure replied. The evening meal was simply scrumptious and they enjoyed French cuisine once again.

Next day, Mr Faure invited the Russian royal family into Notre Dame Cathedral in Paris. The French lady of Paris stood proudly in front of them, like a queen.

'Notre Dame Cathedral has enormous religious and cultural significance,' the French president began to explain enthusiastically. 'It was built 730 years ago and restored through the centuries. The bells of Notre Dame are called Gabriel, Marie, Genevieve and others. Each weigh two or three tons and are made of steel.'

When they entered the holy building, they were transfixed by the ceiling, windows, the walls and the Crown of Christ. It was displayed at that day. The diamond of architecture and sacredness overwhelmed them and they stood quietly, admiring the holy moment.

'It's simply unbelievable that the Crown of Christ was upon Jesus's head before his crucifixion and now it's in front of us. It's a supreme object,' Czarina Alexandra remarked, looking at a circular entity made of gold and diamonds.

'I feel his pain and suffering during crucifixion,' Nicholas replied.

'Czar Nicholas, you will experience agony and distress, like Christ during crucifixion,' an authoritative voice spoke in his head. A worrying feeling of fear appeared in his stomach and he shuffled backwards away from the crown, trying to hide his distress.

'If it's my destiny,' he replied in his head, staring at the crown.

'The Crown of Christ has immense power. I'm delighted that it's in France, it protects our country from disaster, catastrophe and enemies,' Félix answered and his voice echoed against the walls. They all left the building with uplifted spirit; however, Nicholas was very sad.

'What's wrong, dearest?' Alex asked her husband when they came outside.

'I just have a headache,' he replied.

In the morning, Paris was grey and gloomy, the dark clouds burst with torrential rain. The enormous puddles of water filled up the empty streets. Despite the rain, Nicholas and Alexandra visited a little jewellery shop across the road and bought a few souvenirs for their friends and family. Nicholas purchased a sapphire necklace and gave it as a gift to Alexandra. It made them both happier during the gloomy day. Soon after, they thanked Félix Faure and left Paris and went home by their royal train; however, Nicholas never forgot the message from God. He made his mind up not to tell a single living being.

In the middle of December, Czarina Alexandra found out that she was expecting her second baby. It was a lovely surprise for everyone, just before the Christmas festivities. Her pregnancy was straightforward and without complications, because she knew precisely what to expect this time. On a warm and sunny day, 10 June 1897, her contractions began and in a few hours a baby was born.

'Congratulations, Your Majesties, it's a little princess!' the midwife announced loudly, cutting the umbilical cord. The baby was strong and healthy and the midwife gave her to Alex to hold.

'She's so cute. I will breastfeed her as well. Please bring her to me to feed whenever she's hungry.'

'It's not a problem that it's a girl, the girls can play together. The third one might be a boy. Her name will be Grand Duchess Tatiana Nikolaevna Romanova,' Nicholas proclaimed, holding the little bundle. The bells of the churches across the country began to ring in honour of the royal new-born.

The next year, life for Alexandra was quite busy, chaotic and unpredictable, because she had two tiny babies on her mind. It was fabulous that Alex enjoyed being mother and received plenty of help.

On Christmas Day, 1898, Czarina discovered that she was expecting one more child. This time, she began to pray daily that it would be a boy. Alexandra wished with all her heart to give birth to an heir to the Russian throne, but she had two princesses only. People begun to talk in court that she was unable to produce an heir and it made her life a bit miserable.

'What shall I eat to give birth to a boy?' Alex asked her midwife.

'Bananas, mushrooms and salmon, Your Majesty, and you will have a boy.'

No matter how hard she tried, after an easy pregnancy, on 26

June 1899, Alex gave birth to a healthy baby girl.

'Look, Nicholas, she's so gorgeous. She has such a cute little face and large blue eyes, like little saucers.'

'Yes, she has. How would you like to name her, Victoria or Maria?' Nicholas asked in reply.

'Well, before she was born, I thought her name would be Victoria; however, Maria suits her more. She will be christened as Maria Nikolaevna Romanova.'

'And her gorgeous blue eyes will be known as Maria's saucers.'

The bells of the churches and cathedrals across the country began to ring in honour of the royal birth.

Nicholas and Alexandra were delighted at having three healthy little ladies. Alexandra dressed them in similar white dresses and the three of them together looked like pretty angels. Nicholas took thousands of pictures of the girls and placed them all in photo albums. The royal family had a happy family life. The only problem that bothered Nicholas was the fact that he couldn't spend enough time with his family because of his work commitments. On average, they enjoyed roughly two hours a day together.

On 15 November at 7pm, Grand Duchess Olga celebrated her fifth birthday party. She was bright, beautiful and eager to learn how to read and write. She was simply an adorable little girl and everyone found it enjoyable and amusing talking to a little princess. Olga loved horses and simply adored riding her little pony.

Soon after Olga's birthday celebration, Czarina Alexandra realised that she was pregnant once again. She prayed to the mighty God that this time it would be a male. All of a sudden, her back began to hurt. A sharp pain went through her body, one leg had numbness and she remained in bed for the rest of the day. An elderly doctor visited her and prescribed a small dose of morphine to reduce the pain.

'Because, it is your fourth pregnancy, Your Majesty, in quick succession, a nerve in your back is jammed and it causes the pain. It's called sciatica. The pain will disappear in a few days and may reappear again.'

In a couple of weeks, Alexandra had a sharp pain on and off and was on medication. It was terrible for Alex to be in bed all that time; she felt like an elderly lady yet she was only 28 years old.

In April, towards the end of her pregnancy, the baby began to kick non-stop. It was the most active baby she had ever had. Every night, it kept her awake and she developed sleep deprivation and severe headaches. She used morphine more and more often now.

On 17 June, her labour began and it lasted all through the night and in the morning of 18 June, with a last agonising scream, her baby was born. The midwife got rid of the umbilical cord, checked that the baby was healthy, swaddled her and gave her to Alexandra.

'Is it a boy?' she asked her.

'No, it's a little girl. She is full of beans.'

The baby opened her mouth wide and kicked left and right. Czarina cuddled the baby and then gave her to Nicholas.

'I'm not surprised, she kept me awake every night, kicking, pushing and prodding.'

'She's like a little tomboy. We'll see what she will achieve when she is older,' Nicholas laughed. 'Her name is Grand Duchess Anastasia Nikolaevna Romanova.'

He walked with the kicking bundle towards the window and showed his daughter the fabulous sunrise. The bells of the cathedrals and churches began to ring in honour of the royal child. The four girls were the centre of attention of the royal family. They were showered with gifts and attention.

The Empress Maria Feodorovna visited them from time to time to see Nicholas and her grandchildren; however, Czarina Alexandra was not at all pleased with her company. Both queens realised it and the tension between them grew bigger and bigger. When Anastasia was born, Queen Dowager arrived to admire her new-born granddaughter.

'Unbelievable, four girls in a row. Where is the male successor to the Russian throne?' she asked Alexandra with irritation. 'I gave birth to a lad right at the start of my marriage. What about you?'

'Obviously, he hasn't been born yet. You have to wait longer, I'm afraid.' Their eyes met.

'Why do you call girls by their first names, Czarina Alexandra, without titles? It's highly inappropriate for the royal ladies.'

'Well, well, well, they're my children and I am in charge and it's only for me to decide how to greet them.'

The terrible tension continued through each meeting and both of them thought that it might be better not to see each other as often as before. Alexandra presumed that Maria was jealous of her power and family life. Maria, however, just wanted to see her son and grandchildren. Also, as it happened, Maria almost always disagreed with Alexandra with one problem or another. Nicholas was truly irritated about it. He was in between two ladies he loved. Alexandra thought that maybe one day she would stop her mother-in-law appearing as often as now.

On 10 June 1902, Grand Duchess Tatiana turned five years old. The little princess had a strong personality. Even in her young age, if the girl wanted something from her parents or sisters, she would get it. She demanded attention and respect from people around her. Tatiana was friendly with her dear mother and used it to her advantage. The Grand Duchess adored wearing stylish dresses, shoes, hats and gloves. She always looked stately royal and commented if her sisters made an improper mistake. The girls took an endless number of pictures of each other and their parents. They loved photography. Grand Duchess Tatiana very often chose to be photographed, pretending to be a queen, governess or parent.

One day soon after, Prince Vladimir Orlov arrived at Peterhof

Palace in his new silver Rolls-Royce that he had just brought in from the United Kingdom. The cars were, generally, unknown unique electronic and mechanic devices across the globe.

'Wow, this horseless carriage looks impressive,' Nicholas exclaimed, walking around the car parked in front of the castle.

The hot, midday sun penetrated through the leafy trees on top of the vehicle.

'I drove it all the way from England, Your Imperial Highness. It is brilliant, would you like to have a ride?'

'Splendid idea, Prince Orlov, it would be marvellous. I'm so curious.' Vladimir opened the passenger door.

'Please welcome,' Prince Orlov turned a crank when they both were inside the car and the engine started. It rumbled, growled, roared and glided away. They looked at each other and laughed.

'This is simply superb. Can it drive a bit faster?' Orlov increased the speed and drove around the half-empty streets. The Rolls-Royce made a loud noise. Some people stared at the horseless carriage.

'This is fabulous. I would love to show this automobile to Alexandra and my children, if you don't mind, they would enjoy the ride.'

Later, the entire royal family had a chance to be driven around Peterhof town. All of them were very impressed.

'Prince Orlov, would you like to purchase a vehicle or two for my family?' he asked without hesitation.

'Of course, I'd be delighted. Which automobile would you like, Your Majesty? English, French or German?'

'I do not mind; which one's first. Eventually, I'm going to purchase several cars, regardless.'

In two months, Prince Orlov purchased a French Delaunay-Belleville vehicle for the Czar. Meanwhile, he volunteered to be a personal chauffeur for the royal family. He drove them to different meetings and events; everyone was so pleased.

Before long, a French, brand-new, shiny Delaunay-Belleville motorcar arrived first. Nicholas was so delighted. To start with, he spent a few hours a day in his new automobile. Delaunay-Belleville became his favourite car. His second car was a silver Mercedes; it was faster than the French one and Nicholas took it for a long drive. His third car was a stunning Rolls-Royce. It had a powerful engine and royal elegance. The cars had gas lights, a bell instead of a horn and started with a crank. The one problem was that with the cars of this time, they stopped from time to time because of a mechanical problem or a lack of petrol. To solve this problem, Nicholas had a second car following him non-stop, in case of an emergency. The Czar ordered to build a first garage for 20 cars in Peterhof and the second one in the Winter Palace and employed an army of mechanics and chauffeurs. They even had their turquoise uniforms.

Chapter 10
Grigori Rasputin and His Wish

Most of all in his life, Rasputin wished to see a member of the royal family, no matter who. He wanted it so much that he decided to pursue his goal by using the silver card he received from his friend Count Paul Vronsky. He retrieved it out of his deep pocket, twirled it a few times in his hands and began to read.

If your heart desires to find out your future, join the black princesses of Russia at 9 pm every Saturday, their address followed. 'Black Peril' Milica and Anastasia will give you an opportunity to dive into your life and discover the secrets of your nearest future and find out what lies ahead and your fortunate or tragic destiny.

'Tragic or not, it will be interesting to find out what those madams will tell me,' Rasputin said to himself, marching around his room backwards and forwards.

He had already heard about the spiritual talent of black princesses from other people. He knew that they definitely have a mystic power; however, he wanted to be there and see it with his own eyes. Rasputin rushed outside and soon arrived at his destination. It was already dark on the streets; however, because of his pure luck, he knew exactly where it was. Rasputin passed by the security using his hypnotic power and entered the mysterious room.

It was a half-lit room with blue walls, floor and ceiling, two round tables stood in the centre of it; one was green with fortune-telling cards on it and another was blue with a large crystal ball. Princess Anastasia sat in front of the card table and Princess Milica was behind the crystal ball. The comfortable sofas stood along the walls. The smoke was inside the room. A strong smell of cannabis and other burning herbs tickled eyes and nose. Ten or twelve people were inside the room, smoking and drinking wine. Quietly like a cat, Grigori stepped softly and quietly, and slowed down in front of the table.

'Hello, monk,' she said sleepily and softly. 'Sit down, I will tell you your future and past.' Anastasia shuffled the cards in front of him and asked him to withdraw three cards.

'Blood, royal family and murder, plus double attempt.' Rasputin sat straight like a statue without saying anything, only gazing into her eyes. Anastasia stared into the deepness of Grigori's eyes. Her gaze was awfully powerful. Rasputin was in a hypnotic trance. He had fallen into a peaceful and euphoric state of relaxation. His entire past went through his mind like a black-and-white film. The black princess was the first person who put him in a trance. Grigori begun to read her mind in return and discovered a few naughty secrets.

'Sister, come and help. The monk is very powerful,' she asked when he began to uncover her secrets. Milica used her power as well and together they brought him back to consciousness.

'Would you like to look at the crystal ball next?' Milica asked, like nothing happened.

'Of course,' he said and sat in front of the sparkling ball. The princess stared into her crystal sphere, trying to read his future.

'Your name is Grigori Rasputin and you were here to help the royal family.' Her voice was soft and soothing.

'I'm not surprised that I'm so determined to meet them.'

'Where did you come from, honestly?' she asked slowly like a snake.

'I travelled from the future, from the twenty-second century. Do you believe me?' he laughed.

'I'm not going to answer that. Would you like a cigar with marijuana?'

He accepted and all three of them smoked. The thoughts began to mix up in his head, time slowed down, he felt ravenous all of a sudden and he ordered a snack and a glass of red wine. From this point onwards, they became close friends and the sisters promised Rasputin to arrange a meeting with the czar.

'Monk, what is your strongest power?' Anastasia of Montenegro asked Rasputin quietly.

'Healing power,' he answered, looking at her.

'Would you like to work with us as a team?' she asked again.

'No, but you can tell people that the famous monk Grigori is here to treat people with God's help.'

When Grigori left, Anastasia and Milica began to talk about Rasputin. They walked into the other room, full of mysterious items, in order to be private and undisturbed.

'Milica, did you notice that the monk knew about his future right from the start?' She shuffled a pack of cards.

'No doubt about that,' the princess answered. 'Nobody ever reacts comely and quietly to discover about their own murder.'

'The first card he withdrew was blood. Do you know what it means? Luckily, he didn't ask me.'

'No, I do not, Your Highness, the future will show us.'

'Perhaps he knew the meaning all along,' Milica replied in a sleepy voice, yawning.

Czarina Alexandra was truly preoccupied with her strong desire to conceive a boy. When next time she encountered Princess Anastasia of Montenegro, Czarina invited her for afternoon tea in Peterhof Palace.

'I'd love to have a conversation with you, dear princess, regarding my problem I expressed earlier. Please join me for afternoon tea, tomorrow at 2 pm.'

'Of course, Your Majesty, I'd be delighted.'

'Please bring everything you need, goodbye.'

'Goodbye, see you tomorrow.'

Next afternoon, at around 2 pm, Princess Anastasia arrived with all her magic gear. The tea was already served prior to her arrival. The minuscule sandwiches, quiches, cream cakes and eclairs were arranged in a peculiar geometrical pattern. Czarina Alexandra and Princess Anastasia were the only people to eat them. The meal took place in a large reception parlour, the room was sunny and bright. The crystal chandeliers reflected the light. The princess curtsied as she entered the room.

'It's marvellous to see you, Your Imperial Highness,' Anastasia whispered in a quiet and mysterious way.

'I am eager to see you, my dear princess. I wonder, if you can help me to conceive a boy using mysticism and magic.'

'No doubt about that.' She opened a golden case and pulled out a necklace. It rocked from side to side, inexplicably sparkling, reflecting the sunlight.

'Please sit down and do start. What is this mysterious necklace?' the queen asked with boundless curiosity.

'It's a charmed necklace made of a combination of moonstone, fluoride and aquamarine. Those stones by themselves increase the chance to conceive a boy and together with my enchantments, it will produce the desired result and you will have a little baby boy. The charm will work only once, because it's personal.'

'How charming, I'd love to purchase this choker, thank you so much. Hopefully, I will have a son rather soon.'

'Please carry it with you constantly, before and during pregnancy, if you'd like to receive the desired result.' The princess stood up and brought the golden box with the enchanted necklace and placed it gently on a polished table in front of the queen.

'Princess Anastasia, would you mind telling me my future, sweetheart, using your cards?'

'No, Your Majesty, of course I don't mind.' She begun to shuffle her cards. 'Please withdraw three cards – blood, abbot and a child and one more please, the broken crown. This mysterious monk might help you with the child and you may have the crown problems at the end of your reign.'

Czarina Alexandra tried to digest this information, looking down at the four cards on the table.

'Positive and negative. Well, I will have a child and crown problems and a monk might have me to solve them.'

'Yes, it might take place.'

'Anything else you would like to let me know, dear princess?'

'I'm not sure,' she begun to think. 'One more thing, I completely forgot. An elderly midwife, Clara, informed me yesterday that the couples who would like a baby boy should try different sexual positions.'

'That's unusual, thank you for your help, dear princess.'

'It was my pleasure to assist you, Your Majesty.' Princess Anastasia was not ready yet to organise a meeting between Czarina Alexandra and Grigori Rasputin. She thought that the monk might decrease the sister's influence in the royal court.

When Rasputin left the place, he was annoyed that he had to go through the long corridors of the monastery, being a bit drunk. If anyone noticed, he would be out. He tried to be as quiet as he could, like a grey mouse, and stepped quietly towards his room.

'You haven't been out this time of night, have you?' a young monk with blond hair asked him when he was halfway there.

'No, I haven't. One of the monks became ill, so I visited him to make sure that he was recovering.' Grigori reached his room and was pleased that no one else saw him. It was rather inconvenient for him to be in the monastery and live a normal life.

'It's time to buy an apartment,' Rasputin said to himself and closed his eyes.

Next day, the group of monks, including Rasputin, were conducting the church service in the monastery. The church building was full of people. There was a reading of the Bible first, receiving blood and body of Christ second and blessings third. Rasputin gave his blessings to elderly people to reduce their suffering and pain: there was an officer with Parkinson's in his eighties, a lady with dementia, accompanied by her daughter and a young gentleman followed them. Rasputin was fully occupied with his work and he didn't look around.

'You are doing a great deed, Grigori, reducing their pain. Can you pray for me? I'd love to have a son.'

'Of course, I will. What is your name?'

'Nicholas II of Russia,' he received his blessings from the monk.

'I will pray for Your Majesty, as I have never prayed before. You will have a baby boy next, I promise,' Grigori answered calmly and their eyes met. This eye contact formed an attachment. For unknown reasons, Nicholas believed Rasputin hundred per cent this time.

When he returned to Peterhof that evening, he said to Alex, 'I met a mysterious monk Grigori. He promised to pray for us in order to conceive a boy.'

Alexandra was astonished.

'My constant praying has been answered. Hopefully, he's the one who was sent by the mighty God,' she replied, thinking about Anastasia's predictions.

'Conceivably, you're correct, we will see in the near future.'

Next, after meeting the czar, Grigori decided to go on a religious fasting, for seven days straight. He stopped eating everything, except water. The monk locked himself in a cell and began to pray solemnly with passion. Other monks every day delivered him water. Grigori thought that if he prayed with a passion, then God will hear him and the czar will have a son.

After a week of fasting, Rasputin began to visit different apartments, which were for sale at that point. The first flat was a large, old place, which needed a lot of work. The wallpaper was peeling off the walls, there was no bath, only a shower and it was dark and gloomy. The previous owner had died and a new one tried to sell it without renovation. Rasputin disliked it. The second apartment was a bit better. It was cleaner and was sold with newer furniture but Grigori didn't know whether to buy or not to buy. He wandered around it for a long time and couldn't imagine himself being there at all. The third place was a bit smaller, it had a bathroom, it was sunny, clean and cheerful, the furniture was included and it even had a telephone line. Rasputin wished to buy it straightaway.

'The Lord tells me that this place will be the best out of the three you have shown me,' he said to a gloomy young man selling flats. They began to arrange all the documents and, in a few months, the apartment was purchased. On one hand, Rasputin was really sad to depart from Alexander Nevsky Monastery, because it was a holy place and he felt close to God being there. Nevertheless, he was happy to leave the walls of the monastery because of his personal freedom. Rasputin wanted to have a social and personal life, even at night.

The apartment that he had chosen was on Gorokhovaya Street. It had two sunny bedrooms, one sitting room with a balcony, a shabby kitchen, a simple bathroom and a dark front entrance. In one of the bedrooms, he set up a praying corner with Orthodox icons. The furniture was simple, but strong and steady. This simple apartment was the top level he could have ever afforded. He was very proud of his new place. At first, he couldn't comprehend the fact that he lived in St Petersburg.

When he moved in, he spent a whole day just making it habitable for him, moving things from place to place. It was crucial to call his friend Count Paul Vronsky. The red shiny telephone with a white disc and black numbers stood on a wooden chest of drawers. This was the first ever phone call Grigori had made in his entire life. He lifted the receiver, listened for a signal and began to dial a number. Because he dialled an international number, he was transferred to a telephone company, and a telephone lady on the other end asked him what number he wanted to dial. He recited it out loud and was connected to a number in London. After a few long signals, someone replied. Grigori explained what he wanted. Rasputin didn't understand a word; however, he carried on holding. Suddenly, he heard a familiar voice.

'Hello, Count Paul Vronsky speaking!'

'Hello, Father Paul. This is Father Grigori. I bought an apartment. How are you?' Rasputin was flabbergasted that he had managed to hear him.

'Hello, Father Grigori. I'm very well, thank you. I'm glad you bought your apartment. I sold my villa in Petersburg. Fabulous news, I got married a few days ago to Dame Verline Saunders. Our wedding was rather marvellous.'

'Thank you, my friend. Fabulous news. What else is happening around you?'

'I spoke to the czar in Alexander Nevsky Monastery during the church service.'

'Outstanding! You are amazing at climbing up and building connections! Stay on the top. Life is awesome for both of us at present.'

'I'll try my best. I will call you again, my friend. Speak to you shortly.'

'Goodbye, Father Grigori!' The short signals followed and he put the phone down.

Next day, Grigori posted an advertisement on an advertisement wall not far from his apartment to employ a cleaner for a number of hours per week. Three people were interested. The first was an elderly granny, the second a young man and the third was a young lassie in her twenties. He denied the position to the first two people and invited a young female for the interview. The young woman, who knocked at his door, was a good-looking woman. She was simply and modestly dressed and had her brown hair in a bun.

'Hello, my name is Valentina and I am looking for a position as a cleaner.' Rasputin found her quite appealing. Especially her brown eyes.

'Have you ever worked as a cleaner before?' he asked her first.

'Yes sir, here are my recommendations.' He looked at her documents, but he had already decided that he would employ the girl regardless. They agreed on a possible payment.

'Start on Wednesday, next week.' She smiled, thanked him and left the flat. The next few days, when she wasn't there, his mind returned to Valentina, again and again and again. From Wednesday, her work began, and she cleaned for him for two or three weeks. Rasputin liked her more and more, day after day after day. One of the Wednesdays, he couldn't stop himself any longer.

'Have you ever had a boyfriend?' he questioned Valentina when she polished a wooden dinner table.

'Yes, sir, why do you ask?'

'You are so good-looking, sweetheart. I'd be surprised if you don't have one.'

'Not now, but I had one before. He dumped me.'

'Would you like to become my girlfriend, have sex and much fun? I will double your wages, nothing wrong with that.' He came closer and closer. She was a bit scared, but thought that if she didn't agree, he would take her by force anyway and she would lose her job. In the volatile situation in the country right now, to have a job meant being lucky. Any work, even 12-hour shifts in the factory. No one would pay her rent, food and clothes if she had no job.

'Yes, sir, I agree.' She was looking down at the floor boards and he kissed her.

'If you go to the police, I'll say that you wanted it first. Who do you think they will believe, you or me?'

'You, sir.'

Grigori gave her a gentle hug. They kissed a few times, he removed some of her clothes and placed her gently on the sofa. They were moving in unison for a while, until he was satisfied.

'Did you like it, sweet pea? It was so nice, in my opinion.'

She nodded in agreement. From now on, Valentina and Grigori enjoyed each other's company more and more as she began to get used to his sexual demands.

Chapter 11
Czarevich Alexei

In February 1904, the Russian-Japanese war began. Nicholas II was certain that it would lead to victory. His dislike towards Japanese people started after the incident with a crazy Japanese soldier who attacked him during his holiday in Japan in 1891. He underestimated their power.

Soon after the meeting with Princess Anastasia, Czarina Alexandra started to feel the symptoms of pregnancy. She prayed to God daily that for goodness' sake, it wasn't a girl once again. She carried a magic choker in a little pouch, following Anastasia's advice.

In June, Princess Tatiana turned six. She grew into the most gorgeous, cutest little princess with large blue eyes and an adorable smile. She was a natural chatterbox and asked questions non-stop. No one could deny her request, because she was so adorable. Her behaviour was immaculate. She was like a little angel. Everybody was amused when she was a bit naughty, because it rarely ever happened. Most of all in her life, she loved playing with her older sister Princess Olga. The girls had been named by their parents as a big pair. They played together all day long and shared all girly secrets. In contrast, their younger sisters Maria and Anastasia were named a little pair. The girls had a governess and a French tutor, Pierre Gilliard, who gave them lessons in French and other subjects.

Alexandra's pregnancy went very well to start with; however, in the middle of July the sciatica problem returned and Czarina Alexandra started to take morphine for pain relief and remained in her room, staying in bed. She dialled Princess Anastasia's phone number, asking for help and advice.

'I can arrange, Your Majesty, to organise a meeting with Grigori Rasputin, a known healer, if you wish.'

'Please, invite him into the Peterhof Palace, I'll be waiting for him,' she thanked her, said goodbye, put the phone down and closed her eyes.

Alexandra didn't know how long she had been sleeping, when she heard a knock at the door.

'Grigori Rasputin, ma'am,' a female voice announced.

'Please come in,' Alexandra answered. She rested in a half-sitting position. The tall monk in brown robes appeared in the royal bedroom. They looked at each other unblinkingly for a few seconds, without saying anything.

'The Mighty God guided me here for years to assist Your Majesty and reduce your pain,' Rasputin announced firmly, lifting his right arm and releasing the energy. Alexandra's pain diminished immediately and a look of unexpected surprise appeared on her face.

'Very well, excellent job. My pain has disappeared. How did you do that?' she asked the monk, who was still standing in front of the door.

'God has given me the power of healing. I'm sharing it like Jesus Christ used to nine hundred years ago.' His deep dark eyes looked through Alexandra. She suddenly became awfully shy and her face became red all over with embarrassment and she looked away. 'Your eyes…they're so powerful,' Alexandra complained.

'You're really shy, Czarina Alexandra, for the royal family, almost like a child,' he said honestly.

'Yes, I do have that problem. My husband thinks that I am making it up, very often I'm too embarrassed to go there and deliver a speech in front of a massive crowd of people. By our agreement, Nicholas does it instead of me.' She found herself thinking she's talking to him like she had known him all her life. How weird. Alexandra never had a friend in Russia.

'If you ever need my help, Your Majesty, or would just like to talk about something, here is my business card.' He walked a few steps further and placed it on the dressing table.

'Thank you kindly, Father Grigori, I'll be in touch,' and she rang the bell signalling his departure.

'God be with you,' Rasputin said and left the royal parlour.

What an interesting visitor, that monk Grigori Rasputin, she thought when he left.

In three weeks, on 12 August, her contractions began. They were strong and Alex knew that her baby would be born quite quickly. She took some morphine for pain relief, prayed, had a glass of wine and called her usual midwife. The midwife hurried in and in two or three hours of pushing and screaming, her fifth and final baby was born. The midwife cut the umbilical cord, checked that the baby was breathing, swaddled it and gave it to the mother.

'Thousands of blessings, it's a boy, Your Majesty!' she said with a kind smile.

Neither Nicholas nor Alexandra could believe their ears at first. Nicholas took the boy after feeding and carried him around the room for a while.

'His name is Czarevich Alexi Nikolayevich Romanov,' he announced and for the last time in history, the bells of the churches started to ring for the newborn royal.

'The heir to the throne at last,' Czarina Alexandra smiled. The celebration began and everybody was so pleased, especially the little princesses. They called Alexei 'our little baby' and spoiled him rotten.

'Please bring the boy for me to feed, whenever he cries, day and night,' Alexandra gave her orders.

The royal family was thrilled to bits.

The next morning, Alexi begun to cry louder than normal. The baby was fed, changed and rocked many times, but he carried on crying. He cried for a couple of hours in a row and Alexandra thought that it wasn't normal and called a doctor. She supposed that he may have caught a cold or an infection. Alexandra knew babies' behaviour very well by now, because he was her fifth one.

The first doctor arrived, looked at the baby and firmly concluded that nothing was wrong with him. He was just stressed after childbirth and he would be fine in a few days, simply wait and see. He also noticed two tiny bruises: one on his forehead and one on his knee. When the doctor left, Alexandra began to pay attention to the couple of bruises on his skin. Alexi didn't stop crying and his bruises increased.

Czarina Alexandra called another doctor. An elderly man examined Alexi's body and finally said, 'Those bruises are lumpy and the boy is crying more when I touch them. Do you have a history of haemophilia?' he asked Alexandra.

She sighed deeply and covered her face with her hands. In a few seconds, she recovered and replied.

'Unfortunately, I do. My uncle Prince Leopold had this illness.'

'I would like to diagnose this boy with haemophilia disease,' he said with a sigh.

'Is there any treatment?' she asked, knowing the answer.

'Unfortunately, not, Your Majesty. Just make sure he has soft objects around him to avoid new bumps and bruises and aspirin for pain relief.'

When Nicholas came home in the evening, Alexandra asked him to talk to her in private. He knew straight away that something was not right. He locked the door behind him when they entered their bedchamber.

'What's wrong, sweetheart? Why do you look so sad like a thunderstorm cloud?' he asked and came closer.

'Alexi cried for couple of hours for no apparent reason today. I called the doctor and he concluded that it was just going through childbirth trauma and nothing more. He showed me a couple of bruises on his skin, one on his knee and one on the forehead. When he left, the bruises began to grow and Alexi didn't stop crying.'

'Perhaps you're just paranoid about him. He's your first son.'

'No, let me finish!' she yelled. 'The second doctor arrived, touched his bruises and concluded that he has a hereditary disease, haemophilia. The process where the body can't make blood clots. So it causes bleeding and each bleeding can be fatal.' She began to sob.

When the sobs subsided, Nicholas asked Alexandra, 'What does it mean now? How to treat him?' Nicholas didn't know anything about haemophilia at all.

'Of course, you don't know. There is no treatment. Just protect him from bumps and bruises. My uncle Prince Leopold survived until his thirties. He even managed to get married and have two kids.'

'It's good, I suppose. Alexi has a chance to survive to adulthood. I don't want anyone to know that my son has a serious condition. Especially in this unstable political climate, they may use it against me,' Nicholas replied in a serious voice.

'I do agree, let's keep it a secret from everyone,' Alexandra agreed and nodded.

'I will support you as much as I can. Why didn't you tell me about it before marriage?'

'I refused your proposals twice. Do you remember? It was my secret reason. I promised Queen Victoria not to tell anyone,' and she began to sob loudly like a child. Nicholas wanted to comfort Alex, but she pushed him away.

'Don't touch me. I'd like to be alone. I'll stay in my personal bedroom overnight. I might say something now that I may regret in the near future.' Alex stomped out of the room and closed the door behind her. This was the first ever serious argument they had ever had.

He opened the bar and chose the strongest drink out of three rows of bottles in front of him and poured himself a drink.

'Perhaps everyone already knew about this condition during Ernest Lewis's wedding day and our proposal, and no one informed me. Well, I have to accept it like a true gentleman. It's yet another challenge and punishment from God.'

Alexandra managed to rock Alexei to sleep with great difficulty. She hadn't recovered from childbirth yet and was truly exhausted. The argument with Nicholas made her feel low and she wept bitterly half of the night, which resulted in a splitting headache. Maybe it was just the baby blues, she wasn't sure. She took a bit of morphine as pain relief and managed to doze off in a heavy nightmarish dream.

At around 4 am, Alexei began to cry again. Alexandra opened her eyes. They were heavy and narrow. At first, she was confused where she was. Alex's nanny heard him cry and began to change him. The memories of yesterday painfully returned to Alexandra; unfortunately, it was real. She didn't even inform her ladies-in-waiting where she was.

'Good morning, Sonia, I just accidentally fell asleep feeding Alexei,' she lied.

'Good morning, Your Majesty, anything else I can do for you?' Servants never show how much they know.

'Please look after Alexei after feeding, I need more sleep.'

'Yes, of course.' After feeding, Sonia took the crying bundle into another room. The boy did not stop making a loud noise. Only after two or three hours did she manage to rock him to sleep.

'He has been crying for five babies,' she complained when he finally fell asleep.

Both Nicholas and Alexandra came downstairs for breakfast. They chose to breakfast together, just the two of them, that morning without children. A new day put everything in a different perspective.

'Good morning, Your Imperial Majesty, apologies if I said something inconvenient last night.' Czarina Alexandra gave him a smile.

'Good morning, dearest, accept my request for forgiveness as well.' And they gave each other a kiss. 'Please sit down, let's have breakfast, I'm so hungry this morning.' The table was full of croissants, crispy rolls, pancakes, jams and toasts. The tea was served a minute later. The majestic early sunrise penetrated through the goldish brown castle windows.

'After the birth of our son, I'd love to announce a change,' Alexandra said, staring into her cup of tea. 'From this point in time, I wish to participate in political and state-based decisions.'

'Indisputably, it will be marvellous, I'll be delighted to share the state work with you. Fresh mind, fresh decisions, fresh perspectives.' At the beginning of their marriage, Nicholas was a bit upset that Alexandra didn't wish to participate in any government decision-making and activities and now he was pleased with her choice.

'I'd love to begin today, if you don't mind.' Her eyes glistened like a couple of diamonds.

Both of them departed Peterhof in the new Rolls-Royce. Czarina Alexandra gave detailed instructions to Sonia to look after the little one while she was away for three or four hours. It was lovely not to be in the castle for a change and it was a chance to spend more time with Nicholas. It was a great deal to familiarise herself with, and she enjoyed it regardless of her circumstances back home. Unexpectedly, a nervous phone call interrupted her work. The baby was crying and no one could stop him. She had to return to the castle as soon as she physically could.

When she entered the nursery, there was not a crying bundle, but a shrieking bundle. Alexandra picked him up gently and he stopped, but not for long. She brought him into her bedroom, breastfed and gave a prescribed dosage of aspirin. It did make a difference. The bruises he had increased in size. She walked around the bedroom rocking and singing lullabies. A splitting headache pulsated in her head. Suddenly, her eyes noticed a business card from Grigori Rasputin, still lying on the dressing table, where he had placed it three weeks ago.

'Maybe he will be able to stop the bleeding and calm Alexei down?' she asked herself. For the first time in her life, she dialled Grigori's number. No one replied. On the third attempt, he answered.

'Hello, this is Grigori Rasputin speaking!'

'Hello there, this is Czarina Alexandra! How are you?'

'Good thanks, with God's help. It's pleasant to hear you. What can I do for you, Your Majesty?' he replied.

'My new-born son is crying constantly. He's in pain. The doctors cannot assist him. Can you help, Father Grigori?'

'Yes, I can, but I have to see the child first. Do not give him any medication.'

'Very well, I am waiting for you in Peterhof Palace, come as soon as possible. Goodbye.'

'Goodbye.' He put the phone down.

Rasputin ordered a carriage and rushed outside. Very soon, he reached his destination. He was truly delighted to visit the castle again and helped Czarina Alexandra. The weather was so pleasant. The evening castle garden looked simply fabulous. The tall electric lights showed the way.

When he entered the building, a tall blond gentleman guided him all the way to the nursery. The baby was in the cradle, crying again. Alexandra stood opposite him.

'Your baby will stop crying soon. God answered my prayers,' he said raising his arm and releasing the energy when he stood in front of the boy. Miraculously, Grigori's voice and prayers comforted Alexei and the boy fell asleep.

'That's a miracle, the baby has fallen asleep almost instantly, as soon as you came in; it usually takes hours to rock him to sleep.'

Alexandra's nervousness subsided and she stopped temporarily worrying about her son's health. Her headaches vanished and she felt generally better.

'The babies look so pretty when they sleep,' Father Grigori whispered. 'What did the doctors say about his condition?' he asked with great interest.

'First, I would like to appoint you as a personal healer for Alexei and you will swear on the Bible that his condition will remain unrevealed.'

'God bless you, Your Majesty, I'll do anything you wish and keep it a secret.' He retrieved an old dusty Bible out of his pocket, put his hand on it and announced, 'I solemnly swear not to reveal a secret to a single soul even during torture for Father, Christ and Holy Spirit.'

'Fabulous, now it's safe to say. He has the disease haemophilia. The disease where the body can't make blood clots. As a result, a small cut or bruising causes bleeding and each bleeding can be fatal.'

'I promise, the boy will be alive, while I am alive. Don't worry, Czarina Alexandra.'

'I'm delighted to hear that, Grigori Rasputin, please return to the castle each Friday to check up on my son.'

She found it so easy and quite interesting talking to him. Alexandra presumed that he might be her first ever friend in the entire Russia. Because of her shyness, it was quite tricky for her to make friends. The majority of them thought that she was arrogant.

'Yes of course, anything for Czarevich Alexei, bless him Mighty God! First of September, two of my children, Varvara and Maria, will start their lessons, in private boarding school, like little ladies,' he revealed.

'How marvellous, see you on Friday. Goodbye, Grigori.'

'Goodbye, Czarina Alexandra.'

He walked through the castle, admiring the luxury surroundings around him. He couldn't believe that he had secured a permanent position and would come back here every week.

Rasputin left the castle with uplifted spirits. People began to treat him in a different way. He was known before; however, now he was famous. Everyone recognised him on the streets and began to follow him with positive or negative purpose.

Miraculously, Alexei's bleeding stopped and he was calm and quiet for a few days. Grigori's treatment helped somehow. Before Alex's birth, all attention had been paid to the little princesses; however, now the attention shifted towards Alexei. All members of the family focused on his well-being and happiness.

Christmas arrived quite soon; the ground was covered with lovely snow. The royal kids began to play snowballs, ice skating, sledge riding and playing in Peterhof Palace garden. The castle had been decorated with Christmas lights and a wonderful Christmas tree was placed in the ballroom specifically for the royal children. It was the most wonderful time of the year for them. They received hundreds of presents. On Christmas Day, Grigori Rasputin's daughters, Maria and Varvara, visited the royal castle. They truly enjoyed playing with the royal children and Christmas festivities.

The Russian Japanese war proved to be quite unsuccessful: defeat after defeat after defeat demoralised the army. It created a growing pressure among the different groups of people and formed an unstable and dangerous political situation in the entire country.

Czarina Alexandra had an unusually large amount of correspondence that Christmas. She spent almost an entire week replying to it all. One of the letters was from her uncle, Edward VII. She decided to read it first.

Dear Queen Consort Alexandra of Russia, Finland and Poland,

I'm writing to congratulate you and the Russian Royal family for the birth of your son Prince Alexei and wish you all a prosperous New Year and a very Merry Christmas.

The dangerous and unstable political situation in Russia might lead to unforeseen circumstances and tragic events. In order to save the Crown in this unstable time, it might be wise to share the unlimited power and organise the parliamentary democracy and constitutional monarchy in Russia.

In the countries with a sovereign in charge, there is always a dreadful danger of uprising from below. The wisest step is to organise political or social change from above.

As a positive example, the public of the United Kingdom and Ireland are quite content with their sovereign and their political, economic and social current position.

Hopefully, the tensions and complications you are experiencing now will be successfully resolved.

I will be truly honoured to invite the entire Russian family on British soil to the Isle of Wight in the near future.

Yours cordially, Edward VII

After reading the letter, Czarina Alexandra thought that currently, it was not the right time to make any drastic political changes in the country. It was much better to keep unlimited power as long as possible. In her opinion, the royal monarchs did not need to earn love and respect of their citizens, they would receive respect and loyalty from Russian people anyhow. Consequently, an answer was written, keeping this in mind.

Chapter 12
A Bomb Explosion

The winter in Moscow was drastically cold that year. Generally, people were awfully unhappy on the streets. The prices were reasonably high for essential items, like bread, milk and flour. The poorest of the population were starving. The richest people hadn't done enough to help. Therefore, they began to unify into local criminal gangs to steal money and food. Some of the people joined the radical political parties, which promoted terrorism as a tool to solve problems.

Grand Duke Sergei had been appointed as a governor general in Moscow. Usually, he shared political views with Nicholas and supported him in the majority of cases, solving problems swiftly and rapidly for many years in a row. The Emperor was contented with his service.

Earlier, the year prior to it, Grand Duke Sergei was involved in directing and organising the forceful removal of Jews from Moscow. The people from the Jewish community had to leave Moscow in a matter of days. There were families with several children, babies, elderly people, people who had lived in Moscow for more than forty years and single households. The police searched each household, making sure that all Jewish people left their properties. They couldn't stay. The only Jewish people who could remain were ladies who agreed to work as prostitutes.

The crowds of Jewish people gathered on a street before their removal, waiting for transport. The temperature outside was -30°C. The Jewish families were standing outside in freezing conditions for a few hours straight. It was an unfair and horrible process, and it was not surprising that it led to their uprising. Twenty-thousand people had been removed. Both Nicholas and his uncle considered it to be a normal chain of events and thought that nothing would follow. Although there were some people in the Moscow government who wanted to change the date of removal to a warmer day. Grand Duchess Elizabeth was horrified about the entire process and explained to her husband that punishment may come from God.

The constant disturbances and turmoil in Moscow made Sergei call Nicholas and ask for his support and advice.

'Good morning, Your Majesty. How are you and your family?' he began.

'Good morning, Uncle. We are not too bad at the moment, but the situation in Petersburg is truly awful.'

'In Moscow it's the same. Perhaps we need more forceful actions to stop those dreadful disturbances.'

'What kind of actions do you mean, Sergei?'

'Give greater sentences for organising demonstrations and radical political parties. Use the army to stop the uprising and install order.'

'The problem is, Sergei, the majority of the regiments are located at the Japanese border. I don't have enough of the troops to crush this uprising across the entire country.'

'Maybe you can do it in Moscow at least. The city has enough military power.'

'No, I don't think so. I'll just wait and see.'

'Great! Seriously, it will lead to a total disaster. Believe me. I would like to resign from my position in the government.' He raised his voice.

'Splendid. Do so. Thanks for the service Grand Duke Sergei, goodbye.'

'Goodbye.' The short signals followed.

Nicholas could not believe or comprehend what had just happened Even though they were relatives; they had had a strong friendship throughout their entire lives and supported each other from early childhood.

Well, in a couple of weeks I'll offer him a place in a different town, when he's in a more positive mood, Nicholas thought.

He was not at all cross with Sergei and blamed it entirely on the current political climate. However, Sergei had no other way or idea to improve the situation in Moscow and decided to resign; he felt powerless.

Sergei and Elizabeth lived in Moscow in their villa near the Kremlin. Grand Duke Sergei had just retired from his government position. The couple concentrated on the charity work and raising their beloved adopted children, Grand Duchess Maria and her younger brother Grand Duke Dmitri.

Just before Christmas day, Elizabeth and her adopted children prepared three hundred gifts explicitly for the kids from an orphanage in Moscow. The poorest of the poor in their community. Elizabeth, Dmitri and Maria arrived at the orphanage on Christmas day to deliver them. It took several days of work to wrap up all the gifts. They were all placed under the Christmas tree prior to the children's arrival in a main reception room. Each gift contained a bag of sweets, a woolly jumper, a box of pencils and a toy.

'Merry Christmas, children, my name is Princess Elizabeth. Here are my adopted children Mary and Dmitri.' Everybody clapped.

'Merry Christmas, Princess Elizabeth,' they all replied.

'As I can see, Santa has already delivered all the gifts into your orphanage, my dear children, they are all under the Christmas tree. Two boys from each class, please take one box full of presents and give the gifts to your classmates.'

'Two boys, not three, Andrew,' their head teacher stopped one of the boys. The boys handed out the gifts very quickly and soon there were only one or two gifts left at the bottom of each box. Those gifts were for children who were in the sickbay.

'Thank you, boys, for delivering the gifts.'

'Thank you, Princess Elizabeth.' The children unwrapped their gifts straightaway and Elizabeth, Mary and Dmitri were delighted to see three hundred happy faces. It was the best moment of their lives.

Besides, Andre and Elizabeth opened a café – 'Hot Meals for Poor' – a few years prior. The cooks were employed to prepare three meals a day. Anyone who was hungry were able to eat there for free. The food was simple: soup, porridge, eggs or bread; however, it gave a chance of survival for people at rough moments in their lives. Long queues formed into the café in January.

Grand Duke Sergei sponsored or directed the multiple charities, which helped blind children, people in wheelchairs, ex-soldiers, deaf or blind people. The charities delivered food packages, warm clothes and medication right to their personal home address. It was so rewarding to see happy faces and hear the kindest words from them. Both Sergei and Elizabeth observed a dreadful level of poverty and believed that Nicholas and his government could have done more to improve their lives in the first instance.

Moreover, Princess Elizabeth and the nuns from the local monastery organised a special donation for the hospitals to provide medication, bandages and doctors and nurses uniforms. In the nunnery, sisters prepared medication packages and uniform parcels during their spare time and these boxes were delivered to the local hospitals. The wounded soldiers returned from the Japanese conflict and arrived in the Moscow hospitals. The hospitals became overwhelmed. Consequently, those parcels were crucial supplies.

Later in February, the entire family went to a concert and a charity event not far from the house. After the event, all four of them were sitting in a carriage, talking, playing games and laughing. A terrorist with an explosive was waiting for them to pass by. They slowed down the carriage by throwing something large under the wheels of it. It slowed down and stopped. The terrorist looked inside the carriage and saw Grand Duchess Elizabeth, her husband and two adopted children sitting in it. He had never seen such a beautiful lady in his entire life.

Wow, she looks magnificent, even prettier than Czarina herself, Kalyayev thought and yelled, 'Wait, not today, children.'

For a split second, Elizabeth's eyes looked at him and the carriage passed by faster and faster.

Around lunchtime the next day, the 17 February, Grand Duke Sergei and Elizabeth decided to dine together, just the two of them. The children were busy studying with their tutor. Not many people at all visited them during those days because the streets were so terrifying.

'Sergei, sweetheart, please do not travel without your bodyguard. I love you so much and I don't want to lose you, my dearest, love of my life,' Elizabeth pleaded with tears in her eyes.

'If it's the will of the high and mighty, darling, it will take place anyhow, no matter how many security guards I have. I love you, my adorable, thank you for being the most magnificent, delightful and wonderful wife, friend and mother ever.' They embraced and passionately kissed. 'Let's go to our bedroom, right now, I'd love to spend time with you, please.'

In half an hour, Grand Duke Sergei walked slowly out of his front door with a smile on his face, stretched and headed towards his carriage. It had been prepared for him half an hour before. The coachman was just waiting for his master.

'Go to Kremlin, please,' he ordered to him.

The carriage slowly moved away. Sergei was totally alone, without security. For an unknown reason, a feeling of anxiety crept up on him. At 2.45 pm, near the monastery, a member of a social revolutionary party Kalyayev threw a bomb wrapped up in a newspaper straight into the seat he was sitting upon. The carriage exploded into tiny pieces. Sergei died instantly. The front wheels and the metal frame of the carriage with the half-conscious, bloody, burned coachman drove by itself, towards the Nikolsky gate. The driver died three days later in a nearby hospital, never coming back to consciousness.

Later, 15 minutes after the tragedy, Grand Duchess Elizabeth was informed that her husband had been killed in a bomb explosion.

'How frightful, dreadful and horrifying, I warned him today to take a bodyguard, he disobeyed me,' her voice resonated around the house. 'Take me there right now,' she ordered a policeman who was in front of her.

'Of course, Madame,' he obeyed. They were on the scene in five minutes straight. Elizabeth began to give orders to everyone: reserved, cold and heroic. The entire body of the carriage had exploded into miniscule pieces. The splinters of wood, bones, metal, leather, blood, parts of his body, medals and rings were scattered all over the place. There was so much blood on the white snow, as if a pot of dark red paint had been blasted. It looked as if a portal to hell had temporarily been opened.

'He wanted to be buried in his suit,' she explained. 'There is no body to bury. Collect everything you can find,' she commanded and begun to separate his remains with her bare hands from the rest of the foreign bodies and separated for burial and the criminal investigation. The first pile had: fragments of his skull, a few bones of his body, fingers ribs and toes. The second pile had: his medallions, rings and personal possessions. All of it was carefully preserved for burial and the murder investigation.

One of the policemen noticed the fragments on a nearby roof. He climbed up using a ladder and collected a few fragments. His entire finger with a ring had been added to the gruesome pile. Soon, on the same day, all the remains were collected and the investigation began. The murderer was arrested and sent to prison.

When Elizabeth arrived home, she was stunned, like a zombie. At first, she couldn't believe and comprehend that it had truly taken place. She locked herself in their bedroom and began to cry hysterically. She grabbed a pile of letters from her drawer and burned them one by one. It was the entire correspondence between her and her husband. Each letter caught fire, brightly burned for a while and finally shrivelled into the blackness of ash in a fireplace. Soon, all of them were burned. She realised that her social life was finished. Elizabeth uncovered their wedding photographs at the bottom of the drawer. Nicholas II took them with his own camera. They were truly beautiful pictures. She decided to preserve them and put them back in her drawer.

'Would you like to eat anything, Your Royal Highness?' her butler asked her behind the door.

'No thanks, I'm not hungry. Please feed the children,' she replied and began to cry once more.

'You have to be strong,' Elizabeth encouraged herself. 'It is a punishment from God for the Jewish removal, he was in charge of it and once again I warned him, that punishment from God would take place.'

She changed into a plain black dress and began to pray to Jesus Christ. In the darkness of the room, only one candle and the burning fireplace gave the subtle light. She didn't realise how long she had been praying when the telephone started to buzz. Purely by reflex, she answered.

'My sister, dearest, are you there, darling? I have been ringing you for a long time, how are you?' Alexandra asked in a kind and calming tone of voice. The silence followed, then Elizabeth sighed deeply.

'It was petrifying, only several bones remained.' She was glad to hear her sister's voice. 'I must get ready for the funeral.'

'God will give you strength, my dear sister, please don't forget to eat, sweetheart,'

Elizabeth's throat was dry and she was terribly thirsty and she hadn't had a drop of water since lunchtime.

'I suppose I should, shouldn't I?' Elizabeth unlocked her room and rang the bell.

'It's very caring of you to ring me, my kind sister, you must be terribly busy, sweetheart, with your family.'

'You are my closest family, no doubt about that. I'm pleased that you are getting stronger. Please ring me tomorrow and we will talk longer, sweetheart.'

'Until tomorrow, bye.' Her voice was feeble and quiet. She ordered food and water.

'Good night.'

Soon, Elizabeth's housemaid appeared with a tray of food.

'Thank you, Barbara, how are the children?'

'They're alright, Miss, sleeping.'

At the same day, earlier, Nicholas had received a detailed report about Grand Duke Sergei's murder. The bomb explosion hurt him painfully in his heart. Sergei was not only his uncle, but he was his closest friend and personal adviser. His loss was tremendously painful and unconceivable.

'The team of criminal investigation detectives, who captured the murderer and cleared the street after the explosion will be promoted in rank and receive a substantial financial reward,' he announced.

'Yes, Your Imperial Majesty, they will receive their rewards and promotions tomorrow.'

'The terrorist must receive a death penalty, as soon as it is physically possible,' Nicholas commanded.

'Yes, of course.'

When Nicholas returned home, he was really gloomy and grief-stricken.

Rasputin had finished his job and was going to leave the castle. They walked towards each other.

'Hello, Your Majesty, why do you look so sad? What happened?' he asked and began to use his hypnotic power, looking straight into his eyes.

'Hi Grigori, my uncle, Grand Duke Sergei, has been murdered in a bomb explosion in Moscow today.'

'How terrible, would you like to talk about it? It will make you feel better.'

'I'll be happy to talk to you only in private. Let's go to my private wing of the castle, no one will disturb us there.' They entered a medium-sized, brightly lit dining room. 'Sit down, let's have dinner.' He rang the bell.

'I'm so honoured.' He was really proud to have his first meal with the czar.

'Swear on the Bible that the facts and people mentioned during this meal will remain undisclosed.'

Rasputin took out his dusty Bible, put his right hand on it and recited, 'The information during this conversation will stay secret until I die, for Father, Jesus and Holy Spirit.'

The czar's butler entered the room. He gave Rasputin a weird look. He distrusted the man and thought that nothing positive would come out of this union. He had been in service for many years, and used to assist his grandad Alexander II.

'What shall I do for you, Your Majesty?' He bowed.

'Royal salmon please, a bottle of my favourite vodka and crème brulee for dessert.'

'What do you want, sir?' He wasn't pleased to serve him.

Rasputin didn't know what to order and said, 'The same with a bottle of Madeira.' It was his favourite wine.

The butler walked away. Grigori's eyes stared at Nicholas with great intensity, his pupils dilated and contracted whenever he wished. He used his hypnotic power.

'Approximately 25 years ago, Alexander II my grandad had been murdered by a bomb explosion by the people's will. Today, an explosion killed his son Grand Duke Sergei by the Socialist party.'

'How horrible. It looks like God abandoned Russia for some reason.'

'I remember Alexander II, after the explosion. It was horrifying, the blood was everywhere, I was only 13. From this point onwards, I'm truly terrified that it will happen to me or members of my family.'

The butler shuffled in with a tray of food and drinks. Nicholas thanked him.

'I swear to God that you will be alive while I am alive,' Rasputin said and stood up.

'I believe you, as I believed you when you promised me an heir to the throne.' Rasputin filled up two glasses for him and for the czar.

'For a peaceful future.'

The evening was quite successful. Rasputin drank his bottle of Madeira and Nicholas half-emptied his. They enjoyed each other's company.

'Would you like a cigar, Grigori?' he said, opening a golden cigar case with diamonds.

'No, thank you, I'd rather have a cigar with marijuana, they are quite nice.'

After the meal with Grigori, Nicholas was a bit more cheerful. The conversation somehow helped. Rasputin, however, was truly overjoyed and decided to continue drinking in a different place all through the night.

Shortly, Grand Duchess Elizabeth arranged a funeral for her beloved husband in Moscow. It was a really small event, because people were terrified that they might be killed during the service. The funeral was quiet, calm and dignified. There were no uninvited members of the public, only church leaders and the Romanovs. During the funeral, the Grand Duchess was resolute, calm and noble.

After the funeral, Elizabeth visited the prison where the murderer of her husband was detained. She asked to see him in person. The meeting took place straightaway. Ivan Kalyayev sat on a wooden bench behind the bars and a policeman with a gun stood in beside him. The Grand Duchess entered the separate area, which had no furniture. The murderer looked dishevelled, pitiful and angry.

'Why did you kill my husband?' she asked, looking straight at him. She just realised that she had seen him briefly from the carriage window one day before the explosion.

'I killed him because he was a device of autocracy, dictatorship and tyranny. Why did he expel all those Jews from Moscow?'

'Repent and I will ask the czar to keep you in prison indefinitely, instead of the death penalty.'

'Never, I'd rather die for the party and revolution.'

'Well, I forgive you, despite the gore and hatred.'

'You're the most beautiful person I have ever seen,' he replied.

Elizabeth left the prison with uplifted spirits. Forgiveness helped her to lead a normal life. The terrorist was executed in May by hanging.

Chapter 13
Revolution 1905

The first and bloody revolution of Russia initiated in the beginning of 1905. On the frosty day of 22 January, a peaceful demonstration began to deliver a petition to the czar. The demonstration was conducted by a revolutionary orthodox priest named Father Gapon. The priest organised workers and peasants, including women, into a large group. Early in the morning, the group gathered in an open area holding portraits of Nicholas II, singing the national anthem 'God save the King'. The petition was already written prior to this by Father Gapon. The document demanded: better working conditions with health and safety in mind, shortening the working day to less than eleven hours, higher wages and the exclusion of children from long labour hours. Singing and holding portraits, the group marched slowly towards the Winter Palace, demanding an improvement of their circumstances. Their purpose was to deliver this petition to the czar. The demonstrators did not know that Nicholas and his family were away that day in Peterhof Palace.

The crowd trooped closer and closer towards the castle walls. They heard a warning from the soldiers protecting it, that if they come nearer, beyond a certain point, then shooting would take place. The demonstrators disregarded the warning and the gunfire began. The bullets were real, they reached their heads, hearts, stomachs, legs and arms. The wounded or killed people fell down on the white snowy ground in deformed shapes and the snow became red from the blood. Injured people cried for help, moaned and wailed. They were taken to the nearest hospitals. According to the police, 200 people were killed, 500 injured and 6,000 arrested by the police. However, non-official parties reported nearly 1,000 dead instead. The police and soldiers demanded that people disperse immediately. The forces managed to divide the huge crowd into smaller fragments and chased them, arresting them one by one. Father Gapon was gone.

Although Nicholas did not order in person the killing of these demonstrators, they blamed him personally for this awful tragedy. The peasants and workers no longer believed in the kind and all-knowing czar. This day became known as Bloody Sunday. Next day, Nicholas gave a speech in St Petersburg trying to calm people down. Nevertheless, the crowds were angry and sad.

As a consequence of Bloody Sunday, a series of horrible events took place. The revolution continued to develop with a massive mutiny of railway and factory workers, peasant criminalisation and uprising, student revolts, military and navy desertion, battleship rebellions and Polish and Jewish uprisings. The brutal violence erupted almost simultaneously, first across different cities and towns of Russia and then in Moscow and St Petersburg. The defeat in the 1904–1905 Japanese war on the land and at sea influenced the development of the first revolution. As a result of the war, South Sakhalin became Japanese land. Japan proved to the world that it was a strong, rising power. The depressed and wounded soldiers returned from the conflict, angry, hungry and ready to fight. Nicholas II believed, all through the entire Japanese conflict, that it would result in Russian victory; however, he was awfully wrong. His idea was that victory at the Japanese War would bring new land and an increase in political power.

Russian peasants and working-class citizens had been affected the most. They were not allowed to mortgage or sell their land, had huge debts, they had no right to vote, serve in the army or navy, had limited access to education, and worked over 11 hours per day in inhumane and merciless conditions without health and safety in mind. Although serfdom was abolished by Alexander III in 1861, just 40 years earlier, their suffering still took place. Subsequently, they organised into different labour unions: railway workers, factory workers or peasant groups and those unions declared a strike here and there, across the country, which paralysed the normal functioning of the whole of Russia. At one point, the entire railway stopped working and hundreds of factories were on strike, which resulted in rising prices of food and essential items and famine developed in the poorest parts. Some of those jobless, hungry groups of peasants organised themselves into violent and unruly gangs, which looted and burned to the ground the properties of upper-class people. Sometimes they killed or raped their owners and occasionally the owners managed to escape. Some of those groups were captured and sent to prison but a number of them were still at large. Exactly the same had happened 120 years ago during the Pugachev rebellion in

Catherine the Great's reign, when unruly gangs of peasants burned the houses of their masters.

In addition, the hundreds or even thousands of soldiers and seamen fed up after a bloody and brutal Japanese warfare, lost their belief in the Czar and his government. Individually or in groups, they ran away from their regiment or battleship and formed criminal and political groups, which looted the shops, banks and organised bomb explosions.

Polish and Jewish people in Russia had the least privileges out of several nationalities. Geographically, they were not allowed to move from place to place or they were moved by force. Their school education was restricted to the bare minimum. Their religion was not equal to other religions in the country. They were not permitted to vote. The Polish and Jewish communities began to rebel against the czar and his government to improve their depressing and repressive position. At one point, the majority of factories in those communities stopped functioning.

Furthermore, the student population was radicalised by the ideas of Vladimir Lenin, Trotsky and others. They stopped studying and taking exams, organised themselves into groups, joined the radical political parties and began spreading the word of knowledge, helping workers, peasants and ex-soldiers to revolt and revolutionise. Usually, in Russia, students had a disproportionately massive political influence.

The main motive for people protesting in general was the demand to create a parliament and constitutional monarchy. It resulted in an idea to request Nicholas II to sign a manifesto. For example, England, France and the United States had their parliament, democracy, election, president or prime minister; however, Russia had autocratic power controlled by the czar. For a few days in a row, Nicholas rejected to sign that policy; however, at one point, he almost changed his mind. Nicholas organised an emergency meeting in order to sign the document. That meeting took place in his personal office.

'Please, give me all your opinions, to sign or not to sign. So I'll make my mind up,' he asked them all.

'In my point of view, Russia must preserve its limitless autocratic power with the czar in control. The demonstrations must be stopped with an army force. The leaders have to be arrested and protesters will disperse. The Russian people overall understand and obey the strict rules and regulations,' the Queen Maria Feodorovna explained imperiously.

'I do agree with Her Majesty. The autocratic power was provided to me by the mighty God and my father. I must pass it down to generations, it's not mine alone to squander. Regrettably, there are not enough army forces for the demonstration disbursement; however, I'm glad that the regiments are still on my side,' Nicholas answered with a deep sigh.

'For instance, England has a democratic monarchy and the people of England are pleased to have the king alongside their parliaments and prime minister. In my opinion, the democratic monarchy might be the best way forward and it may save the country, our people and the Crown, from a total catastrophe,' Czarina Alexandra stated in a serious voice. The letter from Edward VII at present and Queen Victoria's opinion in the past both influenced her opinion.

'Quite a thought-provoking point of view,' Nicholas remarked. 'Thank you Czarina Alexandra. I will pay attention to your wise opinion.'

'Just to stop even more violence to take place, please Your Majesty, sign the manifesto and the violence on the streets might subside a little and also you may have a chance to save your crown,' Stolypin suggested to the czar.

'With the heaviest shame and regret, I will sign this manifesto, in order to save my crown and people on the streets.' He hesitated and signed.

30 October 1905 was the most dreadful day of his entire life so far. Nicholas thought that he had no choice. It was against his entire upbringing. Dreadful anxiety and apprehension fell on his soul. The signing of the manifesto and the creation of the parliament helped to temporarily stop the brutal violence on the streets. Thousands of people had been arrested for organising the illegal demonstrations and just taking part.

When everybody left his personal office and he was alone, he ignited a King Denmark cigar, stood in front of the window and looked at the empty snowy white garden; salty tears appeared on his face. Nicholas thought that it might lead to something even more dreadful and remembered the message from God. However, the manifesto and creation of a parliament would keep Nicholas on the throne for over a decade.

His grandfather Alexander II signed this manifesto 25 years ago to create a parliament; however, unfortunately members of people's will murdered him with a bomb and delayed the creation of a parliament for a quarter of a century, because his father Alexander III terminated this document.

Twenty-five years later, the first-ever Russian parliament called Duma was elected. The manifesto stated that no law could be established without the approval of the parliament and the czar. It had between 400 and 500 people from different walks of life: landowners, middle-class and workers. The first Duma was known as a parliament of people's anger; it had diverse nationalities in it, and worked without much success and made one law. 15 million roubles were dedicated to people affected by the crop failure. In reality, the Duma and the czar must have a direct consensus to pass laws, easily, without delay; however, the members of the Duma wanted to pass laws which the czar disapproved of completely. So, it was soon dissolved by Nicholas entirely.

'Curse that Duma, it stops me from passing the laws. I will dissolve it, Alexandra. They have no idea how to govern,' he complained and was cross.

'Goodness gracious, the second one might be slightly better than the first one. When will this election take place?' Czarina Alexandra replied to her husband with curiosity in her voice.

'Perhaps, in the next month or two.'

The Duma was dissolved. The election took place and the second parliament was elected. It consisted of working-class, middle-class and a few upper-class people. The second Duma and the czar began their debates. There was no consensus among the members yet again and several members created a plot against His Majesty. The czar thought that the second Duma was even worse than the first one.

'They're terribly useless. It's impossible to function like this. I will dissolve the second Duma this instance,' Nicholas explained to Stolypin.

'How terrible, it lasted only 90 days. Your Majesty, what if we have the majority of people from noble classes in the third Duma? It will be able to make laws without delay.'

'Excellent idea, Pyotr Stolypin. You're so clever. Let's make a plan of how to achieve it.'

The third Duma was majority noble. They managed to accomplish it by reducing the value of the lower-class vote. Pyotr Stolypin became its prime minister.

The third Duma was opened by the czar. He gave a little encouraging speech on stage. The members of the third Duma listened intently and paid attention.

'Congratulations on becoming prime minister, Mr Stolypin.' Everybody clapped.

'Thank you, Your Majesty. I hope the third Duma will be up to your standards this time,' he laughed and walked on the stage. They swapped places.

'At the beginning of my speech, I would like to raise a couple of the most vital questions, in my opinion. The first problem is farming and the second question is the Jewish problem. At the moment, the Russian farmers have collective land, huge financial debts and their income is minuscule. If a plot of land will be given to each person individually to cultivate, each farmer will become a mini landlord and they will gradually pay their mortgage through their lifetime and we will manage to raise their income and pay more tax. Consequently, they will have no reason to rebel and revolutionise.' Everybody clapped and cheered. 'The second question is the Jewish problem. Currently, the Jewish community have no right to vote. They can't freely exercise their religion. Their education is just on a basic school level. People from the Jewish community would like to join the army or navy. Jewish people are hard-working, clever, reliable and they suffer from people of other nationalities. If this situation could be improved in one way or another, the country might receive more people in the army or new doctors, nurses or teachers in a few years' time. Consequently, more tax will be paid by them and Russia will have more money for important projects.' The speech about Jewish people had a mixed effect, both positive and negative remarks.

'My son-in-law is Jewish. Please give them a chance,' an elderly gentleman replied in his croaky voice.

'The Jewish people ordered the execution of Jesus Christ,' someone yelled.

'It was 900 years ago,' the prime minister replied. 'Shall we forgive? Forgiveness is in our religion.'

'It's an awfully complicated problem,' Nicholas replied. 'It might take decades to solve it.'

It was the best Duma so far. They pushed through a lot of laws and managed to improve the awfully dreadful situation in the country. Nicholas didn't want to dissolve it at all. The members of the parliament were generally interested in solving one problem or another. The czar and the parliament worked in cooperation at last.

Nicholas II and Pyotr Stolypin became close friends. The prime minister influenced the czar and vice versa. After the brutal death of his uncle, Nicholas had a gaping wound in his heart. He was determined to build a friendship with Stolypin. Particularly because it was so easy, they worked as a team, laughed and joked together. Not everyone was pleased about it.

On 23 August 1906, the prime minister held a public party on his newly built personal wooden villa on Aptekarsky Island. His guests were talking and drinking wine. Two of his children played on the balcony; 15-year-old Natasha with her little brother Arcady. The majority of adults were downstairs laughing, talking and eating the buffet.

'When I was walking along the street a week ago, without a bodyguard, a passing-by youngster threw an explosive device under my feet. It rolled and rolled in front of my eyes and I thought, it was the end of my life. I rolled on the ground and crawled away from it, as far as I could go, behind the trees. It exploded. My ears got temporarily blocked. Slowly and carefully, I stood up and walked away without a scratch.' Pyotr Stolypin told a horrible story to his guests.

'Lucky survival. God protects you, it's so dangerous on the streets nowadays, do not go out without a bodyguard,' Grigori Rasputin replied.

'Well, it's my personal choice only with or without a bodyguard. What is the purpose of you visiting my house today, Grigori Rasputin? You have an appalling reputation with the girls, haven't you. Do not talk to my daughters.' He crossed his arms and looked a bit cross.

'He is right, my dearest. You shouldn't walk along the streets without your bodyguards or you will be with the angels,' his wife interrupted them, trying to prevent the conflict before it was too late.

'God sent me here to eat and drink wine,' Rasputin answered and piled up a plate full of food. He stood not far from the stairs. The laughing and children's voices came from above.

At this precise moment, three people in military uniform barged in, breaking the door open. The door came off its hinges and hurt and injured an elderly lady. Three soldiers rushed in and ran in three different directions; one went upstairs, one to the left and one to the right. They placed three bags with explosives in different places. The bags made clicking sounds from hell. The awfully horrible, dreadful and horrendous noise broke all of a sudden. Planks of wood flew in the air like matches. Two thirds of the entire building was destroyed instantaneously. Two terrorists out of three were killed on the spot and the third one seriously injured. Twenty-eight people perished on the spot, a few by the direct explosion and a few by falling wood. The children began to cry. Both the prime minister and his wife Olga survived the explosion. When the explosion happened, Rasputin was not far from the stairs and he rescued a 15-year-old girl from the fallen balcony. Her legs and arms were broken and her forehead was bleeding a lot. The boy was rescued by his father. He only hurt his knee.

'What is your name?' Rasputin asked the girl as he carried her downstairs, trying not to trip over the broken and rackety steps.

'Natasha,' she replied in a weak voice.

'Natasha, your pain is vanishing now.' He put his hand on her forehead and released the energy.

'It's getting better,' she whispered and lost consciousness.

'Thank you for rescuing my daughter. I will never forget it.' They rushed her to the hospital.

'God wants her to survive the explosion. Can I visit her in hospital to reduce her pain?'

'Yes, you can, you can come with us now,' her father replied without doubt.

The parents and Grigori rushed to the hospital by car as fast as they could. They informed the police what happened at the property. The police sent a few people there and a number of ambulances. The child was taken to the operating theatre by a surgeon and after this operation she was looked after by nurses in the hospital ward. The prime minister and his wife returned home to find total chaos. The czar was in the building, or what was left of it, giving orders. When he saw them, still alive, they gave each other a hug.

'I'm glad to see you both still alive. I order the entire family to move to the Winter Palace today.'

'Thank you so much, Your Majesty, it's very kind of you.'

'You will be comfortable there after your terrible ordeal, no one occupies it at present.'

On the same day, they moved to the Winter Palace. Nicholas provided servants and extra security for the prime minister. Their family was truly delighted. Except, their daughter was still in hospital and they worried about her survival. Pyotr and Nicholas became even closer after the tragedy. A number of people presumed that the prime minister influenced Nicholas and were truly jealous of it.

Chapter 14
A Blue Room

During the two or three weeks after the explosion, Grigori visited Natasha a few times in hospital to reduce her pain. To start with, her condition was terrible. When Rasputin entered the private hospital room for a second time, she was in bed covered with white bandages around her head and plaster on both of her legs. A pile of books lay on a small wooden table and a crystal glass half full of water was on top of it. A medical nurse sat beside her, ensuring her comfort and well-being. A security guard stood beside a door, guaranteeing her safety.

'Good afternoon, Father Grigori. It's great to see you, no one visits me except you and my parents,' she said looking at him.

'God bless you Natasha, you look stronger day by day. With God's help, you will be out of this hospital in no time.' She smiled.

'Thank you, I'm still in pain, but much better than earlier.'

Rasputin lifted his right arm and reduced her pain using his energy. A nurse began to pray. She didn't know what to think about Grigori's power.

'My pain is vanishing, thank you so much. I always feel better after your visits.'

'Soon, you will be strong enough to use a wheelchair and then will be able to walk, Natasha,' he reassured her. 'God bless you, goodbye.'

'Goodbye, Father Grigori.' He turned around and left the room.

The next day, Nicholas thought about a conversation he'd had with Rasputin recently and what he told him during the meal. The recent circumstances encouraged him to do so.

'You will be alive as long as I am alive.'

'Does it mean when Rasputin is dead, I'll be dead?' A horrible possibility came to his mind.

'Send two security guards to watch over Rasputin's apartment, around-the-clock, a weekly report has to be written regarding it. It should be done in total secrecy, understand?' he commanded to his security officer.

'Yes, Your Majesty, the security guards will be on duty today.'

Those reports would become evidence of Rasputin's terrible and sometimes weird behaviour.

His apartment became full of people, there was drinking, smoking, laughing, using cannabis, singing, dancing and having sex. It was a constant party in his apartment. One of the female followers, Masha, became his favourite friend. She even left her husband and children in order to spend time with her favourite lover, Grigori. She looked like a model, two metres tall with long, curly blonde hair, large blue eyes and a perfect body. The size of his penis, 13 inches long, attracted her attention.

'You are a peasant, but have a royal cock!' she shouted at the top of her voice. Everybody burst into laughter, as they were drinking wine for the second day in a row.

'It must be royal, if it satisfies you seven times a day.'

'I have never had a better lover in my entire life. I must admit, you are great at shagging,' and she gave him a snog.

'What do you call a self-centred cock?' he giggled.

'Grigori Rasputin,' Masha squeaked. Everybody laughed.

'Did you see a statue of my dick on Nevsky, they just erected it with gold and diamonds.'

They all laughed uncontrollably and tears appeared on their faces. Sometimes, a group of girls danced around him in a circle, totally naked. He had sex with each of them one by one, each time having satisfaction. He repeated the action until he reached a state of euphoria. Fortunately, it was the same group of girls who agreed to play by his rules. Grigori loved being the centre of attention.

This kind of reputation of a not-so-holy man was damaging for the royal family.

The neighbours were not pleased about the noise; however, it was impossible to complain. Rasputin just answered, 'If you don't like the noise, purchase a different apartment.' The police complaints were usually ignored, because of Rasputin's direct contact with the royal family.

Grigori also gave everyone their future predictions, using his hypnotic power and mind-reading technique. Rasputin's followers were truly excited to discover their future and past. The personal items, which belonged to him in the past, became valuable all of a sudden. They presumed that those items kept his energy and were able to heal even when he was not around.

People gave him lots of gifts in return: icons, candles, bottles of wine or vodka, even jewellery and food. He always had fresh flowers in his apartment.

'They know that I like bunches of fresh flowers, even in the middle of winter,' he explained to his followers. Most of the year, his children were at private boarding school and did not get involved in his parties.

A few months passed, and on Friday, the entire royal family and Grigori Rasputin had a meal and just relaxed in a drawing room. The children were free to do what they liked. Grand Duchess Olga was busy reading a historical novel in an armchair by the window. Her sister Tatiana stood beside her, looking at the snowy garden. They both were wearing white dresses with pearls, the latest French fashion.

'There is always something terrible happening in the history books, though, our life is so boring.'

'You are right, sister, nothing at all happens to us,' she sighed.

Alexei, Maria and Anastasia were playing hide and seek. Their tutor, parents and Rasputin stood nearby.

'You hide and I seek,' Alexei said in a high-pitched voice. 'One, two, three, four, five, six, seven, eight, nine, ten.' The girls ran away and hid; he looked for them in different rooms.

'I believe Mr Stolypin and his family are safe and comfortable in Winter Palace,' Nicholas remarked.

'It would be lovely to visit them as a family in the near future and have a meal together,' Alexandra answered.

'His daughter, Natasha…' Nicholas began.

'He is in the blue room!' Rasputin yelled and rushed straight there. He saw Alexei standing in the middle of the room, looking for his sisters. Rasputin grabbed him by his hand and pulled him towards the entrance. A heavy crystal chandelier fell down and smashed loudly into tiny pieces, just where Prince Alexei had been standing a few seconds prior. Everybody rushed into the blue room.

'You just saved my son's life, Grigori, thank you,' Alexandra gave him a hug. A terrible thought came to her mind.

'You deserve a financial reward,' Nicholas commented. 'Thank you for saving his life,' and he gave him a small sack of gold coins.

'It's my duty, Nicholas. Jesus protects Alexei. I just saw a vision a few seconds earlier.'

'My poor brother, you could have been killed.' Grand Duchess Anastasia gave him a hug. 'We were hiding in a different room,' she explained.

'I don't want to play anymore,' Princess Maria whispered quietly and large tears ran down her beautiful face and she began to cry at the top of her voice.

'You mentioned earlier that nothing ever happens, it just did,' Grand Duchess Tatiana said, looking at Olga.

'Call the police,' Nicholas ordered loudly to a security guard, who just appeared. He left and a few minutes later a group of police officers marched into the blue room. Everyone told them what had just happened prior to their arrival.

'Would you be able to answer whether it was a deliberate murder attempt or if it was just an accident?' Nicholas asked one of them.

'Yes, sir, the chain that was holding this chandelier will be thoroughly examined and we will give you the answer in a couple of hours in a police report.'

Nicholas received a report shortly, which stated that the weakest link of the chain holding the chandelier broke due to wear and tear. This chandelier was approximately 200 years old. Consequently, no one in particular was responsible for the accident. Therefore, they did not look for anyone in connection. Nicholas sighed deeply and pushed the report away. He couldn't imagine what would have happened if Rasputin wasn't there. He loved Alexei and couldn't imagine the world without him.

When he entered the royal chamber that evening, Czarina Alexandra was in tears.

'What's wrong, darling?' he asked and kissed her.

'Alexei is not safe from haemophilia and from the outside world, he nearly died today,' she snaffled. 'Please do something.'

'What can I do to increase his well-being and security, sweetheart?'

'Increase the number of his bodyguards or an extra child minder.'

Alexandra stopped crying.

'Maybe even a soldier or a navy officer, I will start looking for one tomorrow.' Alexandra gave him a long passionate kiss.

Rather soon, the navy officer was employed to watch Alexei's every move. He had to make sure that the Czarevich would not hurt himself during his playtime and lessons. Also, it gave an extra layer of protection from the outside world. Alexei was wrapped up in cotton wool from head to toe. He was not allowed to climb trees, run fast or do anything that had a risk of falling. The boy realised that the protection was somehow special, in comparison to his sisters, and disliked it.

'My sisters are allowed to play in the woods, but I have to play chess, board games or cards, it's not fair,' he complained to his parents.

'Well, you know the reason why?' It was painful for Alexandra to see him being upset; however, his safety was vital.

One summer evening, Grigori walked out of the castle gates, turned left and walked briskly away from the Peterhof Palace. It was already dark outside. The electric lights from the castle made creepy shadows. The leafy trees created patches of darkness on the footpath. The city park was in front of him. A gentleman in a chequered coat jumped at him when he reached the park. The bushy trees make the path look even darker.

'Did you sleep with Czarina Alexandra, Grigori Rasputin?' he bellowed in rage. His teeth were stiffened together and his eyes glistened with fury.

'Fuck you! No, I did not. You don't shit where you eat. I respect them,' he shouted in response.

'People are saying that you are lovers, is that true?'

'No, we are not, you scared the hell out of me. Who are you and why are you asking?'

'I'm a news reporter working for a local newspaper.'

'Why were you hiding behind the shrubs. I thought you were going to murder me.'

'I want to know the truth. Why are you visiting the royal palace so often?'

'That is none of your business.'

'Perhaps you are in love, but just don't want to tell me the truth.'

'Well it's your choice to think what you want; I can't change your mind.'

'Well, this article will be published tomorrow morning all about you and the Romanovs.'

'Lie, but remember you might be punished by people or God for it.' Grigori put him under a hypnotic trance and walked away as fast as possible.

In the next three days, Grigori bought all the local newspapers in order to read his article, because he didn't know the name of the newspaper. Finally, on the third day, he saw it. A photograph of the entire royal family and Grigori Rasputin was on the front.

The Romanovs were in power for nearly 300 years. For three Centuries, they had had unlimited power. The power in their opinion was given by God. They were symbols of autocracy. They had to lead as an example of virtue, faith and morality. Instead, they invited Grigori Rasputin to the royal court. I wonder why? Is he in love with Her Majesty or is there something else? Grigori Rasputin is not just a holy monk. He is a sexually driven liar, who wormed his way into the royal family, thirsty for power and fame. His presence in court destroys the reputation of the ruling family.

'Rubbish, lies and deceit. I hate it.' He ripped the newspaper in half. The article upset him and he walked into the first pub 'round the corner. Some of his friends were already there. After a number of drinks, the world seemed to be better.

'To be famous is not always great, there is a negative side to it, when they start writing all sorts of rubbish,' he complained to someone in the pub.

'Well, let's go and listen to the gypsy girls sing, they're fab.'

Rasputin nodded and they walked outside, rocking from side to side looking for a carriage.

In half an hour, they arrived into a restaurant on Nevsky with live music in it. The gorgeous looking gypsy girls performed their favourite songs.

'You look so gorgeous today, sweetheart,' Rasputin commented. The singer with dark mystery eyes and long, bushy, black hair smiled in reply.

'What would you like me to sing?'

'Anything.'

'Especially for Grigori Rasputin,' she announced the name of the song.

'I love gypsy music, it touches my heart and soul.' He ordered tons of food and wine, bottle after bottle after bottle. The table where they were sitting was full of people. The restaurant closed at around 2 am.

'Where would you like to go next?' one of his friends asked Grigori.

'I don't want to go home, it's too early. I'll make my way to the brothel tonight, do you want to join me?'

One of the gentlemen agreed and they took a carriage straight to the front door of the most expensive brothel in city. The bright electric light shined through the door, welcoming them on arrival.

The front room had white leather sofas, glass tables with flowers and bottles of champagne and the prettiest working ladies. Grigori welcomed the madam and chose the most beautiful girl in the room in his opinion. She had dark hair and a revealing pink dress. Her breasts were like two peaches.

'Let's drink a glass of champagne for the best night ever with the prettiest girl in this place.'

'Cheers, dearest,' she said in a horsey voice. When the bottle was finished, they walked into a little bedroom and locked the door. The room had one bed and two chests of drawers.

'Take your clothes off, I can't wait any longer.' She obeyed him. He pushed her on top of the bed, went inside her and began to pump, strong, fast and rough. They changed positions, again, again and again for over an hour.

'It hurts, please stop, don't do it,' she complained without success.

He ignored her.

'Shut up,' Rasputin answered, 'or I will complain to your madam that you don't want to satisfy me and you might lose your job.' After that, she kept quiet right until the end.

In the morning, he dressed and checked his wallet to pay for the service. Half of the gold coins had gone.

'I was drunk, but not stupid. I knew how much money I had, did you steal it?' He turned her around to face him.

'I did,' she answered quietly. She couldn't lie. His look was too powerful.

'I don't even know your name. Why did you do it?'

'My sister and her children and I live in the basement and suffer from hunger and cold. I am new to this business. It's my second night.'

'Show me and give me the stolen gold or I will complain to your madam,' he yelled. She took out a little bag full of gold coins from her corset and put it down in front of him.

'I'm sorry,' she said in a horsey voice. 'By the way, my name is Sonia.'

'We'll see if you're saying the truth, Sonia, let's go and if you fibbed, I'll take you to the police station.' He paid for the service and they took a carriage all the way to her place. The street was grey, muddy and dull. The stone buildings were close together. It was a very dim street, covered with stinky rubbish. They entered one of the building's front door and went downstairs through a narrow grey staircase. The light in the cellar showed them the way. They walked into a large room of the basement with grey walls and a stony floor. It had really old, broken furniture, which was jumbled haphazardly around the room. Sonia's twin sister was teaching a child how to read. Three other children ran around the room without any purpose. The children looked pale and thin. They were wearing old and dirty clothes. Only one candle lit the room.

'We were not always poor,' Sonia explained. 'My sister's husband died, he was a soldier in the Japanese war, we had nothing to pay the rent and we were kicked out from the place we used to live in.' Four pairs of hungry children's eyes looked at Sonia and Grigori Rasputin. Their mother stood up and walked towards them. Rasputin couldn't bear the hungry eyes.

'God brought me here today to help your family.' He took out a bag of stolen money and put it on a dusty table. 'I'm not going to report you. Buy some food, clothes and rent another place, I have to go.'

'Thank you, it will be enough for a few months. Thanks for not reporting me to the cops, I wouldn't have done it if I wasn't desperate.' Rasputin walked away with a heavy heart. There were so many hungry children in St Petersburg. It was a city of contrasts. You could admire a golden palace with handles covered with diamonds, gold and emerald rooms and the grey basements, broken jumbled furniture and hungry children in one day.

I'll teach my children to share the food and money with the most impoverished, destitute and penniless people in society, he thought to himself, walking home. The sun was shining brightly, promising a warm and cloudless summer day.

Chapter 15
Grigori and His Influence

When Alexei had no bleeding, it gave immense joy to the Romanov family. Although Nicholas had a severely limited time to spend with his family, he used the majority of it to play, speak or teach his five children. Alexandra had more time than Nicholas; however, very often she had unpleasant, irritating headaches or she worried about her son Alexei and was depressed.

'I wish I had more time to spend with my family, sometimes I wish I wasn't born royal,' Nicholas complained to Alexandra when they were walking along the golden autumn garden. Red and yellow leaves fell down on the ground like a magical storm.

'You're doing your best Nicky, dearest,' she replied and kissed him. Alexei ran slightly ahead with his dog called Joy walking into the deep puddles. The dog barked and wagged his tail. The navy officer followed Alexei non-stop.

The grand duchesses were wearing different coloured bright autumn coats from Britain, with matching scarves and posh hats. Anastasia gave her dog pieces of biscuit. The dog barked and licked her hands and face. She was laughing hysterically, squealing and enjoying it. Maria brought her favourite doll for a walk, pretending to be her mother.

Grand Duchess Tatiana and Olga walked behind them with Mr Pierre Gilliard, practising French verbs.

'I have started to read books in French, Mr Gilliard, it gives me such pleasure,' Olga remarked matter-of-factly.

'I'm so proud of you, the language will remain with you for the rest of your life, dear princess,' the tutor replied.

'I can speak German and English with my parents and French and Russian with you and everyone else.' Grand Duchess Olga beamed, taking her gloves off.

'I know a few words in Spanish,' Grand Duchess Tatiana said loudly. The girls looked at each other and ran away, giggling in a woodland area of the garden. The tutor followed behind them.

'Come back ladies, please!'

'Shall we go and look at our elephant? Oh, please, Father,' Alexei suggested in his high-pitched voice.

'Of course we shall, the winter enclosure probably has been built for it by now, Alexei.'

After a few minutes of walking, they reached an elephant winter enclosure. It was built with glass and wood and it looked a bit like an enormous greenhouse. It even had a heating system built in it, especially for this time of the year. It had an artificial pond in the middle and a few logs for its exercise. The elephant greeted them with a loud noise, lifting its trunk up. The children came closer and touched its dry and rough trunk to say hello. Both Nicholas and Alexandra were delighted to see their happy faces. The elephant lifted an entire log and placed it, as if it was a match, in a different place.

'Good boy,' Alexei praised him. In moments like that, everyone forgot about his illness.

A few months later, when the winter finally arrived and the snow settled on the ground, Rasputin thought about taking a pilgrimage to a holy place.

'I wish to travel to the Ural Mountains and visit a holy place there. Can I have your permission, Your Majesty?' he asked Czarina Alexandra when they were standing opposite Peterhof Chapel.

'Of course you can, but do not be absent for too long, for the reasons you know about,' she answered with a deep sigh, looking at the chapel's golden roof. Alexandra was nervous for Alexei.

Next morning, Rasputin took an early train towards Ekaterinburg. He travelled first-class and shared his compartment with another passenger. The miles of woodland covered with deep snow passed in front of their eyes. The train was quite fast and in three days, Grigori reached his destination. He came out on the ordinary-looking station at a little town not far from the Ural Mountains. He purchased extra food and found a shabby-looking coach driven by one horse.

'Take me to the Ural Mountains in front of the old Catherine the Great mines,' he ordered to the driver.

'Not all the way through, you will have to walk the rest of the way, the path is covered with snow and it's too narrow for a horse to pass through.'

'No problem, I will hike the rest of the way,' he answered.

The heavenly beauty of the ancient peaks covered with deep snow materialised in front of their eyes.

'Why are you going to the mines?' the driver asked Grigori.

'It's a pilgrimage mission, because I'm a monk.'

'Yeah, there is a very old wooden church there, I know about it.'

The mountains dominated the scene, making them look small and insignificant compared to the rocks. In couple of hours, the path became too narrow for a horse to trot through.

'Here, I have to stop,' the driver said loudly.

Rasputin paid, turned 'round and began to walk through the deep snow. There was total silence around him, he couldn't even hear the birds. Grigori lost track of time and couldn't comprehend how long he had been rock climbing through the icy stones. Suddenly, he saw a cave.

It must be the entrance to the old mine shaft, he thought and walked in.

'Hey, anybody here?' he yelled.

Only the echo replied, reverberating in his ears. Grigori's intuition told him that it was not the right place. The shaft was so old that it was dangerous to walk around there. A broken train track, collapsed roof and deep holes in the ground full of muddy water were a death trap. Rasputin came outside and began to climb. In a few yards, he saw another cave; it was totally empty this time and a few bones were scattered everywhere. He prayed and climbed higher, higher and higher. Finally, he saw the third cave. On his hands and knees and covered with snow, he entered that grotto. It looked magnificent. Precious and semiprecious stones glistened in the walls, floor and ceiling all around him. His head began to spin. He had never seen so many diamonds, rubies, emeralds and amethysts in one place.

'I found treasure,' he said out loud.

All of a sudden, he heard a voice. A dull light reached his eyes. It was an entrance to another cave inside the rocks. He slowly entered and saw a man. The elderly, as old as the world itself, man had a long white beard and long straight hair. He was wearing a black robe and cloak. A shelf with jewellery stood behind him.

'I was waiting for you, Grigori Rasputin,' the elderly monk said in a loud voice. The powerful and electrifying energy was around him. 'I am an evil spirit, my name is Devil Lucifer, I am here to assist you with anything, my friend, what would you like from me?' He laughed with icy hiccups.

'Hello, Lucifer the sorcerer, I would like to obtain more power,' Rasputin roared.

They stood opposite one another.

'More power and what else?' he cackled. They stood, staring into each other's eyes. Lucifer was more powerful than Grigori. The entire life of Grigori Rasputin went through his mind in front of him like a black-and-white film.

'Yes, one more wish. I'd like to find a powerful stone which will protect Czarevich Alexei from bleeding after my death and for other stones for the grand duchesses.'

'Very well, Grigori. Go and mine out the five stones you require, here are the tools.' Rasputin went back to the grotto with the precious stones and dug out one red ruby and four green emeralds, the largest in that cave. He brought them all to the devil and piled them up on the table in front of him.

'I want to have five golden lockets to make with those stones,' Grigori explained.

'I'll put a curse on all of these stones and make lockets for you and you will obtain more power.'

'What will be my payment?'

'Sell your soul to the devil,' he screeched.

Rasputin was silent. He thought about it for a long time.

'Do you think I'll go to Hell straightaway after my death, Lucifer?'

'No doubt about that, my friend Grigori,' he laughed.

'What type of curse will you put on the stones?'

'Protection, of course,' Lucifer lied. The sorcerer changed his mind.

'I agree,' Rasputin finally answered. When the lockets were made, Lucifer put both of his hands above the lockets and pronounced a curse.

A huge amount of energy was released all of a sudden and the rocks crumbled in places around them. Grigori received the extra energy.

'Because you found the stones, the green emeralds will be called Emeralds of Rasputin and a ruby will be called a Ruby of Rasputin. See you in Hell, my friend,' he laughed and gave him the lockets.

The stones sparkled magically in front of his eyes. Rasputin put the lockets in his secret pocket and walked out of the grotto. His soul was heavy for some reason.

'Why didn't I ask anything for my kids?' he asked himself. 'Well, at least the royal children will be protected.' After a few hours of walking, he reached the outskirts of the local town and saw a pub.

'It's time to celebrate.' He ordered a bottle of vodka and food. *I should have asked him about Nicolas Flamel and his stone,* he thought with regret, drinking a shot of vodka. Later that evening, he took a train back to St Petersburg. In three days of travelling, he reached the city; because he was away on holiday, no one was in his apartment.

Rasputin cut five tiny pieces of paper and wrote 'From Grigori Rasputin, with love and protection' on each one, opened the lockets and placed one piece of paper inside each locket.

Next evening, Grigori arrived at Peterhof Palace with the lockets in his pocket. Five children and Alexandra were busy having their photographs taken by professional photographers. Grigori joined them.

'God bless you all,' he declared loudly. 'My trip was quite successful, I brought five gifts for little ones.'

'Lovely to see you, Father Grigori, Alexei was restless last night,' Alex replied.

Rasputin took out five lockets and gave them to the children.

'Look, Mum, they're so beautiful,' Maria answered. 'And mine has a large green emerald.' She put it over her head.

'My locket has a red ruby, instead, why is that Grigori?' he asked with interest, looking at him.

'It's because you are a boy, Alexei,' Grigori coughed. 'Those stones will protect you all from harm.'

'That's so thoughtful of you, Grigori, thank you so much. I know it's not Easter yet, though, I'd love to give you a Faberge egg with the photographs of a miniature portrait of our family,' Alexandra smiled and gave him a gift.

'This is a real treasure,' he twirled it in his hand. 'It's an object of art. Thank you, Your Majesty, I don't deserve it.'

'Don't be modest, Grigori, of course you do. Indeed, I'd like to talk to you in private. Let's go to the portrait gallery, we won't be overheard over there.' They glided through the rooms of the castle holding hands, before they reached the gallery. Paintings from Rembrandt, Leonardo da Vinci, Michelangelo and Pablo Picasso revealed the moments of history in front of their eyes.

'What's troubling you, Alexandra?' he asked quietly when they stopped.

'Alexei,' she whispered back. 'Around three am last night, Alexei woke the entire castle up with an ear-piercing scream. I rushed straight to him. I thought someone had attacked him or another bleeding, but I was wrong, it was just a dream or nightmare.'

'What did he dream about?'

'The entire family standing by the wall, as if to take a picture and suddenly gunfire begun.'

'He might see the future; I see visions similar to those during the night or day and sometimes they are showing the true future and sometimes those dreams are just only empty visions.'

'He cried and no one could stop him, he was truly scared, I have never seen him like this.' Silent tears ran down her face.

'Please don't cry, Alexandra, it may not be a future prediction,' and he gave her a hug. They stood silent for a while. Rasputin decided to hide the truth from the empress.

'I have to go now,' she whispered. 'Thanks for your help, see you shortly.'

He waved goodbye and they both walked in different directions, Grigori holding an egg. Rasputin had seen thousands of those Faberge eggs all over the castle and now he had one of his own.

Rather soon, Czarina Alexandra experienced a number of complaints from different people from her castle regarding Rasputin's behaviour. They wanted him out of the castle. They complained about his manners, behaviour and attitude.

One evening, a nursery maid knocked at her door.

'Come in, who is there?' Alexandra sat ahead of the long table, signing some documents.

'A nursery maid Madeleine, Your Majesty.' Alexandra lifted her eyes.

'Why are you here, Madeleine?' she asked. The nursery maid looked at the floor like a naughty child and began to speak.

'I don't know how to begin,' she mumbled. 'Grigori Rasputin was in the nursery last night around 7 pm and one of the girls was wearing a nightie.' She became red all of a sudden. 'I'm worrying about the girls, it's dangerous, he has such a terrible reputation.'

'Did he do anything inappropriate?'

'No, he just prayed with them.'

'Well, from now on, I'll make a rule. No one will come in the nursery after 7 pm without my permission.'

'Will Rasputin remain?'

'Yes, he will remain in court, but you will go. Thank you for service, leave me,' her voice became icy and cold.

'Please, your Majesty.' Madeleine began to cry, she couldn't understand why, she just wanted to protect the royal children. Rasputin had been informed about the new nursery rule and he started to obey it.

Next summer, Grand Duchess Anastasia turned seven. Czarina Alexandra arranged a small, family-only birthday celebration. A pretty, seven-layer birthday cake with icing and cream was baked specially for this occasion.

'Happy birthday, my daughter Anastasia. I can't believe you are already seven. Not long ago you were just an infant.'

The girl blew out the candles and everybody clapped.

'Thank you, Mother,' she squeaked. 'I am truly delighted, this is the best day of my life,' and she twirled on the spot.

Alexandra wished to spend more time with Anastasia because she supposed that she was too busy looking after Alexei and didn't have enough time for her younger daughter. Very often, Anastasia disobeyed her governess, climbed trees or hid from everyone in order to get her parents' attention. She was like a tomboy.

'Maria, dearest, can you keep a secret from everyone?' she asked her sister during the party.

'Of course, I can, I promise, what is it?'

'I don't like writing and reading,' she said to her sister Maria. 'I'd rather be outside playing with my dog. I like wind, sun, grass and snow.'

'You are so different from me, I'd rather be in the castle to practise painting, piano or reading, but I will keep your secret from the adults, regardless.' The girls giggled and ran away.

The previous year was the highest level of fame for Grigori Rasputin. He had been loved and hated simultaneously. Some people thought that he was a true genius and some people thought that he was a total idiot. Perhaps Grigori had both darkness and light. He was positive and negative to the extreme. For example, when he was in the castle, his behaviour was quite positive. When he was in the pub, his behaviour was quite negative.

The monks and the orthodox church did not accept him as their own, because of his negative behaviour and connections with other sects or religions.

People from the royal court and the distant relatives of the Romanov family did not or could not or would not accept Grigori. Some of them chose to be far away from him and some of them accepted him as he was.

The peasants and working-class people were proud that Rasputin was close to the royal family, because he was one of their lot and had managed to achieve in life. However, they disliked the fact that he became a monarchist and protected the royal family.

People in the parliament began to talk about Rasputin's attitude to the ladies in general, and campaigned to banish him from St Petersburg. Despite all of that, every morning, just before dawn, during summer, autumn, spring or winter, hundreds of fans of Rasputin gathered on Nevsky, waiting for him to arrive. Sometimes, they were totally unsuccessful and occasionally, they had the chance to see him in person.

A number of followers wanted to touch him in order to get their health back.

If I touch him, they thought *with true belief in my heart, I will be healthy again, because he has a power like Jesus.*

A few of them wanted to receive a blessing from Grigori and the majority of people wanted to obtain just an autograph.

'God bless you all.' People clapped and cheered. 'Would you like me to predict the future?' he explained.

'Yes, Grigori. Go on.'

'What does the Bible say about the future?' Everyone was silent. 'One part of Russia will rise against another in a bloody conflict, a kingdom against kingdom and government against government, there will be hunger, explosions, infections and bombs and I promote against this conflict.'

'If there will be a war, when will there be a victory?' an elderly man asked him.

'Decades from now.'

'Can you stop the war, Grigori?' a female voice shouted from the crowd.

'I'll try my best to talk to the czar,' he replied and people applauded.

'Can you predict my future please, please, I'll pay a gold coin,' a tall gentleman asked politely.

'You might not like my prediction, someone is hunting for you and when they will find you, they will try to kill you. Be ready and fight for your life.'

The gentleman became pale and gave him a shiny coin.

'I knew that I was in danger, he is saying the truth.'

The crowds believed or wanted to believe Grigori, because Russia was in crisis and they needed someone to give them wisdom and hope.

Chapter 16
Visit to England and Alexei's Birthday Celebration

In 1909, the Romanovs accepted the invitation from Edward VII to visit British shores. They travelled in their royal yacht, which was surrounded by Russian warships for their protection. The royal yacht was decorated up to the uppermost standards; with golden chandeliers, exquisite furniture and bathrooms, providing the most luxurious service and food. The sea voyage was quite pleasant.

'The weather has been jolly good during our sea voyage, I am so delighted to be on deck,' Grand Duchess Olga admired the schools of fish swimming under water.

'It's been simply marvellous, I do agree. I am truly looking forward to seeing our British relatives,' Grand Duchess Tatiana beamed. The wind blew her hair all over the place, it was so pleasant.

The sisters were wearing their favourite white dresses, white hats and gloves; they looked simply magnificent.

On 8 August, they reached the Isle of Wight. The British royal yacht, named *Victoria and Albert,* transported Edward VII slowly in front of the Russian royal yacht. Nicholas II stood on one yacht and Edward VII on another. The monarchs saluted to each other.

Shortly, the Russian delegation was invited on board *Victoria and Albert.* The simply scrumptious evening meal was prepared for 40 royal guests. Not just one, but two monarchs were to dine that night. Everything was arranged in the uppermost level possible. The British royal family tried their best. The two monarchs sat opposite one another during the meal.

'I'd love to form an alliance, Czar Nicholas, if the war will be upon us,' Edward VII announced loudly.

'It will give extra protection to both our countries; Russia already has an alliance with France.'

'United Kingdom has a strong fleet and army, it might be wise to accept our offer,' Edward VII began to eat.

Even though Nicholas knew that his army might not be the strongest in the world, nevertheless, he didn't want to admit it. One monarch never shows weakness to another monarch.

'King Edward, as you know Russia has a massive army and fleet and I'd love to build an alliance with England,' he responded.

'Much obliged.'

'You're welcome, hopefully this union brings both countries greater levels of defence.'

'Why are you not eating anything, Nicholas?' Queen Alexandra asked him.

'He is on a diet,' Czarina Alexandra replied.

'To be truthful, I have terrible toothache which stops me from enjoying this fabulous banquet. I will just have a bit of wine.' The evening meal lasted until darkness; everyone had a marvellous time.

Alexandra was so pleased that they would stay in Osborne House for a few days. She used to stay in this castle very often, visiting her grandma Queen Victoria. Everything around her reminded Alex about the queen and she wandered around the castle to refresh those memories.

Three days later, in the morning the weather was even more pleasant than the day before, the burst of sunshine penetrated through the balcony door of a luxurious guest bedroom.

'I promised the girls to take them shopping this morning, but I have a terrible headache,' Alex complained to Nicholas when they were still lying in bed in the morning.

'I think they jolly well can do it by themselves.' They kissed. 'I'll send one security officer for their safety.' They kissed again. 'They will not know that he is following them.'

'I love you, Nikki,' she whispered quietly. 'It's truly safe here in England, I have no worries about their security.' They embraced.

'I love you, my beautiful wife, Alex, and my love will last forever,' Nicholas whispered back. It was the best morning they had had for a while and they decided to stay in the bedroom for two extra hours.

When the girls received their permission to go for a walk, they squeaked with excitement. The princesses never had a chance to go anywhere by themselves. It was an amazing opportunity to explore the Isle of Wight. First, they collected seashells on the seashore in Osborne House and built sandcastles with the golden sand.

'I built the best sandcastle ever, look,' Anastasia said proudly.

'I have the prettiest seashells,' Maria showed them. The girls were so delighted. They walked towards a street with a lot of shops.

'I can't believe it, we are free to walk without adults, how marvellous is that,' Maria smiled.

'The streets are safe and people are kind,' Anastasia replied.

The four walked into a gift shop. They spoke English, German and Russian, interrupting each other. They collected a pile of gifts that they would like to purchase and piled them up on the counter.

'Hello, please would you be so kind to sell us all these items,' Grand Duchess Olga asked the lady in front of her.

'I'll be delighted, if you have enough money with you, it will be quite expensive for all these items.' Olga opened her handbag and retrieved a purse covered with pearls; it was full of gold coins. She had currencies for different countries inside.

'Please help me to find the correct British coins, I have never done shopping before in my entire life.'

'How is that possible, you are about 15.'

'We are from the Russian royal family.'

'Of course, little princess, I will help you,' and the lady retrieved the right amount of money and gave Olga her change and she thanked her. The girls came outside with the enormous shopping bags and they had never been so delighted.

'I'm jolly well pleased with all our shopping, I wish we were able to do it in Russia,' Tatiana said with regret when they walked towards their yacht.

Shortly after, the Russian yachts and boats left British waters. Everyone was a bit sad to depart. Before they arrived, Queen Alexandra thought that it would be too overwhelming for them to look after the Russian royal family, but at the end, she was glad they stayed.

On 12 August, Alexei turned five. He was delighted to be on board the yacht during his birthday. A chunky chocolate cake had been baked especially for the occasion, with five candles and white, red and blue icing on the top. His sisters gave him the gifts they had purchased during their shopping spree. It was a wonderful surprise for Alexei.

'Thank you all so much for my gifts, I am so delighted to have such an awesome family.'

'You're very welcome, brother, anything for you. Our shopping spree in England was quite pleasant,' Grand Duchess Olga said proudly.

The fireworks began almost instantly. The rockets and Catherine wheels burst in the air. Alexei truly enjoyed his birthday celebration.

Nearly two years later, Rasputin departed towards his village in Siberia called Pockrovskoe. After a few days of travelling by train, he arrived there. He was glad to see it at last. His wife Praskovia was pleased to see him.

'Hi, great to see you, Grigori. How are Maria and Varvara in the boarding school?'

''Turning into real ladies, they are,' he said loudly and gave her a kiss. 'I missed you, Praskovia.' They embraced. She was happy to see him.

The wooden bungalow was totally rebuilt and looked larger and had better furniture. It had wide, bright windows with flowery curtains, a wood burner in each room and a timber floor. The rooms were decorated with icons, candles and flowers. The house was clean. Praskovia tried her best to improve it. They even had a housemate, who was employed to do washing and cooking. Outside, in the garden, there was a water well, wooden toilet and vegetable patch. An animal enclosure with chickens and pigs stood away from the house and they had a man who looked after it. The ancient pine trees and birch trees grew all over the village, providing shade.

Later that evening, Praskovia cooked a welcome meal for her husband. They invited neighbours and friends. The table was bursting with food. They drank only vodka.

'Praskovia, do you know that your husband is sleeping with other people in the capital and beyond?' one of their neighbours asked her.

'He has enough for all,' she replied.

They burst into laughter. She was honest to Grigori right until the end, despite of his behaviour.

After the meal, Grigori went outside singing. It was already pitch-black. The light from other houses showed him the way. He was at home and relaxed and didn't even take a dog with him. He wanted to visit one of his neighbours. Suddenly, a dark shadow approached him from behind. It crept silently like a cat. The shadow was visible in the moonlight; however, he didn't notice it. The shiny blade of a knife swung in the air and hit Grigori in the abdominal area, again, again and again. The sticky red blood appeared and spread all over the place.

'I will kill you, Antichrist,' the murderer said in a hoarse voice. The figure moved swift and forceful. Half of his face was covered with a hood.

'Fuck you, bloody bastard,' Rasputin bellowed in reply. The man turned around and began to punch his attacker with his fists as fast as he could. His adrenaline kicked in and he didn't detect any pain at that point.

When the wound was big enough, the murderer pulled the guts and stomach out. Everything in front of Rasputin was blurred. He felt awfully sick all of a sudden.

'Alaska, come here!' he yelled. The dog barked and ran towards Grigori. The dog was 18 years old, but was still strong. Alaska crushed the leg of the murderer with his teeth.

It gave some time to Grigori; he put his organs back in the abdominal cavity and begun to walk slowly towards his house, rocking from side to side. The murderer slid a bloody knife into Alaska's heart. The dog died proudly for his master.

'Call the police,' Rasputin said loudly. 'Someone is trying to kill me.' The neighbours heard his voice and barking and rushed to help. They managed to stop the murderer with shovels, hammers and bricks.

The murderer was wearing a black cloak. Rasputin stumbled towards his bungalow. Everything was blurred and the sounds were distant.

'Go now to the police station and I'll give you a gold coin,' Rasputin yelled to a neighbour's boy, who ran towards him.

'A gold coin, for me? I have never even seen one before, I will be back soon,' and he rushed as fast as he could to the police station. The boy had never run faster. The neighbour's boy reported the crime and the murderer was caught shortly. Rasputin managed to reach his house on his own feet and collapsed in front of the door. When the boy returned, Grigori's wife rewarded the boy with a gold coin and they carried him into their bedroom. The bloody trail was following him. When he was in bed, he lost consciousness. A local doctor arrived rather soon. The surgeon performed an operation and gave him a lot of morphine. His wife looked after him all night, changing bandages and praying for him.

'I don't want to go to hell yet,' he whispered, his head turned left and right. 'Alexandra needs me.'

'I'll pray for you the whole night,' his wife replied. His temperature was high and he was unresponsive.

At dawn, Grigori opened his eyes and looked at his wife. She was exhausted.

'Thank you for saving my life, I love you Praskovia,' he whispered. 'What's happened?'

'You were attacked by a crazy beggar woman,' she answered. 'Don't you remember that?'

'Vaguely, I do.' His eyes were heavy and narrow.

'The police said that they will come back to question you, when you are a bit better.'

'Good, where is Alaska?'

'The dog died, saving you.'

'I'd like to bury it in our garden, beside the tree.' He closed his eyes and fell asleep.

'I'm glad I saved a puppy from the previous litter,' she responded with a deep sigh.

From this point in time, Grigori began to recover. He spent two weeks in bed, drinking wine and vodka for pain, relief and boredom. He asked to send a telegram to Czarina Alexandra, informing her what had just had happened to him.

'Your Majesties, Father Grigori was attacked by a beggar woman in Pockrovskoe. He is recovering and with God's help will be back soon,' the telegram informed Nicholas and Alexandra.

'How terrible, hopefully Grigori will survive his ordeal. What am I to do without him? I'll pray for his recovery,' Alexandra said, reading the telegram. She ordered to punish the attacker and investigate the motives.

A few days later, a police report arrived regarding his attack. It stated that a female, who was arrested for this case, was sent to a psychiatric clinic due to her mental health issues. The reason she committed the crime was that someone had paid her to accomplish it.

Three days later, Nicholas ordered to prepare five horses for him and his daughters to enjoy a free ride in the woods among the trees. The brigade of dragoons followed them for safety purposes. It was a bright sunny day. The sun penetrated through the canopies of birch trees, making leaves look all green. They followed the path for an hour, talking, laughing and enjoying the ride. Then they reached a riverbank; it was a narrow, fast, blue stream with a rocky mountain on another side. A brown bear with two cubs searched for strawberries and fruit on the opposite bank of the river.

'That view is fabulous,' Grand Duchess Olga exclaimed with excitement.

'Can you see the bear over there with cubs?' Anastasia whispered and pointed at it.

'Shall we have a picnic right here, this place looks superb,' Grand Duchess Tatiana smiled with her brilliant smile.

'Please, Father, it will be wonderful,' Maria agreed with her sister.

'Yes, we shall, it's a splendid idea, my daughters,' Nicholas replied, dismounting his horse. The girls followed him.

Soon, the picnic was prepared by servants. Everyone enjoyed the meal. It tasted truly scrumptious outdoors after riding, among the trees, chirping birds, buzzing insects and wild animals. They galloped back after the picnic, relishing it even more.

Although Czarina Alexandra had a horrendous, pulsating headache that morning and medication did not help her, she was determined to take Alexei for a boat ride along a canal, because she thought that he might consider himself left out.

The group of ladies including the queen went for a gentle stroll in the private land of one of the ladies-in-waiting, gossiping about the latest news. There were dressed in the most up-to-date French fashion. The group walked along the canal; it was a perfect day.

Alexei with his navy officer marched towards a wooden boat which was prepared for two of them to have arrived along the canal. The sun was shining brightly and green trees reflected in the water.

'I want to be first in the boat,' Alexei said loudly and ran towards it. The boy put one leg inside the vessel and nearly climbed on board. Abruptly, his leg slipped and he hurt his knee terribly badly. Czarevich Alexei screamed from sudden pain and begun to cry. The officer picked up the boy and carried him all the way to his mother. Luckily, she was nearby.

'What's happened?' she asked when the officer with a screaming child came into view in front of them.

'I hurt my knee climbing into the boat,' Alexei shouted through the sobs.

'I'm afraid, we have to go home,' she replied in a hurry. 'Prepare my carriage right now.'

'My knee is getting bigger and bigger,' the boy complained through the sobs when the door of the carriage was closed behind them.

'Drive as fast as you can,' Alex ordered. She was scared for her son's life. When they arrived back at the castle, Alexei went straight to bed. At one-point, the child cried himself to sleep, but not for long. He awoke in terrible pain and a high temperature. Alexandra sat beside his bed.

'Why is it always me?' he sobbed. 'It never happens to anyone else I know.'

'It's a shame Father Grigori is not in St Petersburg; he would have helped you.'

In the evening, the boy developed a cough, refused to eat or drink and became very quiet. His skin was too hot. When Nicholas saw him, he immediately called a doctor. He examined the boy carefully.

'I'm sure he has got an influenza,' he said finally. 'I'd like to prescribe aspirin, plenty of water and a herbal concoction to get rid of the cough,' he explained and pushed his glasses upon his nose.

'I will follow your instructions, doctor,' Alexandra answered with a deep sigh. Honestly, in her heart, she didn't believe that his instructions would be helpful.

Although they followed the doctor's advice as prescribed, at midnight Alexei began to moan. His head turned left and right and he was as hot as a furnace.

'I can't bear it any longer,' Alexandra sobbed and large tears ran down her face. 'I have an idea.'

'What is your idea?' Nicholas asked her. They both looked exhausted.

'A telegram must be sent to Father Grigori, asking for help.'

'Brilliant, I will write it and send someone to the post office this instance.'

'Thank you, Your Majesty,' she replied like a robot.

Father Grigori, Alexei is really poorly and he might not survive until morning, please pray for him, Nicholas and Alexandra,' the telegram stated. One of the servants rushed into the post office and sent the telegram. In three hours, the telegram reached Father Grigori. Because he was poorly, he asked his wife to deliver his reply. In the middle of the night, Grigori began to pray for Alexei.

At around 3 pm, Alexei's condition began to improve a little, his temperature subsided, but he was still in pain. At six in the morning, a telegram was received by the royal family.

'Your Majesties, God saw your tears and heard my prayers, the boy will not die, but survive. I will pray for him, do not give him any medication, Father Grigori,' Alexandra read out loud, and a smile appeared on her tired face.

Alexei opened his eyes.

'Good morning, my leg is so much better today,' Alexei said quietly. He looked healthier all of a sudden and his pain and suffering had diminished. It was a real miracle.

'Bless you, my son,' she kissed him. 'Father Grigori prayed for you, I'm glad you are getting better.' The level of anxiety and depression diminished and Alexandra allowed herself to relax. 'Now it's my turn to go to sleep,' she smiled and closed the door quietly behind her.

Chapter 17
Murder of Mr Stolypin

As soon as he was able to, Rasputin went back to St Petersburg. The large number of invitations piled up on his desk. There was a particular invitation which attracted his attention from Baroness Catherine Orlov. She did not explain her reason why, but invited him for a coffee to talk about her current problem.

Next day, Grigori's carriage stopped in front of the orangey brown estate. A young housemaid showed him the way into the dining room of the luxurious property. A gorgeous looking lady in an emerald silk dress was waiting for his arrival.

'How do you do, Father Grigori?' The lady looked at him from head-to-toe. She looked terribly sad.

'Hello, Lady Catherine, I'm here to help you with anything.' He established eye contact and put her in a mild hypnotic trance.

'Sit down now and I will explain. Would you like a coffee?' Her voice was slow as if she was on drugs.

'Coffee will be nice and what's the reason for your invitation?'

The maid came in and brought two cups, a plate with 12 cream cakes and a pot of coffee. When she left, Catherine began to tell her story.

'Two months ago, I lost a baby, it was a stillborn. I cry all day and have no appetite and am no longer involved in social life and closeness with my husband, can you help me?'

'Jesus tells me that you need to get pregnant again. Where's your husband today?'

'He's in Germany.' Grigori stood up and took her hands in his. His soothing voice put her in a soft cocoon of pleasure. He kissed her again, again and again. It felt wonderful and she didn't resist him. Just in case, he locked the door. Grigori loved it. It was the first sex after his injury and he was very careful. They both received pleasure out of it. At the end, he put her in a mild trance again and they began to talk normally.

'I'm so surprised at what has just happened between you and me, but I feel great, regardless,' Catherine said to Grigori.

'Catherine, you might get pregnant again,' he beamed. 'I will pray for you.'

'If not, wait for my invitation.' They laughed.

When Rasputin was in his carriage, he couldn't stop smiling, because he honestly liked Catherine.

Shortly after the murder attempt, Rasputin made his mind up to visit holy places in Jerusalem. It was a dream of his entire life to see where Jesus died on the cross, his tomb and other relics. As soon as he arrived in the city, his spirit increased beyond belief. He walked around the cathedral, praying, looking at holy objects and collecting positive energy.

'Jerusalem is more holy than Mount Athos in Greece,' Grigori explained to a stranger who stood beside him.

'I do agree, it is the holiest place and I'm delighted that I'm here to see it.'

At the beginning of September 1911, Nicholas and his family with Mr Stolypin travelled by royal train to Kiev. There were ten attempts in total to assassinate the prime minister before; nevertheless, he was determined to travel to Kiev with the czar regardless.

'Presently, it's treacherous in Kiev, it might be another attempt on your life there,' Nicholas warned the prime minister when they travelled by train to Kiev. The dinner was served for two of them.

'I'm not terrified of another explosion, Your Majesty, I'm ready to die for Russia and the royal family.' Peter raised a glass of red wine. The situation in the country was dreadful, but everyone predicted that it might get even more serious.

Next day, after they arrived in Kiev, Nicholas with his two daughters Tatiana and Olga watched the opera called the 'Tale of Tsar Sultan' by Rimsky-Korsakov at Kiev opera house. They watched the performance from the balcony. There were a huge number of security officers present in the theatre. The public was on edge. When Grand Duchess Olga looked at the faces of the members of the public below, she saw angry people and it made her feel a bit anxious.

Those people are able to murder anyone, she thought and her hands became sweaty all of a sudden. The performance began and she did not tell anybody about her thoughts and feelings.

After the second act, Mr Stolypin stood, his back to the stage, holding onto the ramp separating him from the orchestra, talking to someone in front of him. Unexpectedly, five gunshots blasted in Stolypin's direction. One killed his bodyguard. Two went in his chest and two went in his arm. The prime minister stood up, despite the pain, took his gloves off, unbuttoned his covered-in-blood jacket and waved to Nicholas to go back for safety.

'I'm proud to die for the czar and my nation,' he declared in a loud and confident voice. The audience applauded loudly around him. The prime minister was a real hero.

Three days later, Pyotr died and was buried in Kiev where he was killed. It was his wish. Nicholas was utterly grieved and dismayed he had lost his best supporter and real friend. Because of the risk of being murdered during the funeral, the royal family did not attend. Both Olga and Tatiana were shocked by the prime minister's assassination.

Nicholas ordered to conduct an investigation regarding the murder of Mr Stolypin. It was discovered that the revolutionary Bogrov was the assassin. He was hung nine days later.

It was such a terrible loss of life and brain. Mr Stolypin could have pushed through his brilliant reforms and perhaps made Russia stronger in the arena of the world. Nevertheless, after his death, Nicholas promoted Stolypin's Jewish and agrarian reforms. They were successful. He did not die in vain. The prime minister was a true Russian hero.

Almost a year later, Rasputin picked a blonde, good-looking working lady named Marisa, had sex with her and it was not enough for him. He was still bored. After the injury, he no longer could reach that euphoric state of mind, which he used to have in the Siberian sect, no matter how much he drank and how many sexual partners he had. It bothered him. He was hopeful that it would one day reappear.

'Let's go to the casino, I want to play cards,' he whispered in her ear and gave her a sloppy kiss.

'Anything you like, sir,' the girl smiled.

She was wearing a creamy short dress and her breasts were visible. They entered an enormous hall with marble floor, holding hands. The room had a green card tables and snooker tables; it was full of well-dressed wealthy people.

'A bottle of champagne and two cigars with marijuana,' he made his order, and they sat down to play blackjack. At first, he lost 1,000 roubles and then won it back. The game was exciting. The person he played with left the table. It was nearly dawn. Grigori stood up and walked around the hall, looking for a suitable gaming table. Marisa followed him holding a glass of champagne. Unexpectedly, he saw an extremely beautiful young gentleman; he reminded him of Count Paul Vronsky. He wanted to join the table which was nearly full, they were playing poker.

'Hello, gentlemen, can I join your table?' he asked.

'The bids are quite high, if you don't mind,' he replied, looking at his cards. 'Royal flush.'

'Yeah, you are lucky today, what's your name?' They sat down to play.

'I am the richest man in Russia, Prince Félix Yusupov. Who are you?' he replied in his icy voice.

'Grigori Rasputin, royal adviser,' he responded back.

'Your name is known.' The game continued. Grigori forgot about Marisa and all his attention concentrated on Félix instead.

'Full house,' said Grigori.

'Straight flush, I won again,' Félix yawned.

They played until dawn. Grigori lost 600 roubles. He didn't mind that. Everyone stood up. Grigori looked at Félix using his hypnotic power.

'You have powerful eyes,' Félix yawned again,. 'My wife is in Florence, would you like to come for breakfast, Grigori Rasputin?'

'Yes, Félix, I just have to pay Marisa and then I am as free as a bird.'

The three of them walked out of the building drunk and tired. The morning sun shined on the sleepy city. Rasputin paid Marisa and she walked away. The golden carriage, which belonged to Félix, stopped in front of the most luxurious castle Rasputin had ever seen.

'This building is bigger than Peterhof Palace,' Grigori admitted.

'Welcome indoors.' The butler opened the front door and the most luxurious hallway came into view with a marble staircase, rare works of art and even diamond handles throughout.

'This house is as beautiful as the owner,' Grigori said and made Félix smile.

'Serve breakfast for two in the drawing room and do not disturb after,' he ordered to his servant. The breakfast was served almost instantly.

'Do you like both sexes, dear Félix?' Grigori enquired, putting him in a trance.

'Yes, I do. When I was a little boy, my mother used to dress me as a girl in pink princess dresses. From that moment I realised that I like boys,' he answered in a high-pitched voice.

'Princess Félix, you look so lovely,' he smiled. 'Would you like to have sex with me this morning?'

'Yes, please, we'll see how good you are at it.'

They kissed. Then began to explore each other's bodies. It was the most powerful desire in Grigori's life to have sex with Félix. Grigori had never experienced anything like this in his entire life. Félix was a bit drunk and under a mild hypnotic trance. They went upstairs into a guest bedroom and spent two hours in there. Rasputin managed to achieve a state of euphoria, which was higher than a normal orgasm; he was delighted about that. Félix was finally exhausted and fell asleep. Rasputin left a thank you note and went back in his apartment.

When Félix awoke a few hours later, he felt embarrassed. The prince thought that he was used by Grigori. He relaxed in a hot bath for three hours, but it didn't help him. He became angry with Rasputin.

'Nasty beast, I hate him, I do not wish anyone to discover what happened between us. He stinks and his table manners are appalling, he will pay for this, I swear to Devil and God,' Félix yelled.

Shortly after, five royal children sat in front of their desks in their study. Pierre Gilliard stood in front of his students, conducting a lesson. 'There are five oceans in the world: Arctic Ocean, Southern Ocean, Pacific Ocean, Indian Ocean and Atlantic Ocean.' The map was in front of him and he pointed at each one.

'What did Indian Ocean say to Atlantic Ocean?' Alexei asked everybody.

'Nothing, it just gave a royal wave,' Grand Duchess Maria laughed.

'Now, please write a story about your last sea voyage and what you remember about it.'

The children began to write and became quiet all of a sudden. Pierre had become used to the royal children over the years and treated them as if they were his own.

In 1913, a 300-year celebration of the Romanov's power took place in Moscow, St Petersburg and other cities across Russia. The celebration was arranged to highlight the czar and his royal power. The lavish festivities had been organised with gifts, fireworks and royal processions. Unfortunately, both Alexandra and Alexei became unwell all of a sudden. Alexei had to be carried everywhere because of his illness. Alexandra had the chance to speak to the crowds and change their mind about her, but instead she stayed away from them. Consequently, once again people thought that she was arrogant and conceited. At one point, Alexandra fainted during the celebrations and Nicholas caught her. From that terrible moment, Alex stayed away from the festivities.

The election of the fourth parliament occurred and both Nicholas and Alexandra found it challenging to work with the fourth Duma. Alexandra grew closer to Grigori Rasputin and asked for his advice in the government decisions.

'Do you have anyone to suggest to replace the current Minister of War, the current one is not doing his job properly,' Alexandra asked Grigori.

'Yes, I do. He's a person who is not going to criticise Nicholas and his decisions, he might be quite good at fulfilling his task.' Rasputin was delighted that through Alexandra he was able to appoint whoever suited him as government ministers.

A few months later, Queen Alexandra stood in the throne room, totally alone, thinking about a letter she had received earlier. She walked backwards and forwards, concentrating on what she would write in reply. She was wearing a purple long dress and gloves. Abruptly, a loud knock at the door distracted her attention.

'Enter,' her voice echoed in an empty room. Her sister Elizabeth walked in. She was wearing a monastic outfit and her pretty face was solemn. She gave a little courtesy.

'It's lovely to see you, Elizabeth,' Alexandra said coldly.

'Hello, Your Majesty.' They stood opposite each other.

'Do you feel better now after the tragic events?' Alexandra asked with interest.

'Yes, I do, but I'm here for a different reason.'

'What is the purpose you are here for?'

'Someone is planning Rasputin's murder and I know who,' she came closer and whispered in her ear.

Alexandra's eyes became larger all of a sudden, like an owl's eyes.

'Nonsense,' she responded.

'Also, I'd love to let you know that the people in the monastery and I suspect that Rasputin has been sent by the devil or maybe is the devil himself.'

'Absolutely preposterous, I have never heard anything more absurd, my sister.'

'You must remove Rasputin from the royal court, Your Majesty, or something horrible might take place,' Elizabeth demanded.

'Never, you know pretty well why Rasputin has a job in here,' Alexandra yelled.

'You don't have to coddle, indulge and overprotect Alexei constantly, Czarina Alexandra, just treat him as a normal boy, like Queen Victoria used to with her son Leopold,' Elizabeth answered with a distressed scream of exasperation.

'Elizabeth, you have no idea how to look after them because you have no children of your own. It's only for me to decide how to treat Alexei,' her angry voice trembled in the air.

'I made a conscious decision never to communicate with Rasputin in person, in writing or through other people, because it's beneath my dignity and for that reason I'd like to ask your permission to depart from the royal court.'

'Go and never come back, Elizabeth. Go to a monastery and pray there,' she pointed to the closed door.

'Goodbye, my sister, God bless you and your children.' She walked out of the room and the salty tears ran down her face freely, like a waterfall. She never used to argue with her sister so terribly badly.

'Alex is under Rasputin's spell and it's unbreakable, if you give your heart to a holy man, he will take your soul entirely,' she said out loud to no one in particular, walking along the corridor of the castle.

When Elizabeth left, Alexandra ordered to bring her a glass of cognac.

'Everybody is telling me what to do, I simply detest it,' she said sipping a drink. 'I'll do directly the opposite of what they are demanding.' Her face was as cold as a stone.

The Queen Mother arranged a personal meeting with Nicholas. It took place in his office. The situation in the country was appalling and she wanted to improve it. They stood opposite one another. Nicholas was wearing military uniform and Queen Dowager was dressed in black.

'Nicholas,' she begun. 'When I was a ruling empress, it wasn't long ago, the life was so peaceful, people used to dance, show off the latest outfits from French couture and everyone knew that they were safe and protected by state. However, nowadays, bombs are on the streets, people shooting each other and we are all scared to go outside,' the queen raised her voice in a cry of desperation.

'What would you like me to do to make it more peaceful, ma'am?' he quietly answered.

'Please remove Rasputin and Alexandra from power and the situation may improve. He has such an appalling reputation. He's not a healer. He is just a charlatan and swindler, who is preying on your weaknesses and Alex believes him,' she pointed out, using her imperious voice.

'I'd rather have one Rasputin instead of my wife's hysterics.' Nicholas made his decision.

'Can you keep one of my ministers in power, I mentioned previously or now it's Rasputin's job to appoint them?'

'Definitely not, I already answered,' Nicholas raised his voice.

'Do not go to war, because it will drain the country of cash, the army is still on your side and if it suffers from heavy losses and is defeated, the soldiers and officers may stop obeying you. No army, no protection and you may lose your crown,' Queen Maria Feodorovna warned her son.

'Remind you, I am the emperor and it's only for me to decide. The war will take place and no one will stop it. I truly regret to say that I no longer acquire your expertise and advice. Your Majesty, please leave the royal court and St Petersburg.'

'Goodbye, Nicholas, hopefully I will see you again and my grandchildren,' she said in a trembling voice and walked away, slamming the door behind her.

The queen didn't realise that by removing her from royal duties, Nicholas had inadvertently saved her life.

At the beginning of July, the emperor received a telegram from Grigori Rasputin. The monk was in his village in Siberia.

'Hello, emperor, please do not start military actions. I had a prophecy from God that the future war, if it takes place, will bring destruction, bloodshed and failure. Millions of Russian people will die during the conflict. It will lead to starvation of the poor and total chaos, bless you God. Grigori Rasputin.'

Nicholas read the telegram a few times and shredded it into tiny pieces and threw them all over the place. The white pieces of paper landed on the floor like snow drops during the winter.

'The war will take place, it's my decision, he doesn't understand I have an alliance with England and France.'

'Hello Nicky, dearest, how was your day in Duma today?' Alex enquired, when he returned home.

'The day was awfully terrible, the room was full of people, but I felt dreadfully lonely, no one to share my thoughts and feelings with. It's as if a chessboard became suddenly empty around me.'

'I do understand you, so many people died or left and you feel unprotected. I am here, sweetheart,' and she gave him a hug.

Chapter 18
First World War

Archduke Franz Ferdinand of Austria was shot with his wife Sophie on 28 June 1914.

His last words were, 'Sophie, Sophie, don't die for our children.' They both passed away.

Subsequently, Austria-Hungary declared war on Serbia, which led to the beginning of First World War. The triple entente formed between Russia, France and the British Empire. In opposition were Serbia, Montenegro and Germany. Germany invaded Belgium. Russia entered Germany.

'The First World War began. I declare the entire mobilisation of the Russian nation. We are going to fight against Austria-Hungary and Germany,' Nicholas II announced, standing in front of the crowds of people. They cheered and supported him.

Russia had millions of soldiers fighting or reserved for military action; however, the Russian army was exceptionally unprepared. There was a huge distance they had to cover in order to deliver food provision and ammunition to the front. As a result, the Russian army was underequipped with transport, guns, boots and gun shells. The army experienced one awful defeat after another, which led to multiple fatalities, casualties and low morale. They buried the bodies where they fell, as fast as possible, in order to avoid infections.

The wounded soldiers and officers returned from the bloody conflict with severe injuries, which needed immediate medical attention.

'I am going to dedicate a few rooms of the castle for a temporary hospital,' Czarina Alexandra announced.

'That's so kind and thoughtful of you, Mother,' Princess Tatiana replied. 'I'd like to join you and help soldiers as much as I can,' she insisted.

'I think, it's my duty as well, to join you both and help wounded officers,' Princess Olga agreed.

'You both have made the right decision. I'm proud of you, my daughters, real Romanovs,' Alexandra assured both of them.

Shortly, the wounded soldiers and officers had been directed to Peterhof.

Defeat after defeat after defeat led to an emergency meeting between Nicholas, Alexandra and Rasputin. They gathered in the throne room of Peterhof Palace. An enormous map lay on top of a polished wooden table, demonstrating the current positions of the forces.

'I wonder why the army suffers the awful defeats time and time again?' Nicholas quietly enquired.

'The general of the army, Nikolay Nikolayevich, is not the best commander and leader. His poor tactics produce dreadful defeats,' Rasputin specified and stood up.

'Although the soldiers respect him, his strategy doesn't lead to the needed victory, you are right, but who will replace him?'

'Your Majesty, because you are a great leader, if you personally take command of the army, the battles will be won.'

'The soldiers will be more motivated with the czar on the front,' Alexandra added.

'Excellent idea, both of you, I'll take command of the army from today and will inform the Duma regarding my decision.'

'God bless you Nicholas; hopefully it will lead to the needed victory, I will pray for you,' Rasputin replied.

'Alexandra, dearest, you will be in charge instead of me.' Nicholas began to give orders regarding his departure.

When the Emperor left, Alexandra and Grigori became even closer. Subsequently, they made vital state decisions together regarding state ministers and the parliament.

'I don't even know what I would have done without your help and support, Father Grigori,' Czarina Alexandra praised the monk, when they both were walking along the cobbled path with rows of pink flourishing cherry trees.

The first snowdrops, tulips and daffodils appeared all over the garden.

'Czarina Alexandra, I have a prediction.'

'What is your prophecy about, Father Grigori?'

'If I will be killed by a member of your family, you all will be in danger rather soon. If I will be killed by a working-class person, the light will be reasonably good for the royal family.'

'Thank you for your prediction; hopefully, you will be alive for a while.'

'It's my duty, Your Majesty, I am truly happy to help you with anything.' They stopped and looked at each other.

'Spring is finally here, but the problems like snowbells are growing bigger and bigger.'

'It's because of the war.'

'The prices on meat have doubled, bread tripled and sugar quadrupled; the problem is caused by irregularity with food delivery by railway,' Alexandra explained to Grigori.

'The current railway minister has to be replaced with someone active and may I suggest Alexander Trepov.'

'Yes, you may, Grigori, let's give him a chance. Alexander Trepov might normalise the dreadful situation with the food crisis. I will definitely appoint him as a minister.'

The Minister Goremykin worked in cooperation with Nicholas; however, he complained regarding Rasputin and wanted to get rid of him.

I think it's time for Goremykin to go, Grigori thought and complained to Alexandra that he was incompetent and must be replaced.

'Goremykin in my opinion is not doing enough as a minister.'

'Who would you like to suggest?'

'Boris Stermer.'

'It's a brilliant idea, Goremykin will be displaced.'

This dislodgement was truly unexpected for everyone including the replaced minister, but Rasputin was pleased. He was able to appoint the new ministers through Alexandra, as if he was the czar himself.

'Hopefully, the newly appointed ministers will bring a vital contribution to our suffering nation,' Rasputin sighed deeply, kicking the gravel in front of him.

'Unfortunately, the emergency crisis occurred in police and secret police departments,' Alexandra continued. 'Multiple arrests took place, more people commit crimes because of hunger and the war. I need someone clever to solve this problem.'

'What about Dmitry Shuvaev, Czarina Alexandra?'

'I am not entirely sure, perhaps, I'll decide later.'

A couple of months later, Dmitry Shuvaev was placed as secret police minister by Her Majesty.

Both Grigori and Alexandra became increasingly unpopular. The general public suspected that Alexandra and Grigori were lovers. The caricature sketches of both of them together circulated among the soldiers on the frontline, which decreased the already low level of morale of the army.

'They must be lovers, how else would you explain the fact that they spent so much time in each other's company?' one of the soldiers commented, holding a drawing in his hand.

'I wonder why Nicholas doesn't say anything regarding this bizarre love triangle,' the other soldier replied.

'He is scared that his wife will be cross.'

The man burst into laughter. The war was with Germany and the fact that Czarina Alexandra was a German-born princess, made the general public suspect that she was a German spy, together with her lover Grigori Rasputin. They supposed that they sent vital information regarding the force's location and military plans to the German government, and because of that the Russian army suffered many fatalities and defeats.

Rather soon, Czarina Alexandra, Grigori Rasputin and the two grand duchesses Tatiana and Olga walked into a local military hospital, full of sick soldiers and officers. Father Grigori was wearing a black robe and Czarina Alexandra and her daughters were wearing nurses' uniforms. They looked dignified and solemn. The hospital was lit was electric light throughout. The walls of the hospital ward were brilliantly white and the rows of beds stretched across the spacious hospital area; each bed had one patient. The injured had multiple gunshot wounds, a few men had head injuries, a number of sufferers had broken arms, legs or ribs. The wounded moaned, yelled, wailed and cried from pain and some patients suffered silently. Most of them had blood-soaked red bandages. The heroic nurses ran from patient to patient, changing the bandages and helping during surgical procedures. Alexandra, Grigori and the two grand duchesses began to help them, changing bandages, helping to reduce their pain, giving medication and just talking kindly to the patients.

'What is your name?' Olga asked a patient with a head injury, who suffered silently from his wounds.

'My name is Victor, I am 8 years old. I had been shot during the battle,' he whispered. 'I know I'm going to die for Russia and our nation.'

'Be strong, you will survive. I will pray for you and your name will be remembered in history,' Grand Duchess Olga replied.

'I'm too weak to survive, I know that,' he whispered. 'Thank you so much for your kindness, what is your name?'

'My name is Olga,' she quietly answered.

'You are so beautiful, Olga. I always imagined my future bride looking like you.' His face contorted with pain, he lost consciousness and died in front of her eyes.

'Goodbye Victor, I will write about you in my diary.' Olga closed his eyes and attended to the other patient.

Father Grigori used his energy to reduce the pain of the wounded soldiers and officers.

'With God's help, your pain disappears,' he said raising his arm in front of a patient with broken ribs.

'What is your name, brave soldier?'

'My name is Bogdan, I have broken ribs and suffer from gas poisoning,' he explained.

'I see, you will survive and return home shortly,' Grigori gave a prophecy.

'Bless you, monk, thank you for reducing my pain.'

'What happened to you and what is your name?' Tatiana quietly enquired after a patient who had a gun injury in his arm.

'My name is Stefan and I received my injury in battle. When I'm better, I will return to the battlefield. What is your name?'

'My name is Tatiana; do you need any help?' she answered.

'Can I have some water please?'

'I will pray for you and write about you in my diary,' Tatiana said, giving him a glass of water.

'Thank you so much, sister, you look like an angel.'

Both grand duchesses considered themselves to be blessed that they were allowed to help in the hospitals. The ladies mentioned their experiences in their diaries.

Czarina Alexandra had been doing exactly the same job and once again, she thought that she would have been a great nurse if she hadn't been born royal.

A few months later, Rasputin had a clear idea that he would pass away rather soon. It made his level of emotions rather low. He had written a number of letters to Nicholas and Alexandra, informing them of his future predictions. He gave clear instructions to his daughters, as a precaution, as to what to do when he was dead.

In the evening, he went to a pub and had a few drinks. It was not enough. He went to another pub and had more. It didn't affect him.

'Would anyone like to go to the restaurant with gypsy girls, I miss them?' he announced loudly to no one in particular.

'I'll go with you, mate,' someone agreed and they stomped out of the pub, singing Russian songs in a loud baritone voice. When they arrived at the restaurant, the place was already full. However, the waitress gave Rasputin a table, because she knew him. When they entered, the gypsy girls were already singing. He waved hello to them. Grigori's table filled up with people all of a sudden. He was really popular. The man drank bottle after bottle after bottle. The table was bursting with food.

'I love gypsy songs,' Rasputin growled. 'They touch my heart and soul.'

'Yeh, they are. How often do you go to see Czarina Alexandra?'

'Not very often, once or twice a week.'

'Did you sleep with her?'

'Yes, I did, I swear.'

'Prove it.'

'Here you go,' Rasputin flashed his genitalia.

'I believe you.' The man laughed.

'If you do it again, I'll cut it off,' one of the gypsy girls said loudly.

'Anything for you, darling,' Rasputin replied.

When the restaurant stopped working, the man came outside, holding the bottles of wine. Everything was blurred in front of Grigori. He put the bottles down and began to vomit behind the tree. Half an hour later, he took a carriage back to his apartment, because he was too drunk to continue.

Elizabeth collected and sold all her jewellery and began to build an orthodox monastery in Moscow. The monastery was named Marco Mariinsky convent. Elizabeth became its abbess. The monastery had quarters for nuns, an orphanage for girls, a hospital with an emergency department and a kitchen for the poor.

The walls of the monastery were bright white, the buildings looked gracefully magnificent, decorated with orthodox crosses.

Abbess Elizabeth became vegetarian and promoted the charity work as much as she could. The monastery provided work for the nuns. The kitchens, organised by nuns of the monastery, served 300 meals daily to the poorest of Moscow society. The hospital gave treatments for free to the poor. Mothers in childbirth, children with horrific injuries, the homeless with horrible health conditions, the elderly with chronic illnesses and mental health patients received treatment and support in the monastery's hospital. The infirmary also treated the wounded soldiers of Moscow during the First World War.

'If you suffer from health conditions, mental health problems or just need clothes, food and drink, come to our monastery and tell the sisters about your sorrow, grief and distress and we will help you and your children, like Jesus did,' Abbess Elizabeth explained during the service.

The hundreds and even thousands of poor people in distress came to the abbey screaming for help. The kind sisters supported everybody.

The orphanage had 400 beds to accommodate the parentless girls and teach them how to read and write and, of course, orthodox religion education.

'All of you little girls have the choice to become nuns when you are 18 and serve the poor and grief-stricken people of Moscow.'

The girls were obedient and prayed and studied hard in order to show their respect and thank them for the comfort and warmth of the monastery.

'This monastery is the most beautiful place I have ever lived,' a little girl said loudly. 'Thank you so much, Jesus and Sister Elizabeth.'

Elizabeth and the sisters of the monastery truly changed the lives of the poor. They worked so hard to help and support them.

Russia was in a terrible crisis – the First World War, revolution, bombs and explosions. Despite her terrifying experience, Sister Elizabeth displayed true kindness, faith, compassion and generosity to everyone around her.

Shortly after the argument with Nicholas, Queen Maria Feodorovna began her preparations to leave St Petersburg for good. She was in her palace getting ready to depart. The closest people to Maria Feodorovna, her daughter Princess Olga, Prince Félix and Princess Elizabeth were there to support the queen.

'My life became dreadful and miserable when Princess Alex arrived in Russia; my husband died, I'm no longer a ruling monarch and the centre of attention, no one even listens to my advice,' Maria Feodorovna complained to her relatives and closest friends. 'Nicholas just removed me from St Petersburg and royal duties,' she exclaimed in a trembling voice.

'No, he did not,' Félix answered, looking at Her Majesty. His large eyes became even larger.

'I am afraid, it's true. I'm not even allowed to write to my grandchildren and it's partly Rasputin's fault, all because of his mischievousness and wrongdoing.'

'I simply detest Rasputin, Your Majesty,' Félix shouted at the top of his voice. 'I'll do everything in my power to get rid of him.'

'He must be banished from St Petersburg, I do agree with you, Prince Félix,' the queen replied.

'Where would you like to depart, my poor godmother?' Félix asked with real curiosity.

'I may settle in Kiev to start with,' Her Majesty answered. 'I'd love to go on holiday first: Britain, France, Germany, of course Denmark. Far, far away from gossip and crown problems,' she smiled.

'Princess Irina and I will visit you in foreign countries, Your Majesty. We are your trusted mentors.'

'Thank you for your support, Prince Félix. Maybe I will organise a coup with the help of a loyal army and put my son Kirill on the throne instead of Nicholas. What do you think, my boy, about this idea?'

'I am on your side, Your Majesty. In theory, it's possible. Why would you like to organise the coup?'

'Because of the appalling, dreadful and horrifying situation in this country. I love Russia and Russian people are fond of me, I'd love to recuperate this nation.'

'That's a brilliant idea, I just have one question, will there be enough army forces on your side for the coup?'

'No, I don't think so. In reality, it will be terribly difficult to find the loyal military forces, especially in the mess we are in, although I suggested it. In truth, I'm not going to accomplish this plan.'

'The plan was amazing in my opinion,' Félix replied.

'I may return to the plan in the future, but not now. I must go, my train will take me to Kiev. Thank you for being loyal, goodbye.'

'Goodbye Your Majesty.'

When the Queen disappeared behind the door, the deafening silence hung in the air.

Czarina Alexandra received a letter from Nicholas, that there were terrible defeats happening one after the other at the front.

'Death and destruction are ubiquitous and the soldiers and officers stopped obeying me and entire battalions deserted from the army. I don't know what to do.? With love, your Nicky,' Nicholas wrote in desperation.

Czarina Alexandra wrote a reply and asked her lady-in-waiting to send it as a telegram, as soon as possible.

'You have to be strong, my dearest, like Ivan the Terrible or Peter the Great. Show them your true power and bless you Jesus, with love, Alexandra.'

This telegram was delivered shortly to Nicholas. He couldn't wait to come back and see his family.

Unfortunately for Alexandra, one of the letters she wrote to Grigori Rasputin was lost and ended up in the wrong hands.

'It's so, so lonely without you here, Grigori, and I miss when you whisper in my ear the words of wisdom,' one of the ladies read out loud, when their group were sitting around the table.

'What words of wisdom?' Everybody laughed. 'She misses him, they are in love.'

'Grigori and Alexandra, it sounds romantic.' The ladies giggled.

As soon as Nicholas II arrived home, his family welcomed him in front of the front door in Peterhof Palace. The children rushed to Nicholas to give him a hug. He really missed them all dearly. Shortly, they had a fabulous family dinner, everyone was trying to say what happened when he was at war.

In the evening, when Nicholas and Alexandra stood alone in their bedroom, Nicholas begun to question Alexandra.

'Alex, did you sleep with Rasputin?' He was cross.

'Of course I didn't, what a ridiculous question,' Alex had an honest appearance.

'Everybody is talking about it. Rasputin himself admitted it during a restaurant meal.'

'Maybe it was his double, not him, but whatever he said, I am innocent, do you believe me?'

Nicholas remembered his mistress Matilda, how she betrayed him with two other people when they were in love. Nicholas thought that if Alex wasn't honest, it would have hurt him, but her eyes looked so innocent.

'I hate sharing, I believe you.'

They gave each other a hug and stood like this for a few minutes.

'I love you, Nicholas.'

Alexandra was accused of being a German spy and now Rasputin's lover. It was difficult to bear, but she was pleased that her husband believed her.

Chapter 19
Unkillable Monk

Despite the bombs and explosions on the streets, the fourth Russian Duma gathered every day. They managed to push through a few laws and regulations. People in the parliament could not or would not stop talking about the legendary mystic monk Grigori Rasputin. Vladimir Purishkevich gave an encouraging speech regarding Rasputin.

'Grigori Rasputin is a devilish force, who negatively influences the royal family. Being so close to Czarina Alexandra, the monk is able to appoint and dismiss the ministers, as it pleases him, and even postpone the work of the parliament itself. His attitude to the ladies of any social position is appalling. The innocence of our daughters must be protected. Grigori's connection to the royal family is so robust that he must be removed only by force.' The members of the parliament clapped and cheered.

Félix sat on the front row and listened intently, trying not to miss a word of this inspiring speech.

'I'm going to murder Grigori Rasputin and save Russia and the royal family from this devilish force,' the prince decided and his face contorted with fury.

A few days later, Félix organised a meeting between Grand Duke Dmitri and Vladimir Purishkevich in the local café in order to plan Rasputin's murder. The three of them gathered around the table in a corner of the café and spoke quietly about their secret plans.

'What is the easiest way to kill him?' Félix whispered.

'Poison him like a rat with cyanide cakes,' Dmitri replied. 'I will be in charge of the poisoning part.'

'Give poisoned wine to make sure that he is definitely dead,' Vladimir suggested.

'When he passes away, we will roll his body in a rug and throw it over the bridge,' Félix squinted.

'Gentlemen, don't forget a heavy object to hang on his neck in order for him to sink right to the bottom of the River Neva,' Dmitri said quietly.

'When would you like to murder him, Félix Yusupov?' Vladimir asked.

'The best day for me will be 30 December. My wife will be away in Crimea, so she will not disturb our secret plans.'

The gentlemen shook hands and marched out of the café. No one seemed to notice what they were discussing there. The assassination could not take place in Rasputin's apartment because of the czar's security watching his flat twenty-four seven.

At the end of December, Félix phoned Rasputin. The phone rang loudly many times.

'Hello, this is Rasputin speaking.'

'Hello, Grigori, it's Félix. I would like to make an appointment because I have a problem,' Yusupov requested.

'What problem?'

'It's a secret, I can't tell you, it's too embarrassing.'

'I will help you, I promise. When would you like to organise this meeting?'

'30 December in the palace, you have visited previously. My wife Irina and I will be there and we will have a party.'

'Of course, Félix, my friend, I will be there. See you shortly.'

'Goodbye.' He put the phone down. 'Fucking twat and bastard, I loathe him with all my heart.'

On the morning of 30 December, Rasputin woke up with a feeling of despair. In order to get rid of it, he called his friend Anna and asked her to come 'round and enjoy some time together. She came and spent an entire morning with Grigori. When she left, Rasputin started to get ready to visit Félix. Abruptly, a loud knock at the door interrupted him.

'Who is there?'

'It's Félix, would you like to have a lift by car?' Félix answered. He thought that Rasputin may change his mind to visit him and decided to give Grigori a lift in person. Otherwise, all their preparations would be useless.

'I'm glad to see you, Félix, you look pretty as usual.' Rasputin put on his fur coat, hat, boots and gloves, locked his front door and they walked downstairs.

The Porsche was waiting for Félix with his personal chauffeur, who opened and closed the doors for both of them.

This is your last journey by car, Grigori, Félix thought and sniggered.

The streets were covered with a deep layer of snow in the capital and looked festive.

'Something is bound to happen, I have a feeling of anxiety today,' Rasputin explained to Félix.

'I promise you, we are going to have a fabulous party.'

The snow began to fall. Both gentlemen came out of the vehicle and entered the side door of the castle and ran downstairs in a soundproof basement room. The gramophone music played loudly, giving an extra festive atmosphere.

The basement was lavishly furnished. A silver serving plate with 12 strawberry and chocolate cakes with cyanide stood on the table opposite the door. Each cake was cut in half and cyanide crystals placed in the middle. Because the crystals were white, they were not visible and both halves of the cakes were connected back together again. The plate looked completely untouched. Three extra plates with the leftovers of the same cake were on the table, to demonstrate that someone already had eaten from those plates. Five glasses of Madeira wine with cyanide at the bottom of each glass stood beside each plate. Three bottles of poisoned Madeira wine stood on the table.

'Sit down, Grigori, my wife Irina is not here yet, she's getting ready.'

'Yeah, it takes forever for the ladies to be prepared.' Grigori picked up a cake and began to eat. Soon, he drank a lot of poisoned wine and the majority of the cakes disappeared.

'Félix, what is your health problem?' Rasputin questioned the prince.

'Don't worry about it, it's better now,' Yusupov sniggered.

'Nice cakes, Félix,' he said with his mouth full.

'Cheers.' Félix lifted his glass of wine, pretended to drink it and put it back on the table.

'Cheers.' When the majority of the cakes and wine was gone and Rasputin stopped eating, Félix asked, 'How do you feel now, after all this wine?'

'My head is heavy and it's a bit hard to swallow, but other than that I am all right.' Rasputin laid on a leather sofa to relax.

'Excuse me, I just heard a noise, wait a minute,' Félix said and went upstairs to see his associates. When he entered a drawing room, Dmitri and Vladimir were there, playing cards.

'Is he dead yet?' one of them asked impatiently.

'No, not at all, he consumed all the cakes and the majority of wine, but he's still fit as a fiddle, what shall I do?'

'Kill him with a gun,' Dmitri suggested.

'Yes, of course, I'll be back shortly.' He ran downstairs as fast as he could, holding a revolver. Félix silently entered the basement room. Rasputin was standing in the middle, holding a bottle of wine, drinking it slowly right from the bottle. When he saw Félix with a gun, Rasputin walked towards a statue of the crucified Jesus and stared straight at Félix with a deafening silence, calm and quiet as if nothing happened at all.

'I'm going to kill you, fucking monk,' Félix shouted and pointed straight at his heart.

'Why are you killing me, Félix?'

'To save Russia and the royal family from your presence and the dark forces you represent.'

'Don't kill me, Félix boy, the Czar Nicholas, Czarina Alexandra and Prince Alexei need me to be alive. There is a prophecy that they are alive as long as I am alive.'

'I don't believe in prophecies, you're just a charlatan and liar, Grigori Rasputin, and I will kill you,' he yelled and his gun began to shake in his hand. Rasputin laughed loudly.

'If you kill me, dear boy, you will never see Russia as it is. Millions will die and Russia will change beyond recognition.'

'I will fire the gun and our secret will die with you and no one ever will find out about the sexual connection between you and me, Grigori Rasputin.'

'It was pleasant and we can do it again if you like, Félix?' Rasputin tried to put Félix under a hypnotic trance, but somehow he resisted.

'Never,' he shouted. 'I'm in control now, not you.'

'I'd like to go and see Pockrovskoe, my family, fans and Siberia, they all will miss me.'

'Go to hell, Grigori, it's time.'

'I'd like to go to the restaurant and listen to gypsy songs, would you like to join me, Félix?'

'Die.' The gunshot ricocheted with a deafening sound, then one more. Straight in the heart. Rasputin's body rocked and fell down on top of the fluffy polar bear skin.

'Is he dead yet?' Félix walked around the body. 'What a strange feeling, there was a strong man in front of me and now he is just a dead body. How easy it is to kill someone, let me check.' He bent down and checked his heart beat. Rasputin's eyes opened and he began to crawl towards him.

'I will kill you, fucking Félix,' he yelled and began to strangle him with all his remaining strength. They rolled over and over, fighting; the dishes, plates and furniture fell down on the floor, smashing all over the place. Finally, Félix stood up and ran upstairs to speak with his associates. Rasputin raised up and began to walk slowly and quietly, holding onto everything. The bloody trace followed him everywhere. He opened the door with a diamond handle and it became covered in blood.

Diamonds and blood, how weird is that, Rasputin thought walking up the stairs and opened the outside door, the one he had entered earlier. He walked through the snowy yard, away from this place to freedom.

Félix ran into his drawing room, panting.

'Félix, did you kill him?'

'No, he's still alive.'

'What were you doing there together, reading poems?' Dmitri laughed.

'I shot him twice in the chest, but he is still alive, fucking bastard.'

'I'll take my gun and finish the monk, wait and see,' Purishkevich replied firmly.

All three of them ran downstairs towards the basement and realised that Rasputin had run away. They saw him escaping the property. Purishkevich raised the gun and fired four times, three times he missed and one went straight in his head. Rasputin rocked and fell slowly on the snowy ground.

'He's definitely dead now,' Purishkevich answered and ran towards him.

Together with Félix, Purishkevich rolled the body into a rug and tied him up with a strong rope. The car was already prepared. They put the body in the car's boot and drove away slowly.

'I think I can hear noise,' Félix said to his friends when they were driving slowly away from his property.

'You just imagine it, buddy,' Dmitri chuckled.

'Hopefully, you are right,' Félix sighed deeply.

'Please drive slowly, so the police will not suspect anything,' Dmitri grumbled.

When they reached the bridge, they came out of the car and took the body out. The three threw the body over the bridge and it splashed in the icy water. Luckily, the water wasn't frozen solid. It was three am at night.

'I have three joints of cannabis from Egypt, would you like to smoke, gentlemen? You deserve it,' Félix sniggered. They all agreed and began to smoke just beside the car.

'Do you know what, gentlemen, we forgot to put a heavy object on Rasputin's neck, so he will float.' Everybody burst into hysterical laughter.

When they finished smoking cannabis, they drove towards Rasputin's property in order to bring his fur coat, hat, gloves and the key back to his apartment, to show that he was there all the time, sleeping.

After that, the group went back to the crime scene and burned objects covered with blood in the fireplace in the basement. There was so much blood everywhere, that they couldn't possibly clean it all the way. They had no experience of cleaning. There was blood on top of the snow and Dmitri tried to cover it with a shovel, but not very well; the blood was still visible.

It was morning of 31 December, a New Year celebration considered to be quite an important family event in Russia. Rasputin's daughters Maria and Varvara were staying in their father's apartment. They both had a small winter break from the boarding school. It wasn't unusual for Grigori to be away for the entire night, so they were not worried about him, until that evening. The girls sent a telegram to Pockrovskoe, making sure that he had not returned there without telling them. In the morning, they received a reply from their mother.

'Grigori is not in the village yet, if he appears in a few days, I'll let you know. Please inform me when you find him. God bless you all, mother.'

The girls began to ask the neighbours and friends whether anybody knew of his whereabouts. No one seemed to tell them anything reasonable.

'Let's look through his telephone notes and address books, maybe we can find something interesting,' Maria suggested to her sister. It was a difficult task. There were so many notes scattered haphazardly all over his desk. They rang a few numbers and asked without any success.

'If he's not going to appear by tomorrow morning, we should call the police,' Varvara stated firmly. Her sister nodded in reply.

'Mary, do you know what I find a bit strange in this situation?'

'What?'

'His key is here, hat, gloves and coat, but one pair of his winter boots is missing.'

'That's bizarre.'

The next day, the sisters called the police and registered Rasputin as a missing person. The policeman questioned the girls about what they knew of his disappearance. They told the policeman everything, they already knew about his sudden departure and a criminal investigation began.

Grigori was supposed to visit the royal palace at the beginning of January. It was agreed between Rasputin and Czarina Alexandra a few days prior. He simply did not appear. It was rather strange, because if he was too drunk or unwell to visit them, he usually informed them through a phone call.

'The holy man was supposed to visit Alexei this morning, but for an unknown reason he did not,' Alexandra informed Nicholas.

'He might be unwell or drunk and will let us know when he will turn up,' Nicholas answered.

'I hope you are right. There was an assassination attempt on him previously, not long ago.'

A few days passed and there was no phone call or telegram from Rasputin. Consequently, Nicholas telephoned Rasputin's apartment and Varvara answered that he hadn't been at home since 30 December. As a result, Nicholas called the police and asked them to search for Grigori's whereabouts. Nicholas also ordered to provide him with information from the security officers who were watching the monk's apartment. From the reports, he discovered that the last two people who visited Grigori were Ann and Félix and then he vanished in the middle of nowhere.

Could it be Félix? Nicholas thought and informed the police. He remembered that Grand Duchess Elizabeth informed Alexandra that Félix was planning to assassinate Rasputin and no one believed her.

Suddenly, a fisherman found a single boot floating near the bridge. Mary and Varvara identified that the boot belonged to Grigori. The police began to search the area and shortly discovered Rasputin's remains. The biopsy was performed on his body and it was revealed that the traces of water were in his lungs, he had multiple gunshot wounds and crushed genitalia. Consequently, he died from drowning and gunshot wounds. Nevertheless, the cause of death stated assassination. The next day, when Nicholas was busy working and didn't want to have any meetings, Alexandra was grief-stricken by the death of Grigori Rasputin. She wept openly and was totally inconsolable.

'There are ministers waiting for an appointment, Your Majesty, would you like to see them?' someone asked Alexandra.

'No, I am grieving, I'll see them tomorrow,' she sobbed.

'But they have a really urgent message for Your Majesty, regarding revolution.'

'Do you understand the reply?' Alex answered coldly. The man left the room.

Shortly after the body's discovery, the police questioned Félix Yusupov. All the logical traces pointed towards him.

Félix was woken up with loud knocks at the door and shouts; it was a police investigation team. The door was unlocked and the group of policemen entered Yusupov's palace loudly. They walked around the palace searching for clues.

'Where were you on 30 December, Félix?'

'I was in Crimea with my wife Irina,' he answered shortly.

'The chauffeur stated that he gave you a lift there and back to bring Rasputin here.'

'Well, Rasputin left after the meal.'

'Your servants heard the shooting, who was shooting here? There is a lot of evidence, bullets and blood.'

'It was a British secret agent.'

'Yeah, right, I put you under house arrest for Rasputin's murder. Why is there blood on the snow?'

'The dog was shot by accident by my cousin four times removed.'

'I certainly believe you, Félix. Who are your associates?'

'Grand Duke Dmitri and Vladimir Purishkevich.'

'Now you are speaking the truth, Félix.'

Both gentlemen were arrested shortly and placed under house arrest.

Félix was annoyed and disappointed to be under incarceration. Never in his life had he had a limitation of freedom. Félix made a plan.

'Irina, sweetheart, darling, please pack a suitcase full of diamonds and luxury items.' He gave her a kiss. 'We are going to escape abroad, as soon as possible.'

'Of course, Félix dearest, where would you like to go, my love?'

'France or England,' he whispered. 'We are leaving at four in the morning.'

'It will be ready tomorrow, my love.'

Next morning, quietly and carefully, Irena and Félix went downstairs into the servants' quarters and walked out of the labourers' entrance and a black carriage took them to the train station. Unfortunately, when they entered a second-class area of the train, a policeman arrested the escaped couple and put Yusupov back under house arrest. Félix and Irena were truly disappointed.

Soon, the czar ordered to confiscate one of Félix's castles as a punishment for killing Rasputin. Luckily for Félix, it wasn't a tremendous distress, because the Yusupovs had several castles only in St Petersburg and a few across Russia.

Rasputin was buried in a picturesque area near St Petersburg. Alexandra herself chose a place of burial in a small orthodox chapel. It was a quiet private memorial, only the Romanovs and Rasputins were invited, because of security reasons. Everyone around was scared of being murdered.

'What are we going to do without Grigori? Alexandra asked Nicholas.

'Exactly the same, darling, he always said believe in yourselves and everything will be fine, that God will protect you all.'

Next day, Nicholas left to fight the Germans and left Alexandra to govern instead of him. The situation in St Petersburg became treacherous. The revolution begun.

Forty days after the funeral, an ex-fan of Rasputin and an elderly man he used to drink with, Stefan, witnessed a strange scene. Rasputin, alive, walked towards him with a bottle of wine in his hand, he was wearing a black robe.

'Stefan, buddy, would you like to visit gypsy girls with me?' he said loudly, attracting attention. 'I came back to life and that's it.'

A dreadful chill went down Stefan's back.

'Nn-nn-next time, perhaps, I'll let you know when.'

He began to walk in a different direction. Other people witnessed his unforeseen resurrection. The city was buzzing about it.

Chapter 20
Revolution 1917

Nicholas II lost control of the army, the soldiers and officers stopped obeying his orders and thousands of armed people, entire regiments and battalions deserted and the czar became totally powerless. The revolution began. The strikes occurred simultaneously across the main cities of Russia – Kiev, Moscow and St Petersburg – and people came out on the streets with illegal protests and demonstrations. The dense crowd stayed on the streets. Moreover, thousands of armed soldiers and officers joined the strikes across Petrograd. Furthermore, the factory workers, female suffragettes and railway workers rose across the country to join the uprising.

Nicholas ordered the armed forces to disperse the crowds; however, because there were so many people on the streets already protesting, gunfire here and there didn't make any difference. The people carried on remonstrating. At this point in time, the czar and his government couldn't do anything to stay in power; it was too late.

The first Bolshevik party leader Vladimir Lenin was against involvement in the First World War and wanted to withdraw Russia from the conflict. In the newspapers and on the streets, he campaigned against the war.

'Millions of Russian people died during the war, follow me and I'll make sure that Russia is out of this bloody conflict,' he proclaimed enthusiastically. People were starving and had no interest to fight and they listened to Vladimir Lenin.

'Yeah, we are tired of this chaos, do something,' they shouted.

Crowds of people followed him, cheered, clapped and joined the Bolshevik Communist Party.

'Land and bread to everyone!' Lenin yelled, raising his arms in the air. People believed him and thousands of them joined the Communist Party.

When Alexander II was assassinated by the terrorist organisation Narodnaya Volya in 1881, Lenin's brother Alexander was executed. A few terrorists were pardoned, but not him.

'I swear on my life that they will pay for my brother's execution,' Lenin said to everyone who listened to him. At that time, no one believed that he was capable; however, decades later, he became the most prominent leader of the Bolshevik Party and always wanted to accomplish his promise.

In March, the royal train was prepared, waiting on a snowy platform. Nicholas II walked in, with a sad expression on his face. Georgie Lvov followed him, holding a dark red folder.

'Take me to Peterhof this instance, I must see my family as soon as possible,' he ordered to a train assistant.

'Your Majesty, the road is blocked by crowds, we have to make a U-turn,' he replied.

'How long will it take me to get there?'

'Anything, up to 12 hours.'

'It doesn't matter,' he sighed. 'As long as I see them at the end of my journey.' When both gentlemen sat down opposite each other and the locomotive moved slowly screeching its wheels, Nicholas thought about his current situation, looking at the passing surroundings – it was terrible. He knew that nothing positive was waiting for him in this volatile and explosive state of affairs. He was alone on the chessboard, a lonesome king, without protection, even his relatives had deserted him. *Not long until the checkmate,* he thought. Abruptly, the train stop. A deafening silence hung in the air.

'We can't go further.'

'Why?'

'This road is blocked as well.'

'Find another way, it's an order,' Nicholas raised his voice.

'Your Majesty, have you thought about your abdication? It might be the right time to sign the documents.' Prince Lvov placed a red folder in front of Nicholas. It had three copies of the abdication act.

'Yes, I'll sign it to save Russian and my family.'

First, he read through and signed one copy in favour of his son Alexei. Then he changed his mind and signed another copy in favour of his brother Michael. Nicholas placed both documents inside the dark red folder and gave it back.

'Thank you, how are you going to use your free time, Nicholas?'

'It would be absolutely wonderful to spend more time with my family – visiting an orthodox church with my children, enjoying outdoor activities, photography, gardening, hunting, sailing and going on holiday abroad.'

'Hopefully, Nicholas, you will be able to achieve your dreams.'

Finally, the train moved again slowly; it was dark outside.

Next day, after the czar's abdication, a provisional, emergency government was created by Georgie Lvov. It began its work immediately. On the morning of the previous day, when Nicholas was on the train, Czarina Alexandra was woken up by sobbing children. They had a blotchy rash, high temperature, coughs and sneezes.

'What is happening to me?' Alexei asked his mother.

'Nothing serious, it's measles, don't worry and stay in bed.' All five of them were ill.

'Mother, why are you still healthy?' Alexei asked, coughing loudly. 'I had measles when I was a child, so I'm immune to it.'

'You're lucky.' When all the children were fast asleep, one of the security officers came to Alexandra.

'The castle is under attack, Your Majesty, what shall I do?'

'Fight.'

'Do you have any plans to escape?'

'No, all five of my children are sick with measles, I can't possibly go anywhere at all, especially since Nicholas is not back yet.' After a few hours of fighting, the officer returned.

'Bad news, Your Majesty, they broke into the castle.'

'That's horrifying, where is Nicholas?'

'I don't know, ma'am.'

When the soldiers entered the castle, they ordered for the royal family to remain in the building. Furthermore, they asked to turn off the electricity and running water to make it as uncomfortable as possible for the Romanovs.

'Ma'am, there is no light anywhere in the castle. I checked, it's scary in the darkness,' Maria said to her mother.

'Don't worry, darling, just use the candles and I will ask for the gas lamps in the corridors to be lit.'

Alexandra felt uneasy about someone else being in control of the castle, but because of the children she went through it with great dignity.

'God sends us a punishment, so we have to go through it with eminence, sweethearts,' she encouraged her sick children.

Nicholas returned to the castle the next morning. Alexandra was pleased to see him and they gave each other a hug.

'Yesterday, I signed an act of abdication and I'm no longer the czar,' he burst into loud sobs.

'The main thing is that you are still my husband, Nicholas, and we love each other.' They stood together for a while, as still as statues.

'How are the children?'

'They have measles and their hair is falling out. Except for that, they are absolutely fine.'

'What about the castle?'

'The soldiers broke in and now they're in control, they cut off the electricity and water.'

'Do you have an escape plan, darling?'

'Well, do you remember George V sent an invitation to our family to stay in Britain for a while, if we were in grave danger?'

'Yes, I do.'

'So, yesterday I received a letter from George saying that he withdraws his invitation, because the king is scared of an uprising in his own nation.'

'Alexandra, darling, we are totally alone now, we have to rely on ourselves and God.'

'I will pray for all of us,' Alexei entered the throne room, yawning, his face was covered with a red rash.

'Hello, my parents, why do you both look so sad?'

'The act of abdication was signed yesterday, so we're not the ruling family any longer.'

'So, will I be the czar?'

'No, you will not, it was signed in Michael's favour.'

'That's awful, why didn't you ask me first? You are always doing that, I hate you!' The boy burst into tears.

'It's because of your illness, Alexei, you will understand in the near future.'

'Excuse me,' Alexei turned around and run faster towards his bedroom and slammed the door.

He fell on his pillow sobbing. He couldn't comprehend why life was so unfair to him; haemophilia, awful restrictions and now no crown.

About a week later, the children's hair continued to fall out in patches. At one point, the decision was made to shave their heads. This was particularly stressful for the young ladies. They cried incessantly for a few days.

'Your hair will grow back, Anastasia, stop snivelling, please.'

It was stressful for Alexandra to see her daughters bald. All four princesses had gorgeous hair before contracting measles.

When the children felt a bit better, their tutor Pierre remained in the castle and gave them lessons every day, according to the schedule.

'Pierre, please take a picture of all of us bald, it will be interesting to see the difference on a photograph,' Olga asked her tutor.

When the photograph was developed, the idea came to Maria.

'Shall we write a letter to our grandma, informing her about the measles and our shaved heads?'

'Of course we shall, Maria, and I will ask someone to post it for us,' Alexei agreed.

Dearest grandmother,

We hope you're safe and well. All five of us had measles, it was truly awful. Our hair fell out in patches and our heads were shaved.

All five of us look a bit awed and bizarre on that photo we've posted. Do you agree, Your Majesty?

How is your holiday in Crimea?

Lots of love from your grandchildren,
OTMA

The letter was posted shortly. Alexei asked someone to do it for him. Because of the war, it took three months to reach Crimea. It was delivered to Queen Maria Feodorovna and she was tremendously delighted. Maria read the letter over and over again and kissed it.

'God bless you all, my grandchildren, I hope to see all five of you again,' the Queen began to write the reply straight away and posted it the same day.

Back in Peterhof, Kerensky was in control of the castle and in charge of the safety of the royal family. First, he had a conversation with Nicholas about their safety and security. Kerensky was a wise leader and truly wanted to provide a guarantee of survival for the royal family; at least, when he was in charge.

'Shall we go for a walk?' Kerensky asked Nicholas in Peterhof Palace.

'Of course, we shall.'

They walked through familiar gardens, but Nicholas had a strange feeling that he was not in charge any longer, even in his own property.

'All phone calls in and out of the castle will be recorded from now on,' Kerensky said in a hurry.

'Yes, Mr Kerensky, if it's truly obligatory,' Nicholas replied quietly.

In reality, he thought that it was infringing his privacy, but he didn't say anything.

'The post in and out of the castle will be checked by the security officers,' he carried on talking.

'Why, is it terribly essential?' Nicholas asked in reply.

'It's only because of security reasons,' Kerensky insisted.

'Wil there be a guarantee of me and my family's personal safety?' Nicolas asked and sighed deeply.

'Yes, but only when I'm in control. Please be ready to depart if necessary, in a matter of hours,' he promised.

'Thank you, Mr Kerensky.'

Both gentlemen shook hands. It was unusual for Nicholas to receive orders from other people and he thought that it would be unwise to argue his position, because Kerensky and his soldiers might create more ridiculous rules. Life in the castle would become even more unbearable. The castle became full of soldiers; they wandered around the castle, moved objects from place to place and entered the rooms without knocking. Alexandra disliked the circumstances, as well as her husband, but they couldn't do anything about it.

The next day, Alexandra invited her chambermaid Nina into her personal bedroom. She locked the door behind her.

'Nina, darling, do you know how to sew?' Alexandra whispered quietly in her ear.

''Course I do, Your Majesty, why are you asking?' she whispered back.

'The situation in Petrograd is so awful that we might have to depart to a different place in a matter of hours, Kerensky said, so I'd love to know how to repair my children's clothes by myself and teach my children.'

'It's a brilliant idea, Your Majesty, you never know when sewing skill might be useful.'

The next day, the lessons began and Alexandra invited Olga, Tatiana, Maria and Anastasia to learn how to sew. In three or four weeks, the ladies were marvellous at stitching and it distracted them from the gruesome reality. When the lessons finally stopped, Alexandra gave Nina a tiny gift.

'Thank you, Nina darling, you are a real brick, I will remember your kind heart,' Alexandra smiled.

'It's my pleasure, Your Majesty,' Nina began to cry. She had worked in the castle for many years and she realised that there were just a number of weeks left and the royal family may depart. She was sorry not for losing her job, but for not being able to see the royal family on a day-to-day basis.

Almost one month passed without any major events. Kerensky was wondering how to punish Grigori Rasputin even after his execution. An idea came to his bright mind.

If Rasputin is to be cremated, he thought, *he will not be able to appear in front of the mighty God on judgement day with all the rest of the blessed souls. Consequently, he will end up in hell, as stated by priests in the orthodox religion.* He was sure that the monk deserved it.

Subsequently, Kerensky ordered his soldiers to exhume the body of Rasputin and cremate it as soon as possible. The body of the holy monk was exhumed out of its grave and set on fire. It burned for hours. The ashes were placed back in the grave; however, the public were told that the ashes were scattered.

'Ought to lose his job,' one soldier complained to another, 'even after death, they can't leave him be.'

'He was a powerful monk; even two or three hundred years ahead, people will talk about Grigori Rasputin,' the other soldier growled.

Moreover, Kerensky also realised that the act of cremation meant that no one else could disturb the grave of Grigori any longer to steal or excavate his body in the future.

In contrast, after the cremation, Nicholas, Alexandra and Rasputin's wife and daughters were truly saddened by this weird act.

When the sewing lessons were completed and Alexandra and her daughters knew pretty well how to sew, Alex invited the princesses into her personal bedroom. The door was locked behind them. Alex opened a silver case full of diamonds in front of them.

'Golly gosh, the diamonds are so magnificent,' Grand Duchess Olga commented.

'Yes, they are,' Tatiana smiled. 'I'd love to go to a ball.' Her eyes sparkled like sapphires.

'I wish we could, sweetheart, darling,' her mother answered quietly. 'We are all here for a secret mission.'

'What mission, ma'am?' Anastasia asked, pointing her finger in front of her lips. 'It sounds so mysterious.'

'Our mission is to sew all these diamonds into five corsets for Olga, Tatiana, Maria, Anastasia and I, and two vests for Nicholas and Alexei.'

'Goodness gracious, what is the real purpose for making the most sparkly vests and corsets in the entire world?' Maria asked with interest.

'It will allow us to carry all those diamonds with us when we are away from this castle, without raising any awful suspicion from weird strangers. Our suitcases could be searched easily and they could be easily stolen.'

'What can you use the diamonds for?' Anastasia questioned her mother.

'The diamonds could be sold if necessary, to buy food, train tickets and clothes.'

'Is there another purpose for wearing corsets and vests covered with diamonds?' Olga enquired quietly.

'Yes, it's a good question; it is protection, the vests are bullet-proof.'

'I'd love to start sewing today.' Anastasia smiled.

'Remember, grand duchesses, it's a secret, it's private and confidential from everyone except the seven of us,' Alexandra whispered quietly. Soon, the sewing started and all five of them worked hard to complete the deed.

Time passed by. One day, Kerensky entered the castle with the terrible news that the political instability and volatile situation in Petrograd had worsened and that it was no longer safe for the Royal family to remain in Peterhof Palace.

'I suggest we move to the Siberian town called Tobolsk. It's quiet out there and safe,' Kerensky explained to Nicholas.

'At this precise moment in time, I'll go anywhere, because Lenin and his associates might plan to liquidate us.'

'The departure will take place tomorrow morning. You'll travel by boat,' Kerensky informed Nicholas. 'One suitcase per person only.'

'One suitcase per person, it's not enough, surely,' he replied with irritation.

'Those are my rules.' The silence hung in the air.

'We all will be ready tomorrow morning,' Nicholas finally stated.

The suitcases had been prepared the day before. No one truly wanted to depart. The family was getting ready as if they were robots.

'Please, put your corsets on and never take them off during the journey there, to maintain your dignity,' Alexandra gave orders to her children.

'I don't want to go anywhere at all,' Alexei complained in a low voice, his voice began to break and sound lower.

'We will be safer there,' Alexandra encouraged him.

The next morning, the family, the tutor, the doctor and the other people who accompanied them gathered all in one room with their luggage.

An officer stood in front of the door letting them out one by one into a closed carriage. The children walked through the door first, then Nicholas, followed by Alexandra.

'One suitcase per person, not two,' he said to Alexandra.

'It's not a suitcase, it's a handbag,' she said firmly. It looked like a silver box with handles.

'You have to leave it behind.'

'No, it was given to me by Queen Victoria, please let me take it, it's a memory.'

'You are not going anywhere then,' he carried on arguing.

'Let me through now.' Alex was cross.

'Maybe you should leave it behind, Alex, please.' Nicholas looked straight in her eyes. 'The main thing is we will be together and you will remember Queen Victoria in your heart.'

'It's so unfair.' Alex put her silver case with handles on the table and walked through the door with her suitcase and Nicholas followed behind her with his.

When they arrived in port, the sun was already up and they all marched in total silence along the street. Kerensky walked behind them; he was armed. Suddenly, gunfire broke out on the street and Kerensky retaliated. He was nearly shot; the bullet passed millimetres from him. The group rushed to the port. Soon, they boarded a boat. The captain welcomed them.

The trip by boat was boring and uneventful. The family amused themselves by praying, learning, reading, playing cards and simply doing nothing. Alexandra became unwell with splitting headaches and sciatica. The medication did not help and she remained in bed for days on end, suffering in pain. Alexei was fine, almost to the end of the journey, but his bleeding started right on the last day of the trip.

A letter from her Majesty Queen Maria Feodorovna, addressed to her grandchildren, arrived at the castle a few days after they left. It was added to the pile of post on someone's table. The post addressed to the Romanov family was not redirected to them.

Chapter 21
Massacre

The Romanovs arrived in Tobolsk on 12 August. It was a quiet suburban municipality. The town looked green and beautiful. It was unquestionably a safe place for the royal family. The summer day was warm and welcoming. They passed by the cathedrals, monasteries and were driven towards the Kremlin of Tobolsk. A white stone spacious governors building on 10 Mira Street welcomed them upon rival.

'How wonderful, this building looks roomy and comfortable,' Alexandra said to her children.

'Optimistically, all of us will be quite content living here,' Nicholas replied.

The royal family with 45 other people registered into the governor's building on the same date.

Luckily, indoors, the house was as good as outdoors. The building had a reception hall, dining and sitting rooms, study area, a spacious kitchen with servants and a number of bedrooms upstairs. Nicholas and Alexandra received the master bedroom of the house. Of course, one couldn't compare it with a royal bedroom at the palace, but it was clean, comfortable and had nice furniture. Alexei had his own room just next door. He quite liked it. Maria and Anastasia shared one room and Tatiana and Olga shared another. The royal ladies were generally pleased with the arrangement. The tutor, doctor, chef, cleaning ladies and chambermaids had their own bedrooms. No one complained about anything during or after arrival. The windows were wide and they let in a lot of light.

As soon as they settled in, the rules were given by the officers. In general, the people in that house were kind and treated them like royalty, with dignity and respect.

'The family is allowed to go for a walk once a day in the courtyard,' one of the soldiers announced loudly.

'Could a priest visit this property?' Alexandra asked with interest.

'Possibly once a month upon request.'

'That's lovely,' Alex said quietly. Because she was a religious person, Alexandra was in distress the most from not being able to go to the church whenever she wished. Alex compensated for it by reading a Bible.

Besides, the children had suffered the most; they were not able to go for a walk as often as they wished. The boundaries were too suffocating for the young souls. All of them became paler and quieter all of a sudden. Luckily for the children, Pierre Gilliard continued their education with increasing dedication and provided his lessons in the most interesting manner to compensate for the loss of freedom. They studied French, English, Russian, Spanish, literature, geography, history, drawing, science and etiquette. The lessons distracted them from the dreadful reality and they learned with increasing pleasure.

In addition, Nicholas suffered from anxiety and depression, because there was no post and he was not able to communicate with the outside world on a day-to-day basis. The local newspapers did not provide enough news. Consequently, he compensated for it with writing in his diary, describing everyday activities and events in bright and vivid details.

In this free time, Alexei loved playing board games and chess with his sisters and walking up and down the stairs in order to exercise. Tatiana and Olga both read all the books in the building. Even the books that their mother did not let them read.

One sunny morning, all seven members of the family enjoyed breakfast together. The food was simple, but good – bread, milk, eggs, porridge, butter and cheese.

'It's fabulous outside, it's a shame we have to stay indoors,' Tatiana complained, looking at the bright sunshine penetrating through the window.

'Sometimes, I imagine myself running through the field free, like a tiger, finding pleasure in jumping, running and hiding. I'd love to enjoy sunshine, wind, snow and rain,' Anastasia exclaimed enthusiastically.

'Yes, I agree, one hour a day being outdoors is not enough, surely,' Alexei agreed with his sisters.

'We'll see what I can do, I will ask tomorrow whether we can increase our time outside. At least the soldiers in Tobolsk seem reasonable,' Nicholas promised to his children.

'Thank you, Father,' Alexei answered. The children could not comprehend why all those restrictions were impressed upon them.

Three weeks passed without major events. It was particularly grey outside and gloomy, the sky was covered with dark heavy thunderstorm clouds, the bright zigzags of lightning flashed repeatedly on and off.

The rumble of thunder growled like a crazy giant. The rain poured down non-stop. Alexei was bored, he went up and down the stairs to spend his free time. This time, he brought a toboggan with him. Alexei laid down on it and let go his hand. The toboggan tumbled down the slippery stairs, making a lot of racket. When it stopped, the boy was badly hurt. Nicholas rushed to help him.

'Alexei, what's wrong?'

'Nothing serious, I have just been tobogganing downstairs and injured myself badly,' he explained.

'Why did you do it? You must have known that it's highly dangerous.'

'Because I'm bored.'

After the injury, Alexei went straight to bed. He was so poorly that he couldn't walk any longer and began to use his wheelchair to move from place to place. Nicholas looked after his son as much as he physically was able to.

'Before, you said that it's God's wish for me to be the czar, and now, it's no longer His wish, why?'

'Perhaps, God has another purpose for all of us?'

'What is that purpose? What are we going to do next?'

'We may all go abroad to England, France or Denmark.'

'I hope you're right this time,' Alexi sighed.

'I'll pray for our family and your recovery, son.'

Alexei spent the majority of his time in bed and his recovery was slow and painful. Nicholas asked for a priest to visit them to pray for Alexei and his recovery. The priest came and everyone had a communion.

'God be with you.' The young priest gave a silver spoon of wine and bread to all members of the royal family.

Shortly after, the terrible news came through for the Romanovs that the communists had seized power with Lenin in control. Immediately, Vladimir Lenin began his negotiations regarding peace with Germany. When the peace treaty was signed, the First World War ended for Russia.

'I truly regret that I signed the act of abdication,' Nicholas said to Alexandra. 'I worry about my family and their safety. I am concerned about Russia and what will become of it.'

'Grigori gave his predictions that there would be the First World War, revolution and total chaos and Russia will drown in blood,' Alexandra shivered. 'So far it has come true.'

'He also gave his predictions that my last journey will be by train,' he sighed deeply with a tragic expression.

The winter passed by rather quickly; the spring came with all its beauty to Tobolsk.

Both party leaders, Lyon Trotsky and Vladimir Lenin, agreed that the Russian royal family had to be executed in its entirety; however it would be tricky to accomplish such a dreadful task in the town of Tobolsk. As a result, it was decided that the family should be moved immediately to a more secluded, Red Army area called Ekaterinburg, where they could hide the buried bodies easily without delay. The urgent telegram came to Tobolsk that the family must be moved on 12 April.

When Nicholas received this information, he was truly saddened,. The ex-czar didn't want to travel to Ekaterinburg. Nicholas was terrified that his family's lives may become even more unbearable over there.

Despite his concerns, the bags were packed and on 12 April the family travelled by train to Ekaterinburg. All members of the family had sober expressions, even the children. They spent their time playing cards. Nicholas walked into the first carriage to talk to a train driver.

'Take us to Moscow instead of Ekaterinburg,' he ordered to the driver. Nicholas presumed that he and his family might find help and support from White Army members in Moscow.

'Yes, of course, Your Highness, it doesn't make any difference for me which way we go. I need to contact the control centre first,' the driver agreed. The train gradually changed direction towards Moscow. The ex-czar prayed for the success of his idea. For a few hours, the train journey was smooth. All of a sudden, the train was stopped by members of the Communist Party with guns, revolvers and pistols. Apparently, the driver reported it to the control centre and they informed members of the Red Army. They entered the train and ordered the train driver to change direction towards Ekaterinburg. Nicholas was annoyed and disappointed that his plan hadn't worked. At least, he had tried to change it.

The family came out of the train onto the grey and dusty platform, holding their suitcases. Members of the army followed them. The group walked slowly towards the house of special purpose, Yepatiev's house. Nicholas carried Alexei in his arms. They all dragged their feet on the dusty road with gloomy expressions and were truly exhausted. Grand Duchess Olga nearly fell; shuffling her feet, one after the other, she tripped. Pierre rushed to assist her.

'Don't help her or I'll kill you!' Yurovsky yelled with a devilish smile on his face. Pierre disobeyed his orders and assisted the Grand Duchess.

'Be careful, Pierre, he is serious about his death threats,' Nicholas interfered.

'Yeah, be fucking careful,' the soldiers laughed. 'Or I'll murder you, right here.' He put a gun in front of his face.

'I'm not scared to die for the royal family,' Pierre said confidently. 'I am not frightened of you and your soldiers at all.'

'Get out now,' he shouted in rage. 'You have one minute and if you are still here, I will shoot you.'

Pierre Gilliard pulled along his suitcase, said goodbye to the royal family and especially the children. He waved and began to walk in a different direction. When he turned the corner, he took a cab and ordered it to go towards the train station, then boarded the train all the way to Sweden. He was a Swedish citizen. Pierre was truly terrified for the royal family. What would become of them?

The house of special purpose was a small four-bedroom house. It was surrounded by a tall wooden fence. The house looked gloomy and uninviting with its whitish grey walls. The group walked upstairs using a creaking staircase. All four bedrooms were small and unattractive. Nicholas, Alexandra and Alexei had the first room. The royal couple had a double bed and Alexei had a single bed. The four grand duchesses had a second room. There was only one double bed to share. So one girl had to sleep on the floor. The girls took it in turns. There were eight other people remaining, looking after the royal family, including Dr Botkin. Four of them went into one room and four in another. There was a shortage of linen – pillows, duvets and blankets – which was rather inconvenient. Luckily, all of the soldiers slept downstairs. A basic reception room served as an eating area. There was one toilet upstairs and one downstairs and a dirty kitchen. This arrangement was too crowded and uncomfortable for the royal family. They had never experienced anything like it.

Anastasia looked at a window in the girl's room and tried to unlock it to let the fresh air in. The window was locked. All of them were locked in the house as a precaution.

'Don't look at the windows, it's not a hotel for you,' one of the soldiers bellowed.

'It's not a hotel, is it a prison?' Anastasia asked with irritation.

'Kind of, I will ask to paint the windows over, so the world will be unreachable and will increase your suffering in the house of special purpose,' he laughed. The windows were painted over soon and it was impossible to see through the white paint.

'Mum, the toilets are terrible in this house and there is no toilet paper at all,' Maria complained.

'You can solve this problem, sweetheart, by tearing out the pages from your diary.'

'What a strange idea, Mother, I wouldn't have thought of that, you are simply genius.'

'No, it's just a life-experience.'

When Alexandra visited those toilets, she was simply terrified of the obscene drawings on the walls of her and Grigori Rasputin. She brought a box of paint and painted them over; however, the drawings appeared again and again and again.

At the same day when everyone was downstairs waiting for a meal, Yurovsky took the opportunity to make his rules clear. He entered the room and noisily interrupted their conversation.

'I want you all to understand that escape from this house will be punished by death on the spot, is that clear?' They nodded in profound silence. 'One one-hour walk a day in the backyard.' Nobody wanted to argue with Yurovsky and he left the room, slamming the door behind him.

Next day, the post arrived. The family was so pleased to receive it. It was addressed to Nicholas. The letter looked normal. It was written in French. They all gathered in one room, curious about its contents. Nicholas unfolded it and began to read. Everyone was listening intently.

'The White Army is attacking Ekaterinburg right now. When our mission is successful, we will rescue you and your family,' Nicholas carried on reading. When he finished, the letter was set on fire. The letter gave a bit of hope to all of them. Unfortunately, it was a trick, it was written by the communists.

In the morning, everyone was waiting for breakfast but it simply wasn't served. At noon, they began to wait for lunch and it was finally prepared at 4 o'clock in the afternoon. When the royal family sat down to eat, half-drunk soldiers walked around the table, swearing, asking stupid questions and commenting about everything.

The food was terrible; dark brown bread, dry and mouldy cheese, pickled mushrooms, mushy peas, boiled eggs and pickled herrings. The food was jumbled up on top of a wooden table.

'I am not eating that food, it's so awful,' Alexei said loudly.

'Just try a small mouthful, please?' Alex answered.

'No, it's not for me, thanks. I used to eat crabs, lobsters and beluga caviar, and now dry cheese, mushrooms and herrings.'

'I am not hungry either,' Olga agreed with Alexei.

'I don't have any cutlery,' Tatiana complained.

'Eat with your hands, like this,' one of the drunken soldiers shouted and picked up a piece of cheese from the table and put it in his mouth. He looked at her in a bizarre way.

'Do not talk to me in this manner,' she glared at him. 'I am royal-born,' Tatiana yelled in dismay.

'I'm just trying to help,' the soldier walked away holding a bottle of vodka.

'Please use my unused cutlery, dear sister,' Alexei said kindly and passed her his knife and fork.

'Thank you, brother,' Tatiana gave him a little smile. They were talking in small phrases and the conversation did not flow at all, it was so tense at the table. When the royal family left the table, the soldiers consumed all the leftovers as fast as they could.

The days passed by. Nothing was good in the house of special purpose except the weather. June came and it was time for Maria's birthday. One of the soldiers brought a little birthday cake as a gift especially for Maria. The princess was delighted. It even had a candle on top.

'How wonderful, the soldier is so kind,' Maria smiled. Everyone sung happy birthday and just for once the Romanovs were happy and content.

As soon as Yurovsky discovered that one of the soldiers had disobeyed him and brought one of the princesses a birthday cake, he ordered to remove him immediately.

'The entire group of soldiers is too soft and fluffy, I will change them all into tougher guys,' he decided. The new group was given better ammunition and guns. All of them were ex-criminals.

'Wait and see fucking now,' Yurovsky sniggered and lit a cigarette.

The grand duchesses were not scared of soldiers, because they had protected the royal family their entire lives. Moreover, the princesses looked after sick and wounded soldiers in the hospital and they remembered it as the best time of their lives.

The next day, the new group of soldiers woke them up at 5 o'clock in the morning. The group was armed, drunk and constantly glared at the ladies. The new soldiers ran upstairs and yelled as loud as they could. 'Suitcases and room search, open all your suitcases!' They searched through all their possessions and took whatever they liked. Alexei sat in his wheelchair.

'It's mine,' Alexei said to a soldier, who took his golden watch lying on a dressing table and pocketed it.

'Nothing is yours now, it all belongs to the Communist Party, boy.'

'Please don't argue,' Nicholas suggested. 'It's not worth it.'

They had emptied the half empty suitcases and the search had stopped.

In the evening, Nicholas went to see Yurovsky in person. His office had a school table, two wooden chairs and a picture of Lenin on the wall. Notebooks were scattered on the table and a gun laid beside him. Yurovsky was sitting in one chair smoking a cigarette, when Nicholas came in.

'Hi, Yurovsky, I would like to talk to you about my family.'

'Yes.' The smoke went everywhere.

'What are your plans?'

'I am waiting for a message from the government, then I will know what to do,' he inhaled.

'My wife would like to see a doctor and a priest. Is that possible?'

'No, she can't see a doctor, but I can arrange a priest,' he exhaled and pushed a box of cigarettes in front of Nicholas. 'Help yourself.' He pulled out one cigarette and began to smoke.

'Thank you, Yurovsky.'

'I can't believe I'm talking to the ex-czar; tell me what did you do for Russian people, ordinary people?'

'I worked awfully hard my entire life.'

'Apparently not enough,' he inhaled. 'The White Army is battling for this town, that's why all of us can hear a lot of gunfire on the streets.' He pushed his cigarette in the ashtray and walked out of the room.

Shortly after, Yurovsky received an urgent telegram from Vladimir Lenin. It stated: *'You can proceed.'*

Urgently, Yurovsky gathered all his soldiers in his office to explain the entire plan of action regarding the royal family.

'First, you must count all the pieces of jewellery they are wearing right now and write it down on a piece of paper. Nothing should be unaccounted for,' he ordered to his soldiers. They walked around the house counting the pieces of jewellery. Who was wearing what and how many.

'Alexandra – diamond earrings, set of two.' For rather bizarre reasons, no one noticed their activities. When the list of jewellery was completed, they proceeded to step two of their murderous actions.

Upon His ex-Majesty's request, an orthodox priest came to visit them. An elderly man with a white beard in brown robes entered the house of special purpose. He conducted Holy Communion.

'The body of Christ,' he announced. 'God be with you.'

'For the Father, Son and Holy Spirit, amen,' Alexei replied.

The entire family was taking communion. They looked solemn and dignified, standing in a line waiting for their turn.

Alexandra spent the majority of her time in the house of special purpose reading the Bible, praying and writing in her diary. The last words she wrote in her life were: *'Friday, July 17, 1918,'* in preparation for the following day.

Her husband Nicholas wrote in his diary for the last time in his life: *'The weather is good.'* Nicholas realised that he was losing control, although he didn't want to show it in front of his wife and children.

His oldest daughter Princess Olga became quiet, depressed and withdrawn. She sobbed bitterly for hours on end into her pillow, refused to eat and stayed in her room.

'I wish I would have married earlier,' she sobbed. 'My life could have been better than here.'

Their second daughter Princess Tatiana found her distraction in reading. She read all the books in the house of special purpose. Even the novels her mother did not advise her to read.

Their third and fourth daughter, Maria and Anastasia, found their distraction in each other's company. They talked to each other non-stop, played games and made up stories.

'Maria, sweetheart, if you would like to go to the ball and meet your true love, please put your best white dress on, in your imagination, a golden necklace, a pair of sparkling shoes and diamond tiara and take a ride in our stunning silver royal carriage with me. We will go to the ball and dance with the most handsome kings and princes and we both will fall in love.'

'A fabulous idea and the gentlemen will propose to both of us.' The girls' eyes sparkled like diamonds.

On the same day, Nicholas, Alexei and Anastasia went for a walk with his dog Joy.

Alexei loved playing with Joy. He chased the dog on his wheelchair, laughing and stroking his fur. At moments like this, the boy forgot where he was and enjoyed the moments of happiness. That day, Anastasia joined him with their mum's cocker spaniel. There was a lot of barking, laughing and fun.

In the evening, the irritating soldiers sung obscene songs about Rasputin and Alexandra, right beside the window, so everyone could hear their tuneless voices.

Nicholas and Alexandra ignored them. They both decided to spend time, privately, in their bedroom. Alexei went to play cards with his sisters and the couple had a moment of privacy. They lay down beside each other, holding hands.

'What do you think will happen to us, dearest?' Alexandra whispered quietly.

'I will take you to the Isle of Wight and we will walk along the beach, holding hands.' They kissed passionately.

'I love you forever, I want you so much.'

'I love you too.' They had the most wonderful time together. When they stopped, Alexei knocked at the door. He returned and fell asleep almost instantly. Both Nicholas and Alexandra stayed awake, the gunshots beside the window stopped them from sleeping.

In the middle of the night, a loud knock at the door woke everybody up.

'Who is there?'

'Dr Botkin, Your Majesty. Yurovsky has ordered to move the family to a different location for safety reasons, because the White Army is getting closer and it's dangerous to remain in this house.'

Everyone got up, dressed, and took all their belongings and animals. Nicholas carried Alexei. Alexandra carried her cocker spaniel. Yurovsky led everyone downstairs to the basement. It was a small room without furniture. A single electric lamp lit it.

'What are we waiting for?' Nicholas demanded.

'The transport is delayed; probably the driver is drunk.'

'Bring two chairs, one for Alexei and one for Alexandra,' Nicholas ordered. The chairs appeared shortly. Alexei and Alexandra sat upon them. The three girls were standing behind the chairs and Anastasia stood slightly to the left, separate from everyone. Nicholas was shielding Alexei, standing right in front of him.

Yurovsky with 11 men entered, holding a piece of paper and a pistol in both hands. He was sweating profusely, he was scared. One of his men refused to do the job, so there were only 11 men beside him. He unfolded his piece of paper and began to read.

'Because you broke the law against Russia, you are all sentenced to death by the Communist Party and Vladimir Lenin,' Yurovsky said and began to shoot. The 11 men joined him. Hell was unleashed.

'What, what?' Nicholas answered turning towards his family, seeing them for the last time in his life. His blood splashed Alexei. In the last second of his life, he remembered blood and seven roses, it was a sign from God; seven roses represented the seven members of his family. The bullets ricocheted against Alexei's sisters and did not harm them. The bullet-proof corsets saved their lives. Then, at 2:30 am, it suddenly became extremely difficult for the murderers to see anything in the surrounding smoke. The group of killers decided to go outside to talk and wait for the smoke to subside. One of the soldiers began to vomit, because it was too ghastly, horrific and gruesome to see. The moaning, crying and wailing was excruciating. When they entered the room, the smoke cleared and they saw that only Nicholas and Alexandra and a couple of servants were dead.

Yurovsky pointed straight at Dr Botkin and killed him instantly.

Blood and brains splashed like a gruesome fountain. Yurovsky turned to Alexei and shot him non-stop for a long time. The bullets ricocheted from his bullet-proof jacket which kept him alive.

'Fucking bastard,' he shouted with irritation. Yurovsky shot him in the head and he slid down beside his father, definitely dead. Then he walked towards the four girls. They screamed in terror in front of him. He shot them all one by one, and used knives until it became so quiet. Anastasia kicked, punched and hit the most, fighting for her life, but what could she do against 12 murderers?

'Oh, thank goodness, I'm still alive,' Anastasia screamed. She was covering herself with a diamond cushion.

'No, not anymore,' Yurovsky shouted. He reached satisfaction from each murder. His face contorted with rage.

Suddenly, Anastasia opened her eyes, sat up, screamed in terror and covered her eyes with her hands. They killed her instantly. The bodies were rolled into sheets and carried in a lorry to the woods. The diamonds were discovered at this point. There were nearly 10 kg of jewellery. It was piled up on Yurovsky's desk. The jewellery was covered with blood and remains.

For nearly two days, for one reason or another, the group couldn't find a suitable burial place. Finally, the group dug one grave and Nicholas, Alexandra, Olga, Tatiana and Anastasia were buried in it. Sulphuric acid was poured on top of their remains before burial. For unknown reasons, Maria and Alexei were buried in separate graves nearby in the woods and their bodies were burned in the fire before burial. Yurovsky was satisfied with his gruesome job. Regrettably, it was the shocking and barbaric end of the 300-year dynasty of the Romanov's reign.

Epilogue

Lenin and Trotsky had a conversation regarding Princess Elizabeth. They stood by the River Neva near Smolny, looking at passing-by boats.

'Do you think Elizabeth must be executed? She is a holy person,' Trotsky asked with interest.

'Of course, she must. Virtue, righteousness and faith in control is more dangerous than a tyrant czar for the communist revolution,' Lenin replied. He was scared that he and his party might lose political power and one of the Romanovs would be in control once again.

Consequently, in July 1918, Elizabeth was taken to Alapayevsk together with the nuns from her monastery and a group of Romanovs, including Grand Duke Sergei. They stayed at a school for a few days and then, on 18 July 1918, were transferred into the woodland area with an abandoned mineshaft. A group of armed communist soldiers followed them.

'Why are you killing us?' Grand Duke Sergei bellowed loudly, in order to attract someone's attention.

'Lenin's orders,' a soldier grumbled.

'I bet you don't even understand why, you are just following orders like cowardly sheep,' Sergei carried on talking.

The soldier pointed the gun at him and shot him right in the head.

'For Lenin and revolution!' the soldier shouted.

Sergei's body fell on the ground. They grabbed it and threw it straight in the shaft.

'Now it's your turn, Elizabeth,' he yelled and pushed her alive into the mineshaft full of muddy water. Elizabeth broke a few bones, but she was still alive when she reached the bottom. Then the other members of the group were thrown into the mineshaft alive. The mineshaft had a bit of muddy water at the bottom of it, but not enough to drown them. Elizabeth began to sing orthodox hymns.

The soldiers threw grenades into the mineshaft. They exploded violently, but only injured one person.

Heroically, Elizabeth carried on singing orthodox hymns for a few hours on end. Her angelic voice sounded sweet and holy. It only irritated the soldiers and they put a lot of dry wood into the mineshaft and set it alight. When all was quiet, the communist soldiers left.

Three months later, all the bodies were discovered – surprisingly, in relatively good condition – and were buried in Jerusalem and China. Grand Duchess Elizabeth was proclaimed a holy martyr by the Russian Orthodox Church abroad. She truly deserved it. Elizabeth was a real hero.

Approximately two years after the royal murder, a girl walked along the street in Berlin, Germany, her eyes were in tears and face covered with horrible scars. Desperate, she turned left towards a bridge across the Rhine and carried on walking, occasionally holding on to the bridge's railing. Awkwardly, she climbed on top of the railing and put her legs on another side of the bridge, still holding onto the metal barrier.

'Stop, don't do it, talk to me, I will help you,' a young man in his twenties marched towards the girl.

'I don't need your help.'

'Climb back then by yourself, if you don't,' he insisted and gave her his hand.

Still crying, the girl climbed back on the safe side of the bridge.

'You are awesome, well done,' the young man said quietly and at this point two policemen behind him arrested her. They brought her to the psychiatric clinic nearby. The girl refused to tell them her name and they registered her as an unknown person.

The girl was fast asleep in bed when the doctor gently touched her hand.

'Hello darling, what is your name?'

The lady opened her eyes.

'I am Grand Duchess Anastasia Romanova,' she replied.

The doctor's eyes widened.

'Oh, poor darling, how did you survive?'

'It was awful, I don't want to talk about it.' And she rolled over, facing the hospital wall.

When the doctor walked away from his patient, he decided to contact the Queen Maria Feodorovna and the tutor Pierre Gilliard and inform them that Anastasia was probably alive. He found their phone numbers and spoke to them both over the phone separately. They both were keen to see the mystery patient and identify whether she was truly Anastasia Romanov.

Pierre Gilliard lived in Switzerland and boarded a train to Berlin to meet with the probable princess. This appointment was made and Pierre entered the hospital door with both happiness and anxiety.

If she's a true princess, I'll be delighted, he thought. *If she is an impostor it will make me even more sad.* He entered the doctor's room and a young lady sat on a hospital bench in her dressing gown with bare feet.

'Hello, Your Highness Anastasia, do you remember me?' he asked in French. 'I am surprised how terribly thin you've become.' He looked straight into her eyes. The lady was still and silent.

'Do you recognise her?' the doctor asked Pierre with great interest.

'I am not sure, it seems to me that she doesn't understand French but her hair, eyes and feet are strikingly similar. Both girls have a particularly unusual shape of feet.' The tutor spoke Russian, English and Spanish and there was no reaction to any of the languages.

'She might be after a trauma,' the doctor said and they decided to have another appointment.

Regardless, the patient got better treatment after this visit than an ordinary person would have received.

A couple of weeks later, the Queen Maria Romanova entered the hospital building. She arranged an appointment with the doctor to see the mystery patient.

If it's my beloved Anastasia, I will be the happiest person in the world, she thought and opened the door of the hospital.

The doctor was awaiting her arrival. He bowed and they both entered a private room. A young girl stood in front of them in a long nightdress and bare feet.

'Hello, Anastasia, sweetheart,' the Queen said, looking at her very carefully. 'Do you remember me, I'm your grandma,' she spoke Russian.

The young lady stood as still as a statue.

'Is she the real Anastasia?' the doctor asked.

'I will talk to you in private,' the queen replied.

'I am Anastasia,' she said in German. 'Believe me, please don't leave me.'

'I will stay,' the doctor smiled.

'Goodbye, Anastasia,' the queen answered and they both walked towards the doctor's room. When they both were in the doctor's office, the queen began to speak.

'It's an impostor, I swear. If she was the real Anastasia, I would have given her a kiss and a hug. I miss them terribly badly.'

'Oh no, I'm so sorry, Your Majesty, what do you think about her feet?'

'Yes, I suppose both ladies have the same feet, but I am certain she's not Anastasia.'

During her lifetime, the unknown girl was known as Ana Anderson. She lived in Germany and the United States. When she died, a lock of her hair and some body fluid was given for DNA testing and it was identified that she was a polish factory worker, Franziska Schanzkowska, and she was not related to the Royal family.

The Queen Maria Feodorovna received the awful news about the murder of Nicholas and his family when she lived in Crimea. She did not or could not or would not believe it.

'The communists are lying, nobody has seen his body yet, so he might be still alive, my poor Nicky, bless his soul.' It was too painful for her to admit the truth. Shortly after the appalling news, the queen arranged with the British royal family for 17 Romanovs to travel to England on board the powerful battleship called HMS *Marlborough* for safety. Queen Maria was invited by Queen Alexandra to live in one of her royal palaces. The invitation was gladly accepted.

Later, she moved to her native Denmark. The Russian community of immigrants in Denmark gave Maria a chance to accept the Russian crown; however, she declined the offer. The queen was respected by the Russian people and right until the end, they asked her for help and advice.

Maria Feodorovna died on 13 October 1928. Her wish was to be buried near her husband in St Petersburg. It wasn't possible; however, in September 2006, she was reburied in Saints Peter and Paul Cathedral in St Petersburg. Finally, she was near her beloved husband Alexander III. They were reunited in death.

Pierre Gilliard returned to his native Switzerland and taught French there. He wrote his memoirs regarding the royal family and their assassination. Pierre supported the murder investigation and assisted them as much as he could. He died in 1962, four years after a car accident.

After the communists obtained power during the revolution, the ballerina Matilda Kshesinskaya and her son Vladimir moved to Crimea, because it was impossible and gravely dangerous to stay in Petrograd. Matilda's house in Petersburg was occupied by communists.

'They turned my house into a pig farm,' she laughed.

Luckily for both of them, Matilda managed to obtain the tickets on a train, which travelled away from Russia with great difficulty. The train was totally full. Their luggage was on their lap and it was too difficult to walk along the train without stepping on someone's bags. They all slept on the train overnight for safety reasons; the air was stuffy and it was bitterly cold.

'Mother, why we are travelling third-class, don't you have enough money to buy first-class tickets? Vladimir moaned to Matilda.

'Vladimir, dearest, if I didn't buy the third-class tickets for us, I would have travelled on the roof of this train. It's a life-saving journey and do not complain.'

'I understand, Mother, I thought we'd run out of money as well,' the boy responded with irritation.

'Do you know that Grand Duke Sergei was killed in a mineshaft in Alapaevsk and Nicholas and his family were murdered in Ekaterinburg? If we had remained in Russia, we almost certainly would have been assassinated as well.'

Deep in her heart, she still loved Nicholas and Sergei. It was so tragic for her to bear both losses.

Soon, they boarded a boat and reached the French coast. Easily, they managed to receive French visas and citizenships and remained in France for the rest of their lives, but they never forgot the train journey.

After the murder of the Czar and his family, Prince Félix Yusupov and Princess Irena secretly packed their bags with the most valuable items: a suitcase full of diamonds, two paintings by Rembrandt, three paintings by Leonardo da Vinci, a pair of earrings which previously belonged to Queen Marie Antoinette and a number of archaeological items of value from a pharaoh's tomb.

When the bags were packed, the couple, under the cover of night and in an unidentifiable vehicle, travelled to the train station and took a train to Crimea. From there, on board the British warship *Marlborough*, they travelled to the United Kingdom. Both of them were so delighted when they came on board and were safe from the Russian revolutionists.

'Félix, please tell us about the murder of Grigori Rasputin.'

'I'm proud to say, gentlemen, I killed Rasputin,' Prince Félix answered. He was boasting about it his entire life.

Shortly, they reached British shores and lived in Britain for a while. Then moved to France and not for long to Italy. The valuable items were sold and helped them to sustain their lavish lifestyle.

Soon after the revolution, both dark princesses Milica and Anastasia, with their husbands, went to Crimea and then in 1919 came on board the British warship *Marlborough*. Just to be on board this military vessel was the biggest magic they had ever achieved in their entire lives. The sister's ability to predict the future, helped them to survive the dangers of the revolution. The sisters gave predictions to other people, including the royal family; however, the predictions were unfortunately forgotten by them.

'Predict my future please, Princess Milica,' Prince Félix asked one sunny day, when they were heading towards Britain.

'Of course, it will be my pleasure,' she begun to shuffle the cards.

Both Milica and Anastasia continued to be popular among their circle. Their dark magic was the way to keep and sustain their lavish lifestyle. The princesses lived in England, France, Italy and, of course, Montenegro.

The revolution left Grigori Rasputin's children in different locations. Grigori's daughter Varvara, moved to Moscow and died there in 1925 from an infection. His son Dmitri was sent to Salekhard by Stalin and the authorities and he died in that town in 1937 from dysentery.

His oldest daughter Maria, however, was the luckiest of them all. Following her father's advice, she married Boris Soloviev. The couple went to Vladivostok and then to Prague. In Prague, they opened a Russian restaurant; however, business was terribly slow. Then they were invited to Vienna, Austria, where their second daughter Maria was born. Next, the family settled in Paris, where Boris soon passed away. Following his death, Maria found a job as a dancer, because of her famous name. Maria Rasputin published three memoirs about her father, describing him as a real angel.

'The negativity about my father was entirely made up by communists,' she wrote in her memoirs. 'He was a great man with a real Siberian soul and true generosity.'

Later, Maria was invited to work in a circus, staging her father's tragic murder. In December 1934, she went to London with a touring circus. After, when the circus was still on tour, she went to the United States and married Gregory Bernadsky. She lived first in Miami and then in Los Angeles, California, where she died. At the end of her interesting life, she had two dogs

Yusu and Pov, named after Prince Félix Yusupov. The pets reminded Maria of her father's murder. In the last days of her life, Maria claimed to be psychic. In 1947, her youngest daughter Mary married an ambassador of France. Hard work and awesome achievements.

Rather soon, the second communist leader Leon Trotsky received the jewellery from the murder of the royal family, particularly the lockets from Grigori Rasputin. For that reason, there were several assassination attempts on his life. Unlucky for him, in 1940, he was finally slaughtered by a Spanish gangster, who used an ice axe to kill him. The murder was ordered by Joseph Stalin; he managed to get rid of him. It was a purely political murder. Moreover, Trotsky's daughter Zinaida Volkova committed suicide in Berlin in 1933. His granddaughter Alexandra died in labour camp in the 1930s. His first son Lev Sedov died from complications after an appendicitis operation in 1933 with KGB involvement in a French hospital. It was a presumed poisoning. His second son Sergey Sedov died in 1937 during the prison uprising and the son's wife and children were killed. Finally, all his relatives were rehabilitated after the collapse of Soviet Union and miraculously, a surviving grandson Esteban Volkov built a museum in his memory in Spain. The question is, was it only Stalin's fault or the lockets of Grigori Rasputin that contributed to all those deaths?

Miraculously and unexpectedly, in 1979, the Romanovs' first grave was found in the Soviet Union with Nicholas, Alexandra, Olga, Anastasia and Tatiana and members of the royal entourage. It was way too early for the start of a murder investigation and their bodies were left alone. Only in 1991 were the bodies exhumed and the investigation started. They performed DNA tests to identify the members of the royal family. The tests confirmed that the remains were genuine. Consequently, the discovered members of the royal family were buried in St Petersburg in Saints Peter and Paul Cathedral on 17 July 1998.

'It's a historic moment,' President Yeltsin said in his speech. The members of the British royal family and the other Romanovs were present during their burial.

The already-buried royal family members were canonised by the Orthodox Church in 2000 and they became holy martyrs.

Lastly, the two other children of Nicholas and Alexandra were finally found: Maria and Alexei in 2007. DNA tests were performed on the burned remains and it was identified that they were truly genuine. However, because the other members of the family were holy martyrs, it was incredibly important for the

Orthodox Church to make sure that they were truly genuine. The church members do not believe it. Consequently, Maria's and Alexi's remains are in an archive for the near future.

Is there a political reason why? It might be connected to sanctions and the poisoning of Boris Nemtsov and Alexi Navalny. Well, history will show us in the near future.

It would be fabulous for the entire Romanov family to be finally reunited in death in Saint Peter and Paul Cathedral in St Petersburg.

Quotes and References

Hans Christian Andersen *Ugly duckling,* (11 November 1843), Copenhagen, 'It doesn't matter being born in a duck yard, so long as you are hatched from a swan's egg.'

Lewis Carroll, *Alice's Adventures in Wonderland,* (26 November 1865), Macmillan, 'Off with your head'.

Reference, Wikipedia

Nicholas II of Russia, Wikipedia, Wikimedia Foundation, (accessed 17/10/ 2020). This page was last edited on 17 October 2020, at 10:09 (UTC), *https://en.wikipedia.org/ wiki/Nicholas_II_of_Russia*

Alexandra Feodorovna Alex of Hesse, Wikipedia, Wikimedia Foundation, (accessed 17/10/ 2020). This page was last edited on 12 October 2020, at 19:30 (UTC), *https:// en.wikipedia.org/wiki/Alexandra_Feodorovna_(Alix_of_Hesse)*

Grand Duchess Olga Nikolaevna of Russia, Wikipedia, Wikimedia Foundation, (accessed 17/10/ 2020). This page was last edited on 7 October 2020, at 21:13 (UTC),
https://en.wikipedia.org/wiki/Grand_Duchess_Olga_Nikolaevna_of_Russia

Grand Duchess Tatiana Nikolaevna of Russia, Wikimedia foundation, (accessed 17/10/ 2020). This page was last edited on 7 September 2020, at 12:08 (UTC), *https://en.wikipedia.org/wiki/Grand_Duchess_Tatiana_Nikolaevna_of_Russia*

Grand Duchess Maria Nikolaevna of Russia, Wikipedia, Wikimedia Foundation, (accessed 17/10/ 2020). This page was last edited on 4 October 2020, at 23:52 (UTC),
https://en.wikipedia.org/wiki/Grand_Duchess_Maria_Nikolaevna_of_Russia

Grand Duchess Anastasia Nikolaevna of Russia, Wikipedia, Wikimedia Foundation, (accessed 17/10/ 2020). This page was last edited on 17 October 2020, at 11:16 (UTC),
https://en.wikipedia.org/wiki/Grand_Duchess_Anastasia_Nikolaevna_of_Russia

Alexi Nikolayevich, Tsarevich of Russia, Wikipedia, Wikimedia Foundation, (accessed 17/10/ 2020). This page was last edited on 13 October 2020, at 19:46 (UTC),
https:// en.wikipedia.org/wiki/Alexei_Nikolaevich,_Tsarevich_of_Russia

Prince Leopold Duke of Albany, Wikipedia, Wikimedia foundation, (accessed 17/10/ 2020). This page was last edited on 30 September 2020, at 20:37 (UTC),
https://en.wiki- pedia.org/wiki/Prince_Leopold,_Duke_of_Albany

Princess Alice of United Kingdom, Wikipedia, Wikimedia foundation, (accessed 17/10/ 2020). This page was last edited on 29 August 2020, at 06:44 (UTC),
https://en.wikipe- dia.org/wiki/Princess_Alice_of_the_United_Kingdom

Queen Victoria, Wikipedia, Wikimedia Foundation, (accessed 17/10/ 2020). This page was last edited on 7 October 2020, at 21:42 (UTC),
https://en.wikipedia.org/wiki/ Queen_Victoria

Princess Alice of United Kingdom, Wikipedia, Wikimedia Foundation, (accessed 17/10/ 2020). This page was last edited on 29 August 2020, at 06:44 (UTC),
https://en.wikipe- dia.org/wiki/Princess_Alice_of_the_United_Kingdom

Princess Victoria of United Kingdom, Wikipedia, Wikimedia foundation, (accessed 17/10/ 2020). This page was last edited on 4 September 2020, at 15:09 (UTC), https:// en.wikipedia.org/wiki/Princess_Victoria_of_the_United_Kingdom

Princess Elizabeth of Hesse by Ryan, Wikipedia, Wikimedia foundation, (accessed 17/10/ 2020). This page was last edited on 9 May 2020, at 23:17 (UTC),
https:// en.wikipedia.org/wiki/Princess_Elisabeth_of_Hesse_and_by_Rhine

Alexander III of Russia, Wikipedia, Wikimedia foundation, (accessed 17/10/ 2020). This page was last edited on 15 October 2020, at 04:15 (UTC),
https://en.wikipedia. org/wiki/Alexander_III_of_Russia

Alexander II of Russia, Wikipedia, Wikimedia foundation, (accessed 17/10/ 2020). This page was last edited on 15 October 2020, at 18:23 (UTC),
https://en.wikipedia.org/ wiki/Alexander_II_of_Russia

Catherine The Great, Wikipedia, Wikimedia Foundation, (accessed 17/10/ 2020). This page was last edited on 17 October 2020, at 12:31 (UTC),
https://en.wikipedia.org/ wiki/Catherine_the_Great

Maria Feodorovna, Dagmar of Denmark, Wikipedia, Wikimedia Foundation, (accessed 17/10/ 2020). This page was last edited on 13 October 2020, at 15:54 (UTC),
https:// en.wikipedia.org/wiki/Maria_Feodorovna_(Dagmar_of_Denmark)
King Christiane IX of Denmark, Wikipedia, Wikimedia Foundation, (accessed 17/10/ 2020). This page was last edited on 16 October 2020, at 17:21 (UTC),
https://www.google.com/search?client=firefox-b-d&q=King+Christiane+IX+of+Denmark%2C+Wiki-pedia%2C+Wikimedia+foundation%2C

Grand Duke Michael Alexandrovich of Russia, Wikipedia, Wikimedia Foundation, (ac- cessed 17/10/ 2020). This page was last edited on 8 October 2020, at 03:01 (UTC), This page was last edited on 8 October 2020, at 03:01 (UTC).

Grand Duke Kiril of Russia, Wikipedia, Wikimedia Foundation, (accessed 17/10/ 2020). This page was last edited on 25 September 2020, at 13:52 (UTC),
https://en.wikipedia. org/wiki/Grand_Duke_Kirill_Vladimirovich_of_Russia

Grand Duke Michael of Russia, Wikipedia, Wikimedia Foundation, (accessed 17/10/ 2020). This page was last edited on 28 July 2020, at 16:52 (UTC),
https://en.wikipedia. org/wiki/Grand_Duke_Michael_Mikhailovich_of_Russia

Grand Duke Nikolai Nikolayevich of Russia, Wikipedia, Wikimedia Foundation, (accessed 17/10/ 2020). This page was last edited on 27 February 2013, at 20:58 (UTC),
https:// en.wikipedia.org/wiki/Grand_Duke_Nicholas_Nikolaevich_of_Russia

Grand Duchess Olga Alexandrovna of Russia, Wikipedia, Wikimedia Foundation, (accessed 17/10/ 2020). This page was last edited on 7 October 2020, at 14:01 (UTC),
https://en.wikipedia.org/wiki/Grand_Duchess_Olga_Alexandrovna_of_Russia

Anna Anderson, Wikipedia, Wikimedia Foundation, (accessed 17/10/ 2020). This page was last edited on 2 October 2020, at 09:39 (UTC),
https://en.wikipedia.org/wiki/ Anna_Anderson

Grand Duke Sergey Alexandrovich of Russia, Wikipedia, Wikimedia Foundation, (ac- cessed 17/10/ 2020). This page was last edited on 11 October 2020, at 15:59 (UTC),
https://en.wikipedia.org/wiki/Grand_Duke_Sergei_Alexandrovich_of_Russia

Grigori Rasputin, Wikipedia, Wikimedia Foundation, (accessed 17/10/ 2020). This page was last edited on 11 October 2020, at 21:55 (UTC),
https://en.wikipedia.org/ wiki/Grigori_Rasputin

Maria Rasputin, Wikipedia, Wikimedia Foundation, (accessed 17/10/ 2020). This page was last edited on 26 September 2020, at 18:16 (UTC).
https://en.wikipedia.org/wiki/ Maria_Rasputin

Alexander Nevsky Lavra, Wikipedia, Wikimedia Foundation, (accessed 17/10/ 2020). This page was last edited on 13 June 2020, at 01:34 (UTC), *https://en.wikipedia.org/ wiki/Alexander_Nevsky_Lavra*

Feofan Bystrov, Archimandrites Feofan, Wikipedia, Wikimedia Foundation, (accessed 17/10/ 2020). This page was last edited on 1 October 2020, at 05:01 (UTC).
https:// en.wikipedia.org/wiki/Theofan_(Bystrov)

World War 1, Wikipedia, Wikimedia Foundation, (accessed 17/10/ 2020). This page was last edited on 14 October 2020, at 18:38 (UTC).
https://en.wikipedia.org/wiki/World_ War_I#CITEREFStrachan2003

1905 Russian Revolution, Wikipedia, Wikimedia Foundation, (accessed 17/10/ 2020). This page was last edited on 14 October 2020, at 08:47 (UTC).
https://en.wikipedia. org/wiki/1905_Russian_Revolution

Russian Revolution, Wikipedia, Wikimedia Foundation, (accessed 17/10/ 2020). This page was last edited on 14 October 2020, at 16:47 (UTC).
https://en.wikipedia.org/ wiki/Russian_Revolution

October manifesto, Wikipedia, Wikimedia Foundation, (accessed 17/10/ 2020). This page was last edited on 24 May 2020, at 20:52 (UTC), *https://en.wikipedia.org/wiki/ October_Manifesto*

Dumas, Wikipedia, Wikimedia Foundation, (accessed 17/10/ 2020). This page was last edited on 8 October 2020, at 13:32 (UTC), *https://en.wikipedia.org/wiki/Alexandre_ Dumas*

Execution Wikipedia of the Romanov family, Wikipedia Wikimedia Foundation, (accessed 17/10/ 2020). This page was last edited on 12 October 2020, at 18:11 (UTC),
https:// en.wikipedia.org/wiki/Execution_of_the_Romanov_family Matilda

Kschesinska, Wikipedia, Wikimedia Foundation, (accessed 17/10/ 2020). This page was last edited on 29 September 2020, at 09:57 (UTC), *https://en.wikipedia.org/wiki/ Mathilde_Kschessinska*

Grand Duke Andre Vladimirovich of Russia, Wikipedia, Wikimedia Foundation, (accessed 17/10/ 2020). This page was last edited on 11 October 2020, at 19:09 (UTC), *https://en.wikipedia.org/wiki/Grand_Duke_Andrei_Vladimirovich_of_Russia*

Prince Vladimir Romanovsky Krasinski, Wikidata, Wikimedia Foundation, (accessed 17/10/ 2020). This page was last edited on 21 August 2020, at 18:3), *https://www. wikidata.org/wiki/Q4397363)*

Wedding of Nicholas the second and Alexandra Feodorovna, Wikipedia, Wikimedia Foundation, (accessed 17/10/ 2020). This page was last edited on 29 July 2020, at 07:40 (UTC).page was last edited on 18 September 2020, at 22:50 (UTC), *https://en.wikipedia.org/wiki/Wedding_of_Nicholas_II_and_Alexandra_Feodorovna*

Coronation of Nicholas the second and Alexandra Feodorovna Wikipedia, Wikimedia Foundation, (accessed 17/10/ 2020). This page was last edited on 29 July 2020, at 07:40 (UTC), *https://en.wikipedia.org/wiki/Coronation_of_Nicholas_II_and_Alexandra_Feodorovna*

Khadynka tragedy, Wikipedia, Wikimedia Foundation, (accessed 17/10/ 2020). This page was last edited on 15 September 2020, at 05:52 (UTC), *https://en.wikipedia.org/wiki/Khodynka_Tragedy*

Prince Felix Yusupov, Wikipedia, Wikimedia Foundation, (accessed 17/10/ 2020). This page was last edited on 14 October 2020, at 00:38 (UTC), *https://en.wikipedia.org/wiki/Felix_Yusupov*

Princess Irena Alexandrovna of Russia, Wikipedia, Wikimedia Foundation, (accessed 17/10/ 2020). This page was last edited on 10 October 2020, at 11:37 (UTC), *https://en.wikipedia.org/wiki/Princess_Irina_Alexandrovna_of_ Russia*

Vladimir Purishkevich, Wikipedia, Wikimedia Foundation, (accessed 17/10/ 2020). This page was last edited on 20 August 2020, at 20:21 (UTC), https://en.wikipedia.org/wiki/Vladimir_Purishkevich

Grand Duke Dmitri of Russia, Wikipedia, Wikimedia Foundation, (accessed 17/10/ 2020). This page was last edited on 18 October 2020, at 05:59 (UTC), https://en.wikipedia.org/wiki/Grand_Duke_Dmitri_Pavlovich_of_Russia

Anna Pavlova, Wikipedia, Wikimedia Foundation, (accessed 17/10/ 2020). This page was last edited on 26 September 2020, at 20:49 (UTC)., https://en.wikipedia.org/wiki/Anna_Pavlova

Mount Athos, Wikipedia, Wikimedia Foundation, (accessed 17/10/ 2020). This page was last edited on 17 October 2020, at 12:19 (UTC), https://en.wikipedia.org/wiki/Mount_Athos

Ernest Lewis Grand Duke of Hesse, Wikipedia, Wikimedia Foundation, (accessed 17/10/ 2020). This page was last edited on 1 October 2020, at 03:00 (UTC), https://en.wikipedia.org/wiki/Ernest_Louis,_Grand_Duke_of_Hesse
Princess Victoria Melita of Saxe-Coburg and Gotha, Wikipedia, Wikimedia Foundation, (accessed 17/10/ 2020). This page was last edited on 31 August 2020, at 14:52 (UTC), https://en.wikipedia.org/wiki/Princess_Victoria_Melita_of_Saxe-Coburg_and_Gotha

William II, Wikipedia, Wikimedia Foundation, (accessed 17/10/ 2020). This page was last edited on 13 October 2020, at 17:13 (UTC), https://en.wikipedia.org/wiki/William_II_of_England

Prince George of Greece, Wikipedia, Wikimedia Foundation, (accessed 17/10/ 2020). This page was last edited on 12 October 2020, at 19:11 (UTC), https://en.wikipedia.org/wiki/Prince_George_of_Greece_and_Denmark

George the Duke of York Wikipedia, Wikimedia Foundation, (accessed 17/10/ 2020). This page was last edited on 11 October 2020, at 20:15 (UTC).) https://en.wikipedia.org/wiki/George_V

Olga Constantinovna of Russia, Queen Olga of Greece, Wikipedia, Wikipedia Foundation, (accessed 17/10/ 2020). This page was last edited on 11 October 2020, at 18:47 (UTC).
https://en.wikipedia.org/wiki/Olga_Constantinovna_of_Russia

Eiffel Tower, Wikipedia, Wikimedia Foundation, (accessed 17/10/ 2020). This page was last edited on 17 October 2020, at 23:14 (UTC), *https://en.wikipedia.org/wiki/Eiffel_Tower*

Notre-Dame de Paris, Wikipedia, Wikimedia Foundation, (accessed 17/10/ 2020). This page was last edited on 10 October 2020, at 19:41 (UTC). *https://en.wikipedia.org/wiki/Notre-Dame_de_Paris*

Prince Vladimir Nikolayevich Orlov, Wikimedia Foundation, (accessed 17/10/ 2020). This page was last edited on 7 August 2020, at 14:11 (UTC), *https://en.wikipedia.org/wiki/Vladimir_Nikolayevich_Orlov*

Winter Palace, Wikipedia, Wikimedia Foundation, (accessed 17/10/ 2020). This page was last edited on 15 October 2020, at 20:42 (UTC), *https://en.wikipedia.org/wiki/Winter_Palace*

Osborn House, Wikipedia, Wikimedia Foundation, (accessed 17/10/ 2020). This page was last edited on 17 August 2020, at 21:20 (UTC), *https://en.wikipedia.org/wiki/Osborne_House*

Petergof Palace, Wikipedia, Wikimedia Foundation, (accessed 17/10/ 2020). This page was last edited on 23 August 2020, at 17:49 (UTC), *https://en.wikipedia.org/wiki/Peterhof_Palace*

Princess Malika of Montenegro, Wikipedia, Wikimedia Foundation, (accessed 17/10/ 2020). This page was last edited on 11 May 2020, at 09:12 (UTC), *https://en.wikipedia.org/wiki/Princess_Milica_of_Montenegro*

Princess Anastasia of Montenegro, Wikipedia shall, Wikimedia Foundation, (accessed 17/10/ 2020). This page was last edited on 15 October 2020, at 11:16 (UTC). *https://en.wikipedia.org/wiki/Princess_Anastasia_of_Montene-gro*

(accessed 17/10/ 2020). This page was last edited on 6 October 2020, at 07:22 (UTC). *https://en.wikipedia.org/wiki/Edward_VII*

Ivan Kalyayev, Wikipedia, Wikimedia Foundation, (accessed 17/10/ 2020). This page was last edited on 23 September 2020, at 22:49 (UTC).) *https://en.wikipedia.org/wiki/Ivan_Kalyayev*

Georgy Gapon, Wikipedia, Wikimedia Foundation, (accessed 17/10/ 2020).

This page was last edited on 28 September 2020, at 12:39 (UTC).) *https://en.wikipedia.org/wiki/Georgy_Gapon*

Vladimir Lenin, Wikipedia, Wikimedia Foundation, (accessed 17/10/ 2020). This page was last edited on 18 October 2020, at 12:26 (UTC). *https://en.wikipedia.org/wiki/Vladimir_Lenin*

Aleksandr Ulyanov Wikipedia, Wikimedia Foundation, (accessed 17/10/ 2020). This page was last edited on 18 October 2020, at 11:55 (UTC) *https://en.wikipedia.org/wiki/Aleksandr_Ulyanov*

Leon Trotsky, Wikipedia, Wikimedia Foundation, (accessed 17/10/ 2020). This page was last edited on 18 October 2020, at 03:33 (UTC). *https://en.wikipedia.org/wiki/Leon_Trotsky*

Peter Stolypin, Wikipedia, Wikimedia Foundation, (accessed 17/10/ 2020). This page was last edited on 23 September 2020, at 09:40 (UTC). (*https://en.wikipedia.org/wiki/Pyotr_Stolypin*)

Queen Alexandra of United Kingdom, Wikipedia, Wikimedia Foundation, (accessed 17/10/ 2020). This page was last edited on 8 October 2020, at 11:04 (UTC).) *https://en.wikipedia.org/wiki/Alexandra_of_Denmark*

Dmitry Bogrov, Wikipedia, Wikimedia Foundation, (accessed 17/10/ 2020). This page was last edited on 5 October 2020, at 21:29 (UTC). (*https://en.wikipedia.org/wiki/Dmitry_Bogrov*)

Alexandre Kerensky, Wikipedia, Wikimedia foundation, (accessed 17/10/ 2020). This page was last edited on 18 October 2020, at 03:23 (UTC). *https://en.wiki- pedia.org/wiki/Alexander_Kerensky*

Georgie Lvov, Wikipedia, Wikimedia Foundation, (accessed 17/10/ 2020). This page was last edited on 17 October 2020, at 20:01 (UTC). *https://en.wikipedia. org/wiki/Georgy_Lvov*

Pierre Gilliard, Wikipedia, Wikimedia Foundation, (accessed 17/10/ 2020). This page was last edited on 10 August 2020, at 16:35 (UTC). *https://en.wiki-pedia.org/wiki/Pierre_Gilliard*

Yaakov Yurovsky, Wikipedia, Wikimedia Foundation, (accessed 17/10/ 2020). This page was last edited on 18 October 2020, at 03:38 (UTC). *https://en.wikipedia.org/wiki/Yakov_Yurovsky*

Joseph Stalin, Wikipedia, Wikimedia Foundation, (accessed 17/10/ 2020). This page was last edited on 18 October 2020, at 03:30 (UTC). *https://en.wikipedia. org/wiki/Joseph_Stalin*

Zinaida Volkova, Wikipedia, Wikimedia Foundation, (accessed 17/10/ 2020). This page was last edited on 15 August 2020, at 11:59 (UTC). *https://en.wiki-pedia.org/wiki/Zinaida_Volkova*

Lev Sedov, Wikipedia, Wikimedia Foundation, (accessed 17/10/ 2020). This page was last edited on 25 August 2020, at 21:04 (UTC). *https://en.wikipedia. org/wiki/Lev_Sedov*

Sergei Sedov, Wikipedia, Wikimedia Foundation, (accessed 17/10/ 2020). This page was last edited on 28 February 2020, at 04:02 (UTC). *https://en.wikipedia. org/wiki/Sergei_Sedov)*

Esteban Volkov, Wikipedia, Wikimedia Foundation, (accessed 17/10/ 2020). This page was last edited on 26 March 2020, at 12:48. (*https://www.wikidata. org/wiki/Q1369819*)

Boris Yeltsin, Wikipedia, Wikimedia Foundation, (accessed 17/10/ 2020). This page was last edited on 14 October 2020, at 23:59 (UTC).(*https://en.wikipedia.org/wiki/Boris_Yeltsin*)

Boris Nemtsov, Wikipedia, Wikimedia Foundation, (accessed 17/10/ 2020), (updated). This page was last edited on 14 October 2020, at 23:41 (UTC). *https://en.wikipedia.org/wiki/Boris_Nemtsov)*

Alexi Navalny, Wikipedia, Wikimedia Foundation, (accessed 18/10/ 2020). This page was last edited on 18 October 2020, at 13:46 (UTC). (*https://en.wikipedia.org/wiki/Alexei_Navalny*)

Félix Faure, Wikipedia, Wikimedia Foundation, (accessed 17/10/ 2020), (updated). This page was last edited on 21 August 2020, at 21:33 (UTC), *https://en.wikipedia.org/wiki/F%C3%A9lix_Faure*